Cari's

Commonplace

Book

Purple Rose Ink Publications

ISBN-13: 978-1539697367
ISBN-10: 1539697363

Introduction

It began with my quest for knowledge and my lack of funds to support that curiosity. As I read and researched many topics over the years, I often found myself taking notes. Many people have asked me why I hang on to a whole filing cabinet (or two) of notes. I told them I thought the information might come in handy at a later date.

Although I had heard of Commonplace Book before, it wasn't until I read Lemony Snicket's *A Series of Unfortunate Events* that I was reminded of how valuable these books can be. Klaus kept a Commonplace Book on his adventures to keep track of important clues and bits of information. This gave me the idea to collect my own notes and create my own Commonplace Book. Many of these notes have appeared on Wordpress as part of my Blog. Some are brief descriptions of books I've read or movies I've seen, while others are more detailed accounts of research I've done. My topics of research have varied from favorite authors of fiction and literature to science. Religion, Mythology and Mysticism have also been sources of fascination along with Psychology and Philosophy.

For those of who you who don't know, Commonplace Books are a way to compile knowledge, usually by writing information into books. Such books are essentially scrapbooks filled with items of every kind: recipes, quotes, letters, poems, tables of weights and measures, proverbs, prayers, legal formulas. Commonplace Books are used by readers, writers, students, and scholars as an aid for remembering useful concepts or facts they have learned. Each common-place book is unique to its creator's particular interests.

Some notable examples of Commonplace Books are *"The Promus of Formularies and Elegancies"* by Francis Bacon. The Promus was a rough list of elegant and useful phrases gleaned from reading and conversation that Bacon used as a source book in writing and probably also as a promptbook for oral practice in public speaking. John Milton's Commonplace Book was John *Milton: Complete Prose Works*. Milton kept scholarly notes from his reading, complete with page citations to use in writing his tracts and poems. *Commonplace Book* was published by E.M. Forrester. W.H. Auden wrote A *Certain World*. And H.P Lovecraft a book called *H.P. Lovecraft's Commonplace Book*. In addition to Lemony Snicket; Virginia Woolf, Bronson Alcott and Michael Ondaatje have all referenced Commonplace Books in their writing.

Anyway, it is my hope that these summaries and reflections inspire you to pick up a book I wrote about or to do your own research into some of these subject areas. This Commonplace Book can serve as an inspiration and jumping off point for your own scholarly endeavors.

A Government of Wolves: The Emerging Police State in America By John W Whitehead

Whitehead is a Constitutional Lawyer who sees our Constitutional Rights and Freedoms eroding away in America. Many are oblivious to the fact that America is quickly and quietly sliding from a Democracy to a Police State. His title is taken from Edward R Murrow, who says, *"A Nation of Sheep will beget a Government of Wolves."*

Since the 1980s the Police have become more militant here in the United States. The 1033 Government Program has allowed our civil police forces to arm themselves with military weaponry, which was never supposed to happen. Cities across the USA have become too reliant on SWAT teams for everything, including misdemeanors and non-serious felonies. The SWAT teams, which originated in California in the 1960s, were supposed to be called in for only REALLY dangerous or explosive situations. They weren't supposed to be doing daily drug busts, etc.

Although non-lethal weapons were supposed allow the police to protect without taking lives, they have had potentially more dangerous side effects. The police are more likely to taser non-violent offenders for the tiniest infraction or insolence. They are much more likely to become over zealous with a taser than an actual gun. In fact, police have been known to taser children, pregnant women and the elderly! And the other methods of crowd control border on inhumane torture. Using pepper spray, LEDI or Barf Beamers, Sound Canons, Active Denial Systems that set your skin on fire and tear gas are all pretty awful means of subduing protesters, who often started out acting peacefully enough.

The police have taken to randomly frisking people, violating our bodily integrity that is protected by the 4th Amendment. The scariest loss of privacy is not something we are even aware of on a day to day basis though. The scariest loss of privacy is through surveillance and invasion of our personal technology. Our government is seizing control not through outright violence, but through things like surveillance cameras, biometrics, iris scanners, and facial recognition software and through Mobile Offender Recognition Information Systems.

The TSA was supposed to protect us from possible terror attacks, but it seems as if they have taken to routinely humiliating travelers. Tearing apart random pieces of luggage and patting down innocent people is something that travelers shouldn't have to be subjected to. And now they are talking about the VIPR or Visible Intermodel Prevention and Response teams to patrol high traffic areas such as malls and stadiums as well.

It is true that the United States of America has not always been perfect. We have annihilated the Native Americans, put the Japanese in internment camps and endured paranoia during the McCarthy era. But none of that comes close to what the Patriot Act did in 2001.

Because terrorism has been defined so broadly, it has given the government much more freedom to invade our privacy in the name of security. However, the Patriot Act violates the 1st, 4th, 5th, 6th, 7th, 8th and possibly the 13th and 14th Amendments. Now any act of Civil Disobedience can be considered an act of terror, which isn't right.

The National Defense Authorization Act is not talked about near as much as The Patriot Act, but it is just as damaging. The President can claim marshal law at anytime. He can also hold terrorist suspects for an indefinite amount of time and take away American Citizenship. The NSA keeps extensive records of all the surveillance that has taken place, including many people's facebook, twitter and Google searches. Phone calls and Bank Records are also accessible to the government without a warrant.

Anyone known as an extremist, malcontent, activist, rule breaker, disrupter of the peace or a misfit is being targeted. People whose only crime is exercising their Constitutional Rights are being harassed, arrested and worse. Brandon Raub's case is the perfect example of this. Raub is a Vetter who was placed in a VA psych ward because of things he posted on facebook. He merely voiced his dissatisfaction with the way things were being run by the government and boom! He is quickly discredited as crazy and locked away.

And its not just former military that are being treated like criminals. American school children are being arrested at an alarming rate for merely acting childish. Their Zero Tolerance policies have increasingly been used to treat children like prisoners. Some truant students have had to deal with RFID tags, wake up calls and constant monitoring. Obese students have been subjected to having their movements and heart rate monitored as well. Is this really what we want for our future generation?

Marshal McLuhan declared that fiction has a tendency to predict the future by a generation or so. Some of the films and books that have predicted our impending predicament are: *Brave New World, 1984, Fahrenheit 451, THX 1138, Soylant Green, Blade Runner, They Live, The Matrix, Minority Report, V for Vendetta, Children of Men, Land of the Blind* and *The Hunger Games.*

Whitehead ends with reminding us of our rights. It is important to know them or they will all be taken from us. Here is a brief description of The Bill of Rights:

1st Amendment gives us the right to assemble peacefully and to free speech.

2nd Amendment gives us the right to bear arms.

3rd Amendment gives us the right to keep the military from entering our homes without permission.

4th Amendment gives us right to be safe from any unreasonable search and seizure. The police must get a warrant!

5th Amendment gives us the right to remain silent. It states that we are innocent until proven guilty. Not guilty until proven innocent!

6th Amendment gives us the right to a speedy and public trial.

7th Amendment give us the right to a trial by jury.

8th Amendment gives us the right to NOT be subjected to cruel and unusual punishment.

9th Amendment gives us Popular Sovereignty or the right to choose our government and laws. As Thomas Paine once said, "Law is King." There is no King over our law.

10th Amendment states that we are a federal government that works on the local, state and national level.

What can we do to prevent the United States from becoming a Police State? Learn your rights and don't let them be taken away. It may seem overwhelming and you may feel powerless, but remember what Evie said in V is for Vendetta. She said that the Freedom Fighter is and always will be "all of us."

A Hidden Magic

I read *A Hidden Magic* by Vivian Vande Velde in 1988 when it first came out. I fell immediately fell in love with the subversive fairy tale. It begins with, *"Once upon a time-before kings and queens were replaced by an act of congress and when kissing a frog still sometimes resulted in more than a case of warts-there lived a young and nice but very plain princess named Jennifer."* Jennifer, following proper fairy-tale protocol, fell for a very handsome but very conceited prince named Alexander. When Alexander offends a powerful witch, it falls to Jennifer to save him. In the course of doing so, she meets a wizard and soon wonders if she's such a proper fairy-tale princess after all—a good little princess would love Alexander, but does she? Nope. It is plain Norman who captures her heart. And Alexander? Well, he is just fine with the vain enchantress they ran into along the way.

This book led to my creation of the Hidden Magic Trail. On my walk home from Whitney School I would take a short cut through what once used to be an ally between Fourth and Third Streets It had long since grown over and become part of everyone's backyard. One day I pushed passed the bushes and wandered through the path imagining myself on an adventure like Jennifer. From that day onward I walked home along my Hidden Magic Trail. I would pass by the magic tree which you could practically walk up since it grew at such a gentle slope. There was a small abandoned garden enclosed

10

by stones, which I imagined to be a wishing well. I created a lean-to out of fallen branches from near-by trees and it became my shelter along the trail. Eventually I exited out onto another ally that connected Third Street to Fourth Street. I imaged the gray gravel and pavement was a silver river, winding its way along. I would walk along the edge of my imaginary river and then imagine wading through it or paddling a boat across it to my home.

It wasn't until a couple of years ago that I discovered that Vivian Vande Velde has written a slue of other young adult books. Vivian Vande Velde who was born 1951, Rochester, New York, began writing at age 28, the same year her daughter was born, and has been publishing relatively consistently since. She currently resides in Rochester, New York. Her novels and short story collections usually contain elements of horror, fantasy, and humor.

Among her titles are: *Heir Apparent, There's A Dead Person Following My Sister Around, Dragonbate, Stolen, Cloaked in Red, Curses Inc and Other Stories, Tales From The Brother's Grimm and Sister's Weird, A Well-Timed Enchantment, Remembering Raquel* and *Witch Dreams*. Her book *Never Trust a Dead Man* (1999) received the 2000 Edgar Award for Best Young Adult Novel. I highly recommend *Cloaked in Red*, which is several retellings of the Red Riding Hood Fairy tail, and *Curses Inc and Other Stories*. Both made me laugh out loud.

Academic Attitude

I want to know to know why modern academics feel that anything remotely positive is naïve or flaky? This week I read the book *Top Secret* by Robert M Price. I knew that I'd probably come away charged with frustration and anger and I did. Price attacks all the New Age/New Thought texts in recent history. He explains the basic idea behind such favorites as the Oprah back *The Secret* by Rhonda Byrne as well as Eckert Tolle's *The Power of Now*. He also examines Wayne Dyer, Shakti Gawain, Deepak Chopra, Pema Chodron, Helen Schumann, Marianne Williamson, Neale Donald Walshe, James Redfield, Stephen A Hoellar and Timothy Freke (Ala Carl Jung), Michael Berg and Joel Olsteen. He is an equal opportunity Bigot. New Age, Gnosticism, Christianity, Judaism, Hinduism, Buddhism are all equally discredited. I was surprised; however, what I was criticizing him for—his rhetoric.

I could argue in favor of New Thought or one particular religion, but I don't think I will at the moment.

Price's book is filled with wit and sarcasm. He claims that he used humor as a way to lighten the mood—that he felt it was important not to take the subject matter or himself too seriously. The effect was that it weakens his argument. His comments are passive-aggressive and belittling. He comes off as an arrogant, pompous jackass and that irritates the hell out of me! Once more, other readers will jump on his bandwagon and continue the cycle of cynicism. His book is dark and cynical, which is oppressive in the end.

I have nothing against humor. I use it in my own writing now and again. It can relieve the tension and can be fun. However, humor can also be used inappropriately to deflect weak arguments or deflect attention away from weak arguments I should say. Straightforward parodies can illustrate political points. They seek to entertain first and educate second. Price's book seeks to educate and then entertain. Since the entertainment value is next to nhil, it simply calls attention to itself.

Price sets up his subject and knocks it down. I will give him credit for having covered each topic thoroughly though. He is obviously well educated and intelligent. That does not, however, make him right. He points toward philosophy and seems to put more stock in what they say then what anyone else does. He throws in some bible quotes as well.

It becomes obvious among all the explanations, that Price views Orthodox Christianity as correct. He doesn't spell it out or devote much time to his particular beliefs, but he is very much a right-wing Christian conservative. Conservatives have been backlashing for sometime now against nontraditional methods of practice and nontraditional belief systems. This book is one of the many aimed to dismantle the current effort to demystify Christ and Christianity. It is an effort to bring followers back to the fold—to shepherd lost sheep so to speak.

Some people do fall into traps and end up victims of some bizarre

13

cult. However, many have intelligently taken up the cause of empowering themselves. The church has victimized for centuries. It has hidden information and launched inquisitions in order to quell the fire of freedom. Price appears to be advocating surrendering to the biblical canon under no uncertain terms. Again, my God or no god.

There needs to be a middle ground. I do agree that New Age and Self-Improvement books are watered down versions of other texts and genres. They may not be philosophic or even that realistic at times. Still, I can't concede that they are unholy or evil. They fulfill a need, a deep spiritual hunger in the American Public. Christianity in its canonical and conservative form is failing to engage its followers. These books are not templates from the devil to do evil. They are not all together worthless and devoid of any substance either. They try to empower people by giving them the tools to find spirituality on their own. Some of these tools work better than others. Some people insist on using the wrong too for the job. Still, others do not exercise critical reading skills or common sense for such matters.

It is important to keep an open mind. Disregarding and outright attacking a genre is tragically common and it shows a severe lack of compassion and tolerance on the author's part. Books attacking other books are depressing to read and serve no real purpose other than to preach to the choir so to speak. If he wanted to convince me of something he'd do better to put forth ideas he was for. I've found that arguments in favor of something are often a great deal stronger than against. Positive positions get positive results. Be FOR Christianity, not against all other religions. Be FOR tradition, not against not anything new. Convince me of how wonderful your position is, not how horrible mine is. Don't guilt me into conforming. Don't manipulate the facts.

In the book *True Enough* by Farhad Manjoo, facts are shown to be fluid. We are living in a post-fact society. Opinions and beliefs have overtaken logic and facts in a cultural coup-d-tete. Price would argue that the New Thought authors are at fault for this. But I would argue that it is people like Price that propagate or propel this fragmentation. Being ignorant or intolerant of others leads to closed minds. Being open is considering all sides and evaluating the evidence. Being open does not mean believing everything you hear or read. Despite the pitfalls of a free press, I believe it is important to have options. I shouldn't have to conform to the world view that Price espouses. I have a choice, be it right or wrong. It is up to me to make my own mistakes. I don't have to worry about the church persecuting me because what I choose to believe. I'm not being forced to pretend to agree with beliefs that I am uncomfortable with.

The only problem with this freedom is that people lack the education and the tools to make responsible decisions. Technology has made us lazy. Schools have failed to educate their students. Well meaning self-esteem programs have created a society of narcissists. No one wants to be wrong, but everyone should be humble enough to admit their mistakes. Instead of taking responsibility, we shift blame. Instead of dealing with problems, we tend to seek escape instead.

America's tendency to escape is the subject of another book I recently read called *Against Happiness*. *Against Happiness* is by Eric G Wilson. I resisted reading it at first, thinking it would depress me or somehow anger me. Instead, it was thought provoking. Wilson isn't really against happiness all together. He is against the reckless pursuit of pleasure at the expense of learning the lessons that pain can bring. America is a nation of consumers who pop pills or run up credit card debt to avoid any sense of discomfort. Happiness, Wilson feels, should be hard or earned. I agree with him on that point. Wilson also spends time attacking the worst offenders or the culprits behind this escapist trend. To his credit, he is equally unhappy with "smarmy, warmongering conservatives" and "passive-aggressive pacifist liberals." I'm not sure what Wilson's ideal political stance is if now one can cope correctly.

Overall, Wilson was well-read and often waxed poetically. While had had many valid points, after awhile it was a bit of a downer to read. I cultivate melancholy moods sometimes, but there is a fine line between artistic ennui and depression. It is okay to indulge in an occasional blue or even black mood. However, if those moods fluctuate too wildly or linger too long, then it is time to get some help. I believe Wilson is a bit too willing to prolong those pessimistic preoccupations.

Again, both Wilson and Price are academics. Granted, they probably would view each other with disdain and distrust, but pessimism is something they share. In fact, many of the academic-oriented books I've read are full of sarcasm, cynicism and even mockery toward anyone the least bit optimistic. It is a stereotype scholars feel they have to conform to, I believe. Just as scientists have a reputation for being atheists or agnostic at best, scholars have a reputation for being arrogant and always skeptical. The scientific method and the critical mind set do not require one to be world-weary. So why the **Weltschmerz?**

\

After Ecstasy, The Laundry

After Ecstasy, the Laundry: How the Heart Grows Wise on the Spiritual Path was written by Jack Kornfield and it came out in 2000. Drawing on the experiences and insights of leaders and practitioners within the Buddhist, Christian, Jewish, Hindu, and Sufi traditions, this book offers a uniquely intimate and honest understanding of how the modern spiritual journey unfolds and how we can prepare our hearts for awakening.

"We all know that after the honeymoon comes marriage, after the election comes the hard task of governance. In spiritual life it is the same: After Ecstasy Comes the Laundry," Kornfield begins. "We want to be enlightened as grapes want to become wine. It is natural. Sufis call this "the voice of the beloved." We are born into this world with the song of enlightenment and wholeness in our ears, but we may first come to know it by its absence in our lives.

Inner growth requires the inspiration of angels. It requires diving into the ocean of tears. We may begin our journey to enlightenment in the dark woods. Our messengers of suffering may come in the form of alcoholic or abusive parents or simply a rough family life.

But each time we blame and fight the world around us, we reject and cut off parts of ourselves.

A great loss, crisis or illness tended to wisely will cause our hearts to grow. When disenchantment arises, the very suffering and struggle it causes brings us to courage to question in the face of all odds. Kabir, the Indian Mystic said, "It is the intensity of the longing that does all the work."

To forgive we must face the pain and sorrow of our betrayal and disappointment, and discover the movement of heart that opens to forgive in spite of it all. Overcome any bitterness. Like the mother of the world you are carrying the pain of the world in your heart. Sometimes mercy is learned in the loneliness of our cell, other times we cannot do it ourselves. We need another human being to witness our sorrows—to touch what is closed in us.

You live in illusion and the appearance of things. There is a reality, but you do not know this. When you understand this, you will see that you are nothing. And being nothing, you are everything says Kalu Rinpoche. In the emptiness of self the world becomes transparent, clear, uncomplicated. We realize that our sense of separate self is untrue.

Poetry has a mysterious power in its ability to hold meanings almost impossible to speak directly. Zen writings offer almost no literal description of the stages of enlightenment, only metaphors and images.

Leaving maps and expectations behind in the then end we must turn our hearts in the direction of love and awareness, come what may.

In living form this awakened heart we become bodhisattvas, all servants of the divine.

Permanence is not true freedom. It is not the sure heart's release. Every wise voyage learns that we cannot hold onto the last port of call, no matter how beautiful. To do so would be like holding our breath, creating a prison from our past. All spiritual life in transition from one circumstance to another. These ordinary cycles of opening and closing are necessary medicine for our heart's integration. In some cases though there are not just cycles, there is a crash. As far as we ascend, so far as we can fall. This too needs to be included in our maps of spiritual life—honored as more natural part of the cycle.

Julian Norwich said, "In falling and rising again, we are held in that same precious love." Only to the extent that we let go into change can we live in harmony with those around us and with our own true nature. No matter what the situation, awakening requires trust—trust that something new will eventually be born, trust whatever is perfect. Wise letting go is not detached removal from life. It is the heart's embrace of life itself. A willing heart opens to the full reality of the present.

Though it sounds simple, letting go is really an advanced process. Letting go can be summed up as Not Always So. It is a truth of the heart that we resist what makes us frightened, hard and inflexible, but we if we embrace it we become transformed. And having entered the stream of dharma, the practitioner regularly examines her own and sees this is the freedom one and these are the fetters, the entanglements still to be released in me.

Certain brilliant intellectuals may suffer from ignorance and disregard for their bodies and their emotions. Other people, quite conscious of their feelings and experts in human relationships, may be utterly unconscious of the thought constructs and beliefs that limit them.

The middle path embraces opposites. It rests between them, acknowledging both truths, caught by neither side. Awakening dissolves the labels we have put on our experience. The wise heart brings compassion to imperfection itself. The wise heart is at peace with the way things are. The heart becomes clear and able to understand the world rather than struggle with it.

Before enlightenment we have to live with our body. After enlightenment we still have to live with our body. While we knew that wise sexuality cane bring intimacy, connection and surrender, wise and holy celibacy can do the same. Both choices can be an expression of love and awareness. The Zen master Dinan Katagiri says, "The important point of spiritual practice is not to try and escape your life, but to face it—exactly and completely." No matter where we are on the journey of awakening, our body must be included.

Some people believe that emotions are dangerous. But the emotions themselves are rarely a problem. It is our lack of awareness of them or the stories that we believe about them that creates suffering. Simone Weil, a Christian mystic said, "The danger is not that the soul should doubt that there is any bread, but that by a lie, it should persuade itself that it is not hungry." Awakening to the emotions means to feel them—nothing less and nothing more. It does not require changing our feelings—feelings change all the time on their own. We fear the destructive power of our emotions when we have seen them for what they really are. We confuse allowing ourselves to be aware of them with necessity to act them out.

The emotional wisdom of the heart is simple. When we accept our human feelings, a remarkable transformation occurs. Tenderness and wisdom arise naturally and spontaneously. Where we once sought strength over others now our strength our own. Where once sought to defend ourselves, we laugh…Happiness and love come naturally in letting go of fear.

Our sacred longing is to return to where we are and know the place for the first time. Then we are coming back to our own true nature. In Buddhist tradition, a bodhisattva is a being dedicated to universal awakening—to having compassion and wisdom to all that lives— how ever long it takes.

Against Depression

Against Depression by Peter D Kramer came out in 2005. Kramer examines what depression is, including apathy, guilt and listlessness. He covers the social attitude toward depression as well as the genetic role in depression. He moves on to cover the roll of ambivalence toward the human condition and then addresses the physical aspects and affects of depression.

Adrenal glands release stress hormones and cause the hippocampus to shrink. People who are depressed do indeed think less than people who do not suffer from depression. Overwhelmed neurons can become isolated and die. Excessive production of stress hormones can decrease bone density, cause us to age prematurely and cause us to slowly fail at our ability to bounce back from traumatic events. Depression affects multiple organs and multiple parts of our lives. For example, 60% of patients with heart-attacks also suffered from some level of depression!

He stresses that depression is NOT a normal variation of feeling and should not be except as such. Having a lot of empathy toward others is NOT depression either. There are emotionally intense people who never suffer from depression at all. Depression is, however, characterized by dependency and desperation. Descriptions of depression tend to focus only on the pain and confusion though.

Depression is what settles in stay in your life. It is characterized by its duration more than anything. Every feels one blue once in a while but not every feels blue for weeks, months or years at a time. And those who experience depression are likely to experience more than one episode of it. Those who suffer from it may experience 3, 4, 5 or 6 episodes during their lifetime. Fifteen years later 6% of patients were still depressed. Many were not receiving on-going treatment either. 40% of those who are depressed had another episode two years later. 60% had another episode with five years. 75% had another episode within ten years and 87% had another episode within fifteen years. With each episode the recovery time lengthened as well. On study showed that two years after the initial episode 20% of patients had not recovered. Ten years later 7% were still depressed or depressed again.

Depression has a rate of 38% heritability. If someone in your family has MAJOR depression then that rises to closer to 40% heritability. 60% of people who depressed are also neurotic, but not everyone who is neurotic is depressed. Major depression accounts for 20% of disabilities in women. 16% of Americans will suffer from Major depression in their lifetime. And 6-7% of Americans are suffering from major depression in any given year.

Dysthymia is a low mood for a long period of time without any major depression. It will present itself as a bad attitude more than an illness but still cause lots of issues such as work loss and even suicide attempts.

Ataraxia is known as serene detachment. A person will avoid disruptive passions by limiting his emotional investments. It is barely a state of contentment to ward off depression and involves a sober mistrust of comment and constant awareness of life's pains.

The gene responsible for depression is known as the 5-HTT gene. If the 5-HTT gene is long then you are likely to be okay even if you are abused at some point in your life. However, if your 5-HTT gene is short then you are likely to develop depression at some point in your life.

In the end, nature and nurture play a role. What predicts an episode of major depression? Being robbed or assaulted, facing housing or financial problems, losing a job or even just problems at work, martial problems, divorce and losing a friend can all be triggers. A humiliating loss is the worst possible even for someone prone to depression. Interestingly, cancer patients often get depressed due to their illness. Pancreatic Cancer is associated with particularly high levels of depression. I guess there is a high plasma cytokine levels in Pancreatic Cancer patients which mimics an interferon-induced depression. Anyway, the more depressed you are the more you tend to continue to contribute to your own misery.

Alcoholism tends to cluster in families with depression. The combination of depression and drinking can be twice as devastating as depression alone. Low levels of stress will continue to cause episodes of depression even in the absence any real trauma. However, losing a parent at an early age may not be traumatic if that child has a supportive family and is able to finish high school. If we work to prevent low self-esteem early on then we can also work to prevent depression from developing.

Suicide is less frequent among those who are medicated for depression; however it can make depression worse in some people. Prozac offers protection and can stimulate new cell formation in the hippocampus. Psycho-Therapy is needed in addition to medication for most patients. Talk therapy alone can be successful for those with mild depression.

Why is that we romanticize melancholy? Certainly, Kay Jameson Redfield's book *Touched with Fire* romanticizes it. But Kramer is decidedly against depression. He believes that the evidence linking depression to creativity is shaky at best. He says, *"Romantic poetry, religious memoir, inspirational tracts, the novel of youthful self-development and grand opera and the blues portray depression as an affliction that inspires art and art forms."* Poets and writers in particular suffer from heroic melancholy—suffering for their art. Why is this? *"Depression is becomes a universal metaphor, standing in for sin and innocent suffering, self indulgence and sacrifice inferiority and refinement,"* Kramer says. Grief has become a model for romantic love and it shouldn't be. Depression is not to be blamed on artistic temperaments or poor choices in life.

Many writers suffer from social awkwardness, depression, bi-polar disorder, epilepsy and narcissism. Writing does provide a sort of treatment for depression it seems. Perhaps dealing with depression is a matter of having certain tools at hand and a new way of dealing with difficult emotions. We might come to identify passion with an inner sense of security and confidence eventually. And then when we do not fear depression any longer we might be free to love more generously.

Agnosticism and Atheism

I'd like to take a brief detour into Atheism. I just read *Dawkin's Delusion* by Alestier McGrath and Joanna McGrath. They were writing in response to Richard Dawkins recent book *The God Delusion*.

Dawkins has denounced God and believes it is only logical that everyone follows suite. According to Dawkins, faith is infantile, irrational and down right delusional. Science is all we need and science has disproved the existence of God. Religion is the root of all evil in his eyes. It is the cause of all violence. He calls God: *"a petty, unjust, unforgiving control freak, vindictive, blood thirsty, ethnic cleanser, a misogynist, a homophobe, a racist, infanticidal, genocidal, filicidal, pestilent megalomaniac, sadomasochistic, malevolent bully."*

Dawkins isn't an atheist! He is a misothesist! He doesn't simply believe God is nonexistent; he hates God and religion in general. Dawkins believes that we were once psychologically primed to believe in God. We needed to believe. Perhaps Dawkins has a psychological reason for needing to **disbelieve**. If Nietzsche's philosophy was born out of a super strict Christian upbringing, what created Dawkins hatred? Perhaps he should blame his parents or society instead of attacking religion. Religion appears to be just his scapegoat for whatever is really bothering him.

I have never been a huge fan of orthodox religion, specifically orthodox Christianity, yet I have never given up my belief in God. I have never had a reason to blame religion or God for my misfortunes. I can understand why people lose faith though. Their prayers go unanswered. Every day people suffer and die seemingly random deaths. The world is a cruel place. It is difficult to comprehend how a father-figure could create something and then abandon his children and let them suffer. There is no proof that our suffering is ever rewarded on earth or in heaven. There is no security when it comes to God. Dawkins complaints are common enough and reasonable enough.

The problem is that the God Dawkins described is merely a human interpretation. Dawkins is describing humanity, not a deity. It is human beings that start wars in the name of God. Scientifically speaking, God has remained surprisingly silent. His/Her silence does not prove his/her existence or absence. It merely proves that God does not choose sides or interfere in any obvious way.

Agnosticism makes sense in many ways seeing has there is no actual proof one way or the other. Unfortunately, Agnosticism has been lumped together with Atheism. It is too bad. Orthodox or traditional believers have a tendency to exclaim, "My way or the highway" and "You are either with us or against us!" Many Agnostics choose an alternative view of God, but that doesn't mean that they are godless. Spirituality isn't spoiled by a lack of Cosmic CEO.

Take Buddhism for example. India, China and Japan all have pagan deities. But Buddhism evolved as an all-embracing philosophy. Some Buddhists believe in pagan deities and some in no deities at all and still others believe in just one deity. Buddhism requires certain rituals and practices, which puts it into the religion category. It is also flexible enough to bend to various world views. This particular flexibility is often what makes it appear as a lesser religion. The world is dominated by Judaism, Christianity and Islam because they all have the same roots. Hinduism and Buddhism are not as wide spread and still foreign to most Westerners. Christians often attack Eastern religions without any real understanding or tolerance of them. Again, it comes down to MY GOD or NO GOD. There is no room for nontheism, Pandeism, Pantheism, Polytheism, or Deism in the Christian World-View. Yet, with Buddhism, there is a bit of possibility or room to play.

I am drawn to Buddhism because it is more open, tolerant and compassionate than traditional Christianity. I know that many Buddhists do not believe in God. I do however; believe in a creator and divine deity. My version or vision is more of a transcendental one though. I am not exactly Pagan, but I do believe that other beings are higher or more powerful than us. I love the focus on nature and feminism in Wicca more than anything.

Why do I believe in a higher power or perhaps a deeper power? What gives me faith despite a lack of proof? Why is spirituality and mysticism so important to me?

I've always sensed that something lies beyond my existence. I believe because it makes more sense than not believing. It is an emotional connection, something I cannot grasp in the limit of my five senses. I look at my children and see the miracle of life. I look at the cosmos and see the vastness of possibility in reality. I see patterns and connections. I see meaning. I ask why would anyone deny the possibility of meaning?

Anaís Nin

Intellect and sensuality: Words and actions. Reason and emotions. Lots of opposites coexist here, in my life and inside me. Why am I so drawn to Anais Nin? I think it is because we a lot in common. Not only being raised by a single mother, but the total absence of her father as well. Then there is her passion, her poetic style, her insight, her imagination and her drive to write. On the way home from taking my GRE I read Anais Nin's **Delta of Venus**. I was filled with desire.

I also recently read a book **about** Anais Nin. Many people have called her narcissistic. The author of the book I read was a bit more sympathetic. In her book was a quote from Edward Edinger's book *Ego and Archetype*. *"Narcissism in its original implications is not this needless excessive self-love, but rather just the opposite, a frustrated state of yearning for self-possession which does not yet exist. The solution of the problem of narcissism is the fulfillment of self-love, and not the renunciation of it...fulfilled self-love is a prerequisite to the genuine love of any object, and the flow of psychic energy in general."*

Anais Nin Quotes

Jung: Proceed from the dream outward.

Furrawn: Gaelic word meaning the kind of talk that brings strangers to intimacy.

Anais Nin The Novel of the Future

Dreaming is indispensable to man. Man has to learn to live outside and beyond history as well as in it, or he will be swept like hysterical sheep in its errors. (12)

The dream then, instead of being something apart from reality, a private world of fantasy or imagination, is actually an essential part of our reality, which can be shared and communicated by means of imagery. (23)

Our psychological reality, which lies below the surface, frightens us in a direction, which society's rules and organizations define as wrong or dangerous. When experiencing such fears, the unconscious mind tries to first control the unconscious by repression. When it rebels, it may lead either to madness or life. (43)

One thing is very clear—that both the diary and fiction tended towards the same goal: intimacy with people, with experience, with life itself. (155)

We should have books not for one person, but books for everyone, books which reflect experience and not a fear of it, confrontations and not evasions, which brings awareness rather than blindness.

(172)

In Favor of the Sensitive Man and other Essays

I believe what unites us universally is our emotions, our feelings in the face of experience, and not necessarily actual experiences themselves. The facts were different, but readers felt the same way. (77)

Nearer the Moon

Passion alone does not make a world. (155)

The imagination rules the life, not reality. (172)

One love is more than many if deeply lived. (239)

I live the life of a spy. Spies do not live with their fear. The risk and danger is their climate. They live in tension, of course, alertness, wakefulness. Not trembling. That is how I live. I am aware of the danger, but not afraid. (239)

Diary 1932-1934

Sex alone does not make me a woman…The liberation of the sexual instinct did not create maturity, womanhood. (229)

Diary 1934-1939

Someday I'll be locked up for insanity. "She loved too much." This could be on my tombstone. What I feel intensely and always respond to is the aloneness of the others, their needs. Which love makes the greatest closeness, the fraternal, the friendship, the passion, the intellectual harmony, the tender one, devotion, the lover,

34

the brother, the husband, the father, the son, or the friend? So many kinds of fusion! What annihilates the loneliness? ...Break and shatter loneliness forever! I am never close enough. I want some impossible communion. I must accept intermittence and loneliness in between. (76)

Diary 1944-1947

I am writing not about objective reality, which is photographic, but as people see and feel reality, their reality.

Diary 1966-1974

Freedom means that no one is able to destroy you, enslave you or paralyze you.

(232)

Anne of Green Gables

I first watched *Anne of Green Gables* on PBS in 1985 at my friend Jill Boroom's house. Realizing the mini-series was based upon a series of books by L.M. Montgomery, I was eager to read them. The first book captured my imagination as much as the series did. In fact, I took to giving all the landscapes around me romantic sounding names.

Smiley Road had a stretch the often smelled in the hot summers, so I called it Sewer Sill. There was a part of the road up on a hill that overlooked a valley, hence the name Valley View. And across the road was Lake View. There was a house hidden back behind a bunch of trees which I named The Mysterious Mansion. Not that it was an actual mansion, but I imagined it to be so. I also tried to found the speech she recited about the Lady of Shallot and learned the words to the poem by Tennyson.

I continued on in the series reading *Anne of Avonlea, Anne of the Island, Anne of Windy Poplars, Anne's House of Dreams, Anne of Ingleside, Rainbow Valley* and *Rilla of Ingleside.* I also tried to read the *Emily of the New Moon* series, but couldn't get into it. Later I picked up the *Chronicles of Avonlea, Further Chronicles of Avonlea* and *Kilmey of the Orchard.*

I also imagined that my best friend Jill was like Diana and I was like Anne. We were never forbidden from seeing each other and our relationship held a lot less drama than Anne and Diana's. Eventually she and I drifted apart. However, she remained close to home and got married like Diana, while I went to college, traveled and taught like Anne.

I'm not sure what my favorite book in the Series is. Although I enjoyed her banter with Gilbert Blythe in the first three books, I enjoyed the particular Gothic Romanticism in *Anne of Windy Poplars*. *Anne's House of Dreams*, *Anne of Ingleside* and *Rainbow Valley* were okay. For some reason I connected to *Rilla of Ingleside*. For awhile I toyed with the idea of naming my son Walter after Anne's son who fights in WWI.

However, I must say I disappointed by Kevin Sullivan's follow up to the 1985 mini-series. *Anne of Avonlea*, which aired in 1987, was a combination of *Anne of Avonlea*, *Anne of the Island* and *Anne of Windy Poplars*. It was not a good idea to combine them all into one. I had hoped for him to follow the books more closely. I was even more upset by the third movie in the series, which strayed from the series completely. It had Anne living and writing during WWI. Instead of having her sons go off to war as they did in *Rilla of Ingleside*, she was the one to experience the horrors of war first hand. Anne was supposed to be married, have children of her own and be quite a bit older during the time period they put her in. Instead, it as if no time had passed from *Anne of Avonlea*, which was some twenty years previous.

I still own the *Anne of Green Gables* Series and hope to share them with my daughter soon. She is now the same age I was when I discovered them.

Apocalypse

Apocalypse is the buzz word of the week, perhaps even the month or year. December 21st marks the 13th b'ak'tun on the Mayan Calendar. It is not the end of the calendar itself. The Mayans mention future dates all the way up to the 17th b'ak'tun, which would lead us into 4772 A.D. Each cycle is 400 years long.

I'm not sure how the Mayan Calendar came to be associated with the Christian notion of The Rapture or Armageddon. The Catholic Church does not subscribe to the idea of the return of Christ. However, the Jehovah Witness, and to a lesser extent, the Seventh Day Adventist, have really run with the idea. Edward Irving developed the modern conception of the Rapture back in 1792-1834. Since then the predictions of the end of the world have ranged from 1844 to 2060. Although, the authors of Revelations believed the end of the world to be in their lifetime, many, many lifetimes have come and gone since. And I suspect many more lifetimes will follow December 21, 2012 as well.

Interesting, the word Rapture means *seizure, rape or kidnapping* in French, but in Greek it means *caught up* or *taken away*. Rapture can be ecstasy or torture depending on the circumstances. Armageddon, on the other hand, is a specific place in the Holy Land. It is supposed to be the location of the defeat of the Beast, The Anti-Christ, Satan or The Devil. Some believe that evil will be bound, thus paving the way for peace in future times.

The Norse had their own version of the end of the world. It was the final battle known as Ragnarok. JRR Tolkien borrowed the idea of a final battle with the idea of Dagor Dagorath.

This week I am reading *Apocalyptic Planet* by Craig Childs. He reminds us that our planet, has, in fact, died many times. The earth is ever-ending and always beginning anew. Craig Childs calls attention the original meaning of the word Apocalypse. It come from the Greek word Apokalypsis and means the lifting of veil or revelation. It has been only over time that the word has come to symbolize mass destruction and the end of the world.

When Religion and the wrath of God falter, the destruction is feared to come from natural forces. Recently NASA has taken to releasing words of reassurance that none of the rumored disasters are likely to happen anytime soon. The sun isn't going to explode just yet, the magnetic poles won't flip-flop overnight and the rogue planet of Nibiru is nowhere near crashing into earth. Nor is there any spectacular planetary alignment coming up. It is likely that the 21st will be a normal day like any other.

Atonement

Atonement is the name of the novel by Ian McGowan. I picked the novel up after seeing the preview for the movie on TV. The commercial reminded me of *Damon's House*, so I looked up the book up on the internet. I later got the book from the library. The book was dark in many ways, but did not match my Gothic tone in *Damon's House*. Both books with English Estates and young girls during World War II and both contained love affairs and rapes. Atonement does not address the themes of haunting, madness and murder though.

"Atonement" in *Damon's House* was left for another life time. The novel by Ian McEwan explores the idea of guilt and forgiveness in a subtle way, which ties into the other book I read this week, *God is Not Great* by Christopher Hitchens.

McEwan tends to dismiss the notion the Briony could truly ever make up for her mistake. Even when given the chance to set things right (to some degree anyway) she fails to do so. We see she is sorry, but that isn't enough. Atonement is a Christian notion, yet the novel is devoid of any real discussion of religion. You have to interpret the author's attitude toward God—through his tone and through what is not said. There is no neatly tied up ending, no Happily Ever After. Atonement is not a heavenly matter, but rather and earthly one. There is no hope for relief from the burden the Briony bears. In confusion, jealous, anger and perhaps simply immaturity, Briony makes a huge mistake. She is sympathetic in that she doesn't intend to hurt anyone. Her weakness is the secular sin and there doesn't seem to be much faith in forgiveness. No ritual belief in a savior will put together what she tore apart.

God is Not Great is dedicated to the author's friend Ian McEwan. Although Hitchens and McEwan may not see eye to eye on everything, I would guess that they hold similar views. Hitchen's premise is that religion poisons everything. His book argues that great atrocities have been committed in the name of Yahweh, Jehovah, Allah, God and Jesus. To be fair, Hitchens attacks Hinduism, Buddhism and even Secularism. No belief system is safe from his scathing criticism. The book should have been titled *Humans Are Not Great*! It is true that no one religion has been able to improve humanity perfectly. Every single belief system is corruptible and easily perverted. People always find a way to use religion for power and pain. Nothing is truly sacred or safe. Hitchens comes to the conclusion that religion is at fault, which I do not agree with.

While Hitchens has many valid points and examples to back up his theory, his theory is still fatally flawed. His book is one long rant about all that is wrong in the world. His call for a new belief system is a weak call. There is no solid outline for what he feels might work. The book is more of a political attack on religion. It lacks in the areas of psychology, philosophy and theology. He doesn't acknowledge any of the positive aspects for spirituality. Faith and hope make life much better. Life is harsh and full of dark times, but there are good moments of life. Happiness does exist. It isn't an illusion. A sense of something larger often is a part of that happiness. Can you imagine a world without religion? Can you really fathom the repercussions both good and bad?

For better or for worse, Christianity is perhaps the largest and most influential religion on Earth. It is only natural that Christians are resistant to change. *Lord or Legend* by Boyd and Eddy addresses the recent arguments or developments surrounding the person known as Jesus. I admire that Boyd and Eddy take a very academic and rational approach. The book is logical and well organized. At first it felt unbiased, but then it slides toward Christianity. It is definitely in favor of traditional faith. The authors acknowledge that we don't know everything about Jesus. In fact, all we really can prove with any certainty is that the biblical figure was based on a real person. For Boyd and Eddy that fact is enough to keep the faith. They are not willing to alter their beliefs, despite the inconsistencies in the gospels. At the end of the book, I was disappointed that they ignored the Gnostic Gospels and dismissed the archeological evidence for the Jesus family tomb.

What do these books mean? Why read them when no one can agree and nothing proves affective at the end of the day? Why study Jesus if he doesn't offer atonement for our sins? Atonement is about stopping the isolation and reconnecting. Our shame and guilt make us feel alone. It is forgiveness that connects us and makes us feel at-one with the universe. Resurrection, or the belief in it, offers atonement. Believing in Karma, Responsibility, Self-Forgiveness and Righteous Action also offer atonement. Jesus can be an example, not an out.

Beliefnet Guide to Gnosticism

*The Beliefnet Guide to Gnosticism and Other Vanished
Christianities* by Richard Valantasis came out in 2006. In the
preface he discusses the Dead Sea Scrolls and The Nag Hammadi
Library. Gnosticism is intellectual, intense, spiritual, sophisticated
and audacious.

There are a number of types or divisions. Valentianian believed
more in the allegorical. Marcionite rejected the Jewish Old
Testament Texts all together. Montanist was a Radical Feminist
Pentecostal type of Gnosticism. They were associated with The
Oracle of Delphi or were similar to them. The Donastist was similar
to a terrorist wing.

Some of the non-canonical Gospels that were associated with the
Gnostic Christians are The Gospel of Thomas, Gospel of Phillip,
Gospel of John, First and Second Apocalypse of James, Gospel of
Truth, On the Origin of the World, Pista Sophia and The Gospel of
Mary.

Gnosticism embraces the connection between the physical and
spiritual realms. The spirit, not the soul, entered the spirit realm.
The body submitted to the soul and soul to the spirit or the divine
spark. Hylic is the world of matter. The Psyche was the soul.
Pneumatic means the spirit or air. The Gnostics focused on the
Pneumatic or the Spirit. Gnostics believe in the demiurge or the false
God. The idea of Pleroma is the completeness or perfection or

fullness that we can connect to in the universe. Aeons is Age in Greek.

The Trinity is the Holy Spirit, which is the invisible father, the mother who is Barbelo and the son which is Autogenes and Anthropos the self generated or the human one.

Seth was the 3rd son of Adam and Eve. He is considered the savior by some in that the seed of Seth bestowed immortality. Sethians are comparable to New Age seekers.

Sophia created the monster Yaltabaoth and Yaltabaoth created the physical universe, not God. The real God lies within us and needs us to free him from the bonds of the physical universe.

Hermeticists break through the limited knowledge and gain great depth of knowledge through prayer and meditation. They initiate the brotherhood into spiritual community. Hermeticism played a role in alchemy and the occult and eventually in the New Age Movement.

Neo-Platonism is a sort of Philosophical religion. Nous means knowledge—specifically intuitive knowledge. They believe that diversity and unity coherence in the universe.

Can Love Last?

Can Love Last: the Fate of Romance over Time by Stephen A Mitchell came out in 2002. I read it in 2011. This book is all about romance and its degradation. Romance is closer to falling in love than being in love. Why does romance fade?

Romance fades because it is driven by sexuality and sexuality is primitive in its very nature. Romance tends to degrade into dispassionate friendship or purely sexual encounters. Romance fades because it is inspired by idealization and idealization, but its very nature, is illusory. Romance fades because it turns easily into hatred. Romance fades because nothing stays the same.

Mitchell gives us a case study where Brett felt put off by Betty because he was in danger of feeling something deeply in her presence. It wasn't so much that he hated her, but that he hated her for loving him. Because her loved open up possibilities of his developing feelings for her frightened him. Men sometimes have a difficult time integrating desire and love. They suffer from the Madonna/Whore complex or some variation of it.

We had the sexual revolution of the 1960s and that led to the higher divorce rates of the 1970s. Many assume that marriage is safe and dull, but that is an illusion. Husbands aren't so dependable and wives are not so devoted. How knowable and predictable can another person truly be to us?

In human relationships safely and predictability are difficult to come by. We endlessly strive to re-establish that illusion of permanence and predictability. Love, by its very nature, is NOT secure. But we keep wanting to make it so. Love, Jacques Lacan noted, is giving something you don't have to someone you don't know. Safeness is deadness in relationships.

Love dies or the lovers die commented Harold Bloom in reference to *Romeo and Juliet*. Human beings crave both security and adventure. We crave both the familiar and the novel. We have conflicting desires so how do we reconcile these two different longings?

Romance is filled with longing and intense desire for what we do NOT have. A precondition of romantic passion is lack. Yet romantic love entices us with the security is seems to promise. If only the loves or lovers could find each other and live happily ever after they would be safe and happy right? But we never stay the same. We change and love changes.

Sex is about imagination. Imaging what the other person looks, feels and tastes like is part of the fun. There is a sense of self and a sense of other where sex is concerned. Sex and death are the most private experiences and yet the self is connected and related to others. And new relationships are often productions or re-productions of the old ones.

Love, and those in love, seek control, stability and continued certainty. Desire and those who feel desire seek surrender, adventure, novelty and the unknown. In desire we are searching for both missing parts of ourselves. The most we can hope for is that the illusion of infatuation will be transformed into "liking." Romantic obsession, Freud believed, is the inverse of psychosis. Unrequited love, in which our romantic expenditures are met with no return or response, can return to self-loathing and even suicide.

Desire for someone unknown and unobtainable operates against desire for someone known and obtainable, therefore capable of being lost. Passion arrives in the tension between reality and fantasy. It is safer to fantasize about what does NOT have and therefore can't lose!

Desire and dependency are interrelated. In the case study with Jake we see he has a bitter hostility toward women because they had power over him. He felt emotionally abandoned and so he orchestrated his revenge. Passionate hatred derives from humiliation and endearment to the self or the ego.

The value of contrivance of arousal in porn is what makes one dependent on it. The woman can't make you want her or be dependent on her. If tricked into being attached or coerced into a relationship, then it doesn't count. Both the women of porn and the prostitute serve the "what if" fantasy for men.

The capacity to love over time entails the capacity to tolerate and repair hatred. Guilt and self-pity are a zero-sum game. Control and commitment both play a role in romantic love. Love and then hate may not be initially our choice, but our commitment to continue the relationship is. Just saying "I love you" deepens the relationship.

Romance is not about secrets. It is about cultivating an understanding of your partner and an acceptance and tolerance of their fragileness. It is about appreciating how fantasies can become realities and how we can be happy with what we have.

Casilda

Once upon a time, around 1990, I read a book called *Casilda of the Rising Moon* by Elizabeth Borton de Trevino. I found the book at my local library. It was published in 1967. The cover intrigued me and the tale of the frail, but compassionate saint promised to be interesting. By the end of the novel I felt some sort of mystical connection to beautiful Casilda. I do believe either I was her in a past life or, at the very least, I knew her.

Casilda was the daughter of a Moorish king in Spain. Her first recorded miracle was in 1046. During this time the Muslims or Moors were at war with the Christians. Her father, King Alamun, often took Christian prisoners. Casilda, feeling mercy for them, would bring them bread and water. One day Casilda fell ill and asked to be taken to the healing waters at Castile. Though Trevino does not name it so, it seems as if Casilda had cystic fibrosis. After a long and perilous journey, Casilda reaches the healing spring and regains her health. From then on, she begins healing others. She converts from her childhood Muslim religion to Christianity and lived out her days humbly by the springs. It is said she died praying before the cross. It is not known at what age she died. Some legends say she died young and beautiful while others say she died at age 100.

Casilda had a sister named Zoraida. At the time I read the book my Grandmother was working as a home health care aid and was taking care of an elderly woman by the name of Zoraida. I thought it was a wonderful example of synchronicity.

Anyway, Trevino was born in California, but lived in Mexico with her husband. It was while she was living in Mexico that she first heard the name Casilda. Many of the little girls she met were named after the saint. The name was originally Arabic and means "A Love Song." When Trevino traveled to Italy and Spain she began to research the little known saint. Casilda was canonized due to the local legends surrounding her. Her feast day is April 9th. She is the one to pray to for diseases of the chest and falls from a height. Queen Isabel carried Casilda's relics with her and the people of Toledo called Casilda Little Rising Moon. She was said to have visions and perform miracles, but what she was most known for was her compassion.

Christa Wolfe

Christa Wolfe was a German Author born in 1929. She died in December of 2011. She was born in what is now Poland, but lived most of her life in East Germany. She joined the German Socialist Party in 1949, but then left the party in 1989. She wrote about German Reunification in her first novel *Divided Heaven* in 1963.

Back in 1998, I stumbled upon her work when I read *The Quest for Christa T.* I've since read her novels *Cassandra* and *Medea* that center on Greek Mythology. Her books have given me a good introduction to both German Writers and Feminist Writers. They are worth reading in order to broaden one's horizons, but are also immensely enjoyable as well.

Wolfe writes in a modern style with a focus on the subject/object dualism. She writes more realistic novels than philosophical, but that is not to say her works have philosophical underpinnings. The experiences of her characters are definitely gendered, as she specifically writes from a woman's point of view. Wolf feels that there is a sister-ness among women writers. Logos or Logic is a socially redemptive power in books as well.

Poetics and Aesthetic Structure are important in her novels. There are four parts: Form of a Texture, Structure itself, Story and Question. The gaps in narration are there and arrange consciously.

The Quest for Christa T is about coming into one's self. Christa suffers from **Sehnsucht**, which I identified with quickly. For Christa the future is bleak, but there is hope. Facts are merely traces left by events. The only way for the character and the writer to discover herself and to cope with things is to write. There is a hunger for reality in the novel. Christa digs herself out of fantasies and dreams in order to realize who she truly is.

Kassandra is the re-telling of the Battle of Troy. It is told as a war for economic power and a shift from a matriarchal to a patriarchal society. Kassandra's experience during the Trojan War parallels Christa Wolf's personal experience as a citizen of East Germany: during the Cold War, a police state much likes Eumelos' Troy. Wolf, too, was familiar with censorship; in fact, *Kassandra* was censored when it was initially published.

Medea is among the most notorious women in the canon of Greek tragedy: a woman scorned who sacrifices her own children to her jealous rage. In her novel, Christa Wolf explodes this myth, revealing a fiercely independent woman ensnared in a brutal political battle. Interestingly, *Medea* is told from the point of view of Medea herself and attempts to understand why she did what she did. Instead of condemning her, Wolfe approaches her character with a feminist approach and makes Medea a tragic figure rather than a villain.

Common Sense

This week I've read Susan Jacoby's *Freethinkers* and now her latest books, *The American Age of Unreason.* I've also read Thomas Paine's book *The Age of Reason,* to which Jacoby's title refers.

Everyone should read Thomas Paine. He addresses the topics of Religion and Freedom in a clear and no-nonsense manor. His common sense and rational approach are uncommon in this era of unreason. If more people read Paine then perhaps the current climate of Christian Conservatism wouldn't be so strong. Truly, the extreme Christian Fundamentalists have created an anti-intellectual society. Not only are Americans less free, but they are less intellectual as well.

According to Jacoby, the consensus of Christian culture is an exception. Europe and much of the developed world is driven by Human Secularism. That isn't to say that the world isn't less spiritual or less religious than America. It simply means that the separation of church and state is being destroyed here. We have been leaning toward a theocracy since Bush was elected in 2000. Jacoby also addresses the trend of Junk Thought or Junk Science. Popular articles and books often promote ideas that are unscientific, unsound and downright unreasonable. It is akin to a bunch of people creating a flat world movement in the age of the round world.

Sadly, America's refusal to be reasonable not only affects adults, but future generations to come. All of this opinion-based research and its results have created a failing school system. Literacy has dropped. Even with people constantly emailing, texting and talking, we are losing touch with reality. People in America have lost their ability to think and read critically.

In my own experience, the school systems are so far behind, that it is impossible to teach incoming freshman this key piece of their education. They lack the basic grammar and comprehension skills. Until those issues are addressed, they will not and cannot learn critical analysis.

Paine argued that citizens should question tyranny and theology, as theology has long been a tool of tyranny. Morality need not be solely based on one's religion, but on our common needs as human beings.

Dancing In the Flames

Dancing in the Flames: the Dark Goddess in the Transformation of *Consciousness* by Marion Woodman and Elinor Dickson came out in 1996. It asks who is the Goddess? It is Eve, Lillith, Madonna or Mother Mary, The Black Madonna and Mary Magdalene. We have both male and female energies inside us and men need to get in touch with their feminine sides just as much as women do. Women can be strong to. We have the Crocodile Goddess Timet. She is the Goddess of Death and Devourer of Death. We have the fierce and loving Goddess of Kali who is the Hindu Goddess of Creation. Isis is our Black Virgin Goddess. Men split their view of women into Goddesses and Whores. The Salem Witch trials and Witch Hunts of Europe are proof of this.

Myths from all over the world show women embracing the darkness. Baba Yaga is the Witch of Russia. She lives deep in the dark woods and represents the darkness of the world. The Judgment of Maat in Canaanite mythology represents the Individuation of the Ego. In Tibetan Buddhism there is the idea of the Dakini. It is the energy through which our darkness descends into the Underworld. And Dionysus from Greek myths is to be embraced as well. He not only represents darkness, but fertility and ecstasy. Keep in mind Demeter and Persephone as well.

We also have Chaos Theory and Quantum Physics which suggests that darkness is a huge part of our universe.

The Rose in the Fire is important. The Lotus Rose intersects passion with the divine. T.S. Elliot wrote in the 4 Quartets, "Break, blow, burn and make us new." So we must be like the rose and be will to burn to become new.

Feminine consciousness is the transfigurative energy that can contain the energies of matter, and through the fire of love, connect the energies of the soul.

Metaphor is the language of the virgin. Metaphors can open us up and transform our consciousness. The Dark Goddess is our metaphor for pain and the process of healing. Metaphors about the Dark Goddess can act as our guide and release that dark matter into the light.

The flames of passion in which we dance with food, alcohol, sex, drugs and death are flames in which we may dimly discern one another. It is our reality seen through a glass darkly. Words DO matter. They can hurt and they can heal, so use them wisely.

Our Sophia is connected to Synchronicity. She is our intuitive wisdom. Chaos theorist suggest that consciousness has an emergent property in matter. We can emerge from the chaos. It can make us better and stronger in the end.

Woodman leaves us with the image of Munch's Madonna. She is dancing in the flames. She represents both beauty and horror. She is love in the darkness. She is our guide to healing our pain.

The Dark Nights of the Soul

The Dark Nights of the Soul by Thomas Moore came out in 2004. It is based upon the ideas of St John of the Cross who was a Spanish Mystic and Poet. His approach, as Thomas Moore's approach, is more spiritual than psychological. Moore addresses the world of emotions in a minor key, focusing on the darkness in life and how it can help us.

Sometimes it feels like the darkness is never ending, like being on the sea at night. We are being carried somewhere, but we don't know where. Poetic language is well suited for this Night Sea Journey. Walt Whitman, Wallace Stevens and Ralph Waldo Emerson understand this. Many poets have created their best works in their states of emotional darkness.

Our inner guide can have a temper. The Greeks called it our diamon. This untamed spirit has an effect on people. Living with this diamon in our unconscious can be dangerous if we don't understand it. It is like junk food. It is an easy way to go through life, but it doesn't give you the nourishment you need. You need to follow the advice "Know thy self."

In life we go through rites of passage. Among them are: Separation, Liminality, Reincorporation or Death, Threshold and Rebirth. If we live our lives bottled up as if in a jar our soul will rot and putrefy. We need change! We need to go through the process of catharsis and purge or emotions either by crying or throwing up or whatever. Truly cathartic is meditation and tranquility though. Oscar Wilde once said, "The sea washes away the stains and wounds of the world."

Sometimes we are De-worlded. Our world has ended and is forever changed. Emotional floods and fires can purge out the old and allow room for new growth and this is good. What helps with this transition? Writing in journals, going to therapy, talking to friends, learning photography or doing art.

Angels can be dark. We can identify with the beauty and terror in the night. Identifying with the Greek Goddess Persephone or Hekate can be a good thing as well. Hekate's symbols are the key, the whip, the dagger and the torch. These are keys to the underworld. The whip represents being overwhelmed with pain. The dagger gives her the power to discover her own strength. The torch is literally a light in the darkness. These are all things we need to get through our own dark nights—emotionally speaking.

What are the signs that we have descended into our own under-world? Loss of meaning in our lives, disconnection from self and other and a sense of emptiness. There is a difference between depression and an existential emptying of ourselves. Life is full of ironies, so it is important to see them and keep a sense of humor even during dark times. And we shouldn't mistake cynicism for wit. There is a difference. All emotional negativity is not necessarily depression. Some negativity is healthy, but it shouldn't overwhelm the positive. You can learn to be smart and have fun acting stupid at the same time. When you can laugh at yourself, you know that you have succumbed to depression and descended into the underworld.

People can go through tough times when they are stuck in a love triangle. Triangles aren't all bad though. The love triangle forces you out of couple-ism and reminds you that you are an individual. Your identity isn't solely based in the relationship you are in. The third person in the triangle represents the soul. This person is out of reach and this soul figure keeps you in a perpetual state of wonder. You might not want new love, but this person forces you to savor the presence of this wonderfully impossible love. Through the very difficulty this triangle presents you become a person of enlarged understanding.

It is important to see that marriage too is a sort of madness. Marriage is a sacrifice of self. It is a journey like Persephone's journey. If you get it wrong you end up sacrificing your partner and that can cause untold heartache. Know marriage for its all its beauty and pleasure—but know it also has a dark side. Like turning water into wine, marriage is a process of transmuting. When you get married you will have to plan on going through a transformation.

Sex is more like a ritual. It is our own private opus. It is our process of becoming a human being. The search for the right partner can create a deep longing. Sometimes our quest can even bring us to discover the darker side of sex. There can be pain and danger involved, but sex is really not a big deal so long as it is not in excess or extreme.

Artists are thought to be born under the planet Saturn and their creativity is often thought to be at the root of their suffering. Why? Well it could be because they take rejection so personally. Maybe they are dissatisfied without being a star. They live lives of quiet desperation. The assembly line, the many anonymous and low paying jobs, the enormous financial and political power of the elite—these qualities of a stratified society leave the ordinary person frustrated. We long for a feeling or sense of worth. We imagine winning the lottery or something to take us out of our ordinary lives. In any case, to create means to be created.

Anger is a call to action and helps you confront a situation. Anger is a source of strength to help you tap into that inner power. But beware that passivity can be a form of control. Passive-Aggressive-ness can also be trouble as well. A passive-aggressive person will be silent and uninvolved and makes the relationship insincere.

What is insight? It is discovering the madness in an apparently reasonable situation. Practical intelligence about your life is important to have. Intelligence is often a matter of attitude than schooling. Knowing that the soul is healed more by poetic than heroics is important. Surrender to life, but not to pain. Accept what you cannot change and learn to live as simply as possible

Your dark night can help you find your luminance and let your light shine.

Decoding Reality

In *Decoding Reality*, Vlatko Vedral discusses how our reality is based on how we process information. He acknowledges that sociology; economics, biology, thermodynamics, Quantum Physics, computer science and philosophy all play a role. Vlatko Vedral uses the metaphor of the card game for perception—as illustrated by Italo Calvino in *The Castle of Crossed Destinies*. There are basic bits of information revealed to us by the universe even if we don't understand "the rules of the game." The so-called rules must be interpreted by each of the players. Other players may view the rules differently.

Eventually Vedral comes to the debate of Free Will versus Predestination. His take is interesting. At first he appears to side with the absence of free will. He argues that both nature and nurture are ultimately responsible for our choices. Even the decision to go against our normal thoughts, feelings and actions is not free from constraints. Just when all hope appears lost, Quantum Theory offers a third choice.

Under normal circumstance, even randomness is not random. A 50/50 game of chance like flipping a coin is ultimately determined by external influences. If one had time to calculate velocity and all the other factors, one could actually predict the outcome. When we flip a coin, we are merely lacking enough information to predict with any real certainty. True randomness, Vedral argues, only lies in

Quantum Physics.

In Quantum Physics, information comes in packets of Quanta or Qubits. Qubits have no particular path and can appear in two places simultaneously. The observer can change the outcome, but beyond that, the mechanics of the process remains a mystery. Vedral believes that process is unknowable, un-nameable and unobtainable.

The idea that the understanding of our world and the universe is a paradoxical undertaking is elegantly expressed in the Tao Te Ching. Perhaps the *Decoding Reality* should have been called *The Tao of Quantum Physics*. All in all, the book says that perhaps that there is some grand design or plan at work, but we humans aren't able to grasp that process and probably never will be able to.

The book left me pondering if it was not only possible to understand the process of Quantum Physics, but if it was also possible to understand the process of consciousness or the process of life in general. I'd like to think that individuals and society as a whole could eventually evolve enough to comprehend the incomprehensible. Is enlightenment possible by admitting that there are some things we will never know or is there nothing that we *can't* understand eventually?

Disinformation

Disinformation and **Information** are the yin and yang of *The Illuminatus Trilogy*. Apollonian and Dionysian or Eros and Thanatos would also work. Instead of choosing war, death or drunkenness as their focus, they use the obscure Goddess Eris. She is the Goddess of Discord—a consort of war.

I read *The Illuminatus Trilogy* this week because the *Lost* writers (According to Lostpedia Article) claim that Robert Shea and Robert Anton Wilson influenced *Lost* a great deal. I can easily see why.

I have to wonder if the literature of *Lost* came mostly from the books referenced in The Trilogy or if someone noticed that their favorites were a part of this particular work. It is the chicken or the egg dilemma.

Anyway, I noticed these works appeared in *The Illuminatus Trilogy* and *Lost*: *I Ching, The Epic of Gilgamesh* and *Alice in Wonderland*. Also mentioned were: George Orwell, Ambrose Bierce, Ayn Rand and Aldous Huxley. Then there was also Jung. And let's not forget the names Drake and Venzeti. Of course Madam Blatsvksy and theosophy is an undercurrent in both the *Illuminatus Trilogy* and *Lost*. Lovecraft and Joyce are in the Trilogy but thus far not in Lost.

Another parallel between the two was the mention of the Gobi desert. Shea and Wilson claim that the yellow sign holds meaning in the Gobi desert and Charlotte Staples Lewis is in the Gobi desert when we first see her in her flashback. Ben Linus there in his flashforward.

The 23 Synchronicity is also a crossover. The number 23 is on the Hatch. It is also at the center of *The Illuminatus's* many conspiracy theories.

I noticed one of the character's names in *The Illuminatus Trilogy* is Muldoon. Is this the inspiration for Mulder on *The X-Files*? It would surprise me greatly if Chris Carter hadn't read the Trilogy. The scene or the episode where an agent in the Pentagon claims that all UFO conspiracies are "misinformation" deliberately leaked is right out of the Trilogy!

Overall *The Trilogy* was highly intelligent and densely packed with information. It is a labyrinth of language and an intense amount of information to process—especially in the short amount of time I took to consume it. It would have to be read repeatedly to untangle all of the possible threads or leads. Lucky for me, I've read most of it elsewhere. I don't think I would have been able to skim unless I already understood the framework of references already.

The Illuminati Trilogy was written in 1975. Although Eastern Thought and Gnosticism were known then, they weren't as mainstream as they are today in America. Much of the concepts in the book were tainted by the idea of magic as mayhem. There was more darkness and subversiveness surrounding the occult back then. The New Age Movement and the popularity of Wicca have done much to illuminate these alternative world views. Had the Trilogy been written in 1995 or 2005 the tone would have been much lighter and I would have liked it much better.

Combine this info with the 1980s movie *Repo Man* and *Xanadu* and it gets even more interesting. *Repo Man* is all about aliens and synchronicity—obviously influenced by The *Illuminati Trilogy*. *Xanadu* is a reference to Shangri-La (Also Kublai Khan by Coleridge.) Xanadu, as it turns out, is actually home to the Greek Gods. Olivia Newton John portrays a Greek Muse.

Could the island of *Lost* be Delos, the movable island of Apollo? The three toed statue, The Apollo Candy bars and the fact that Ben actually moved the island in combination with everything else points toward Delos. It would have never occurred to me even with all my reading on myths if I hadn't noticed a website on Lost that suggested it first. The website looked like a book with tabs and hadn't been updated in a long time.

My question then is how are Delos and Atlantis/Lemuria connected? How many of the readings are clues and how many are red herrings? What is information and what is disinformation?

Doppelgangers

Jesus, Oprah and Doppelgangers have dominated this week—reading wise anyway. I read Phillip Pullman's new book *The Good Man Jesus and the Scoundrel Christ* and Kitty Kelley's biography of Oprah this week. Pullman deals with the idea of Doppelgangers and so does the TV show *The Vampire Diaries*.

Pullman's book is part of the Canongate Myth Series, which also featured Jeannette Winterson's book *Weight* and Margaret Atwood's book *The Penelopiad*. Although Pullman's narrative is subversive in many ways, it struck me as traditional in many other ways. He retells the story of Jesus from the nativity scene to the resurrection without deviating much from the biblical version at all. The Nativity Scene is questionable according to historians. Pullman doesn't speculate much on the missing years of Jesus, nor does he suggest that Jesus was married or that he survived the resurrection. The only real change that he made was in splitting Jesus into two parts—doppelganger brothers.

Some historians believe that the Thomas buried in the "Jesus Tomb" may have been Jesus' brother. The name Thomas means twin apteral. Others believe that Thomas may have been the son of Jesus.

Anyway, Pullman may or may not believe that Jesus had an actual brother. The presence of the brother is more metaphorical than anything. He means to show that the man Jesus and the Myth of

Christ are two different people. Jesus was a real historical person who was not divine or perfect. The myth of Christ the Savior is what the Christian Church was founded upon and Pullman believes that to be a bad thing. He seems to admire then man Jesus and his message of peace, love and tolerance. It is the corrupt church Pullman despises.

Interestingly, The Myth of Christ is largely the apostle Paul's doing. The Apostle Paul is the one who fashioned the events of gospels to fit his message—his vision of a savior. While Pullman does not point directly to Paul, the character of Christ could easily be Paul. I do not believe that Jesus became Paul, as one author suggested, in a way they are brothers or doppelgangers. Jesus and the Myth of Christ are always mistaken for each other—forever entwined in history as they are inseparable in the bible.

The same could be said of Oprah in a way. The Myth of Oprah is connected to the woman, but the woman and the myth are not the same thing. Oprah is an icon and a sort of new age guru. Many of her critics have made reference to the "Church of Oprah" and the "Cult of Oprah," believing her followers to be brainwashed. Kitty Kelley reveals the cold, aloof, insecure woman with dark secrets behind the strong, confident leader. Indeed, Oprah is influential. Many believe that is was her backing of Obama that resulted in his election as President.

While I admire the good that Oprah has tried to do with her power and her millions of dollars, Mother Teresa she is not. Despite her heart being in the right place, she remains disconnected and ineffectual. Oprah is materialistic even though she stresses spirituality. I admire her desire to improve herself and the world, but I do not subscribe to the Myth of Oprah. She offers me nothing I could not discover for myself. I have read only a hand full of her book club selections—the ones that have spoken to me directly. I watch the show only in passing and have read her magazine only occasionally. While I do enjoy her insights and recommendations, I often balk at the expensive items that she raves over. I don't think she realizes that many of her viewers are too poor to purchase the things she advertises.

The problem with those few who are lucky enough to go from rags to riches is that they quickly forget what is was like to be poor. They are fond of reminiscing about how terrible it was to go without, yet they are unable to connect to the poor once they are rich. If money and fame come in the teenage and young adult years, the comprehension of socio-economic factors contributing to poverty fails. To become rich in the formative years breeds a sense of entitlement. To become rich after the age of 30 is more likely to create a sense of gratitude. To raise a child in poverty is perhaps the most eye-opening experience of all. To really understand the failings of society, one must see the system with the eyes of an adult parent trying to care for their loved ones and not being able to.

Anyway, Vampires strike me as rather Machiavellian. They embrace the hunt and relish their control. I have enjoyed the doppelganger back-story in *The Vampire Diaries*. Although, I still don't quite understand why the Petrova Doppelganger exists or how. A double is needed to break the curse of the Vampire and the Werewolf, but why? What power does the mirror image or twin represent?

Dreaming The Dark

Dreaming The Dark: Magic, Sex and Politics by Starhawk came out in 1982. I didn't read it until the reprint came out in 1997. Starhawk wrote the book when Regan was elected and we were on the brink of war with Russia. She wrote it on an electronic typewriter as a 30yr old graduate in a chaotic marriage. At the reprint Starhawk was writing on a laptop with a new love.

"The torture stories and the rage come from the dark. But if you retell the horror without creating the dark anew, you feed it. You do not break the mold," she says. We need to dream the dark process and dream the dark as change. Because the dark creates us.

When we tell of turning dark, Hecates birth-giving darkness, the shadows listen to that also and what we name feeds into the open imaginations that are listening. So their concept of what is narrowly called death can change.

The dark is what we all are afraid of, all that we don't want to see. Fear, anger, sex, grief and death are all apart the darkness of the unknown. The velvet dark is the skin soft night, the stroke of flesh on flesh the touch of joy and mortality.

The question of the dark has become a journey. How do we face the dark on the edge of annihilation? How do we find the dark within us and transform it as our own power? How do we dream it into a new image? Dream it into action that will change the world into a place where no more horror stories happen? Where there are no more victims?

We face the dark with the power of the unseen. The power that comes from within and the power of the immanent Goddess who lives coiled in the heart of every cell of every living thing, who is the spark of nerve and the life of every living breath.

Science killed off God after God sucked the life out of the world. All that is left are the hierarchical patterns of our institutions like the Church, The government and Corporations. All of them embody authoritarian power, all formed in the image of the patriarchal God with his subordinated troops of angels engaged in perpetual war with the patriarchal devil in his subordinate troops of demons.

The Goddess for women means restoring a sense of authority and power to the female body. It means restoring the life process of birth, growth, lovemaking, aging and death that western society has devalued. Women have been identified with the virgin or the whore for far too long. Language distributes power and language conveys metaphors.

Energy is not separate from things. Death is not absolute and not to be feared. Death and life balance each other out. Sexuality is sacred. It is our connection to ourselves and others. We must create justice from the power-within and no longer be victims.

We must guard ourselves and be guardians of the threshold. We must set limits and boundaries, have a sense of honor and a self esteem. Saying no to drugs and alcohol is a start to respecting ourselves. Our guardians are our deeper selves, a place where healing begins.

Hecate is the Goddess of the Crossroads. Maiden Athena is the Goddess of all things wild. Kore became Persephone and Kore is like Isis, Inana and Astarete. Patriarchal society subverts the Goddess Myth and Power of the Goddess. Men are scared by women's power. Men deny the body's dark demands and avoid feeling vulnerable.

Groups have structure even within the sacred circle. There is the facilitator who keeps the meeting focused and moving, the vibes watcher who watched the process, the priest or priestess who channels energy and has a duel conscious, the mediator who is neutral and resolves conflicts when needed as well as the coordinator who keeps things centered and keeps up with all the info.

You can role play when you are together. There is the lone wolf who gives advice but can't commit. There is the Orphan who wants closeness but pushes people away. There is the filler who takes up space and whose opinion isn't valued. There is the princess who is sensitive and competitive. There is the clown who provides comic relief but can be serious when necessary. There is the perfectionist who is the self hater. There is the rock of Gibraltar who takes on thankless tasks and is afraid to show weakness. Then there is the star, the center of the meeting who likes to impress people. It is important to try to equal out the power in the group and delegate responsibility though.

Mirroring begins with the self. All love beings with the self. The root of disease is power. Politics are deeply rooted in our sexuality. Sexuality is the way we have, as adults, to experience this particular dance deep within the caves of the body. For in sex we merge, give away, become one with another, allow ourselves to be caressed, pleasured and enfolded. We allow our sense of separation to dissolve. But in sex we all feel our impact on one another. We see our faces reflected in another's eyes, feel ourselves confirmed and sense our power as separate human beings to make another feel.

The core of identity is their separateness. Pain and the death of victim of violence is not felt by the aggressor. They are not alive to him. Hierarchy itself is sadomasochistic. We see this again and again in the masks of the roles of guard and prisoner, teacher and student, adult and child and master and servant.

An estranged culture breeds sadists and masochists. Gay and Lesbian liberation is threatening because love or attraction to one's own gender un-validates the idea of sex only as a reproductive function.

To honor sexuality is, ultimately, to stop defining ourselves in terms of our sexual partners, to realize that the richness of sexual attraction and experience lies in hues, its infinite shading and only our cultural estrangement restricts us to the three primary colors.

In a monogamous relationship things go in phases. We fall in love with part of ourselves and then fight for power. When we live with someone we ground the relationship in the mundane everyday things. We struggle to see their true selves and not ideal images of that person. We love what is in us and value both ourselves and them.

In our partners we have the mirror where you like what you see and don't want to change it. We have the double that we imagine as our twin. We have the companion for ourselves. We have the one of loving nature and we have lovers who send and receive energy. Advice from Starhawk: Dance! Dance Naked! Dance Together!

My advice? Read this book if you have an interest in nature, sex, Wicca and/or feminism. It is a great book with lots of insights.

Ego and Archetype

Ego and Archetype: Individuation and the Religious Function of the Psyche by Edward F Edinger came out in 1972. I read it in 2000. It proved very insightful and was very influential on me.

Man's consciousness was created to end that it may 1) Recognize its descent from a higher unity 2) Pay due and careful regard to this source 3) Execute its commands intelligently and responsibility and 4) Thereby afford the psyche as a whole optimum degree of life and development.

The Ego is the seat of subjective identity while the self is the seat of objective identity. There is a wholeness, totality and unity of opposites in the self. The center of the self is the axis of the universe is the world navel where God and Man meet. The fact is the conception of the self is a paradox. It is simultaneously the center and the circumference of the circle of totality. However, with Primitives the inner and outer self are not at all distinguished.

M.L. Von Franz discusses the inflated state of the ego. It is a state of childish irresponsibility and dependence. "With this there is often, to a smaller or greater extent, a savior complex or messiah complex with the secret thought that one day one will be able to save the world or have the last word in Philosophy or Religion or Politics or art or something else. This can go so far as to be a typical pathological megalomania or there may be minor traces that ones time has not yet come. The one thing dreaded throughout by such a type of man is to be bound to anything whatsoever. There is a terrific fear of being pinned down, of entering space and time and completely being the human being that one is."

The whole body of Greek Tragedy depicts the fatal consequences of when man takes the vengeance of God into his own hands. Sometimes the Inflated Ego becomes the Divine Victim saying, "No one in the world is as guilty as me." Solipsism enters into this in that there is nothing beyond the self and the self's experience to the inflated ego.

Ophites worshiped serpents. They believed the serpent to be good. The serpent represented gnosis or knowledge. The temptation that condemned Adam was the urge for self-realization and individualtion. That was the birth of the ego. However, the greater consciousness often equaled suffering. Adam and Eve might have been immortal before the fall, but they were also unconscious. The Tree of Knowledge and the Tree of Life in the Hebrew legends were connected. We could only gain access to the Tree of Life if we tasted the fruit of the Tree of Knowledge.

The person with an inflated ego is afraid to make the commitment required to create something real. He would lose the security of anonymity and expose himself to disapproval. He is afraid to submit himself to the judgment by being something defined. This amounts to living in "the garden of Eden" state and not daring to eat the fruit of consciousness. Christians then equate sin with ego inflation

The Garden of Eden is similar to the myth of Prometheus in Greek Mythology. Prometheus tricks Zeus and becomes a Lucifer type figure that creates suffering in the world. Zeus, like Yahweh, withholds fire and knowledge.

The acquisition of consciousness is a crime, an act of his hubris against the powers that be, but it is a necessary crime, leading to a necessary alienation from the nature unconscious state of wholeness.

The early phase of the developing self-ego axis may be identical with the relationship between the parent and the child. At any time during this development, the axis may be damaged or delayed. Psychotherapy offers such a person to experience acceptance.

Cain is an archetypical figure representing the experience of rejection and alienation. His reactions to an excessive and irrational rejection are characteristic of violence. From an inner standpoint there is very little difference between murder and suicide. The only difference is in which direction the destructive energy is moving.

Modern Existentialism can be considered symptomatic of the collected alienated state. Alienation is not a dead end though. Hopefully it can lead to great awareness of the heights and depths of life. Illegitimate children in particular usually have an alienation problem, what might be called an Ishmael complex. The term comes from Moby Dick.

St John of the Cross called these religious experiences *"The Dark Night of the Human Soul."* Kierkegaard called it despair and Jung called it defeat of the ego. All of these terms apply to the same psychological state of alienation. In any case, we find again and again that in all of these religious experiences there is a profound sense of depression, guilt, sin, unworthiness and complete absence of any sense of transpersonal support for one to rest upon. The classic symbol of this state is wilderness sometimes called The Wilderness of Pain.

In Christianity people go to Purgatory to suffer and purge themselves of their sins. The seven deadly sins are all symptoms of an inflated ego: Pride, Wrath, Envy, Lust, Gluttony, Avarice, and Sloth. Catholic Confession gives the individual a chance to unburden self and whatever made him or her feel alienated from God.

Alienation Neurosis in Psychology leads to an inferiority complex. He assumes unconsciously and automatically that whatever comes of himself—his inner most desires, needs and interests—must be wrong or somehow unacceptable. With this attitude psychic energy is dammed up and most people convert to unconscious or destructive ways. Alcoholism, Panic Attacks, Depression, Suicide Impulses are all symptoms of an inferiority complex.

At a certain point in psychological development, usually after an intense alienation experience, the ego-self axis suddenly breaks into consciousness view. As Jung says, one becomes two.

The Sacrificial Attitude occurs when the transpersonal center of the psyche or the ego recognizes its subordinate position and is prepared to serve the totality and its ends matter rather than personal needs. Job in the bible becomes an individual through his trials. Individuation is a process, not a realized goal. You can recover a sense of wholeness.

In the early stages of Psychological Development God is hidden in the cleverest hiding place of all—in identification of one's self or one's own ego. The Process of Individuation in Gnosticism is best represented by the Myth of Sophia, the Goddess of Wisdom. An in Alchemy, the redemption of God is a basic theme. The Alchemical Opus in and of itself is a work of redemption. For the Modern Man a conscious encounter with an autonomous archetypal psyche is equivalent to the discovery of God.

The ultimate goal of Jungian Psychotherapy is to make the symbolic process conscious. Man needs a symbolic life according to Jung. But Modern Man often has no Symbolic life. Man needs a world of symbols as well as a world of signs. Both signs and symbols are necessary, but they should not be confused with each other. A sign is taken of meaning that stands for a known entity. By this definition, language is systems of signs, not symbols. A symbol, on the other hand, is an image.

Nirvana is not an escape from the reality of life. It is rather the discovery of the symbolic life, which releases man from this, "awful, grinding, banal life" which is only succession of meaningless symptoms. Dreams are the expression of the ego-self axis and can help us make these symbols come to light.

To call no man father means to withdrawal all projections of the father archetype and discover it within yourself. To take up one's own cross would mean to accept and consciously realize one's own particular pattern of wholeness. The image of Christ gives us a vivid picture of the self-oriented ego, i.e. individuated ego which is conscious of being directed by the self. The temptation of Christ represents vividly the dangers of encounters with the self.

Christ is both man and God. As man he goes to the cross with anguish, but willingly as part of his destiny. As God he willingly sacrifices himself for the benefit of mankind. Psychologically this means that the ego and the self are simultaneously crucified.

To be aware of individuality is to realize that one has all needs. If you see other people as fragmentations of yourself or your fragmented self in other people means multiplicity and not individuality.

The Holy Ghost is a union of opposites. Father is the self and the son is the ego and the Holy Trinity is the ego-self axis as a whole. It is like Hegel's idea of thesis, antithesis and synthesis. Or in Alchemy Mercury, Sulphur and Salt. Or Mind, Body and Spirit. The Trinity Archetype seems to symbolize the Individuation process, while the Quaternity symbolizes its goal or complete state. Since Individuation is never truly complete each temporary state of completeness or wholeness must be submitted once again to the dialectic of the trinity in order for life to go on.

Embracing The Darkness

Embracing the darkness, The Dark Goddess can be a transformative experience. Always focusing on the bright-side can be a damaging experience apparently. Since it has been cold and snowy, I've stayed inside. Not to mention that it gets dark so early. I've stopped taking the kids to the park after Ana gets home from school. To keep myself busy, I've read mostly. After finishing *The Pregnant Virgin*, I moved onto *Dancing in the Flames: The Dark Goddess in the Transformation of Consciousness*. I followed those up with *Nurture-Shock* and *Bright-Sided*.

There have been many books recently criticizing the self-help genre. Most of those books are biased. Barbara Ehnreich's book is refreshingly balanced. Although skeptical of much, she doesn't appear to have a particular agenda. Ehenreich gets out there and investigates and interviews and researches. She doesn't just complain. She attacks one specific problem and focuses on it. The underlying issue seems to be summed up by Zig Ziggler, *"It is your own fault. Don't blame the system. Don't blame the boss. Work harder and pray more!"* But what happens when it isn't your fault? Where is the call to right social injustice? Blaming yourself for all of life's misfortunes can have a very depressing and damaging effect.

I think of my own struggle with poverty. A typical guru might say I wasn't focusing hard enough, visualizing long enough or deserving it enough. The lack of cash flow is simply of not attracting it or feeling worthy of it. As much value as I place on personal power, some things are beyond our conscious control. There are socio-economic factors at work that can be difficult to overcome. That is to say, eventually we will be better off, but not because of magical thinking. A positive attitude will keep us working hard to achieve a better life, but it won't create a better life all by itself.

Ehenreich talks about her own battle with cancer. She found the efforts of everyone around her to remain cheery in the face of illness, and possibly death, a bit disturbing. The focus on the bright-side of cancer made it difficult to deal with the all-too natural feelings of frustration, anger and fear. There is a place for love and support, but it isn't always a realistic approach. Ehenreich wondered if the correlation between healthiness and happiness was one of causation or not. Are people healthy because they are happy or happy because they are healthy? There are not real conclusive studies on mind-over-matter, or what some people call magical thinking.

I am not sure one can reverse a terminal illness or manifest themselves new material possessions. I do believe we can find meaning in our obstacles, misfortunes, setbacks and even tragedies. Our power comes not from controlling the events in our lives, but in learning to understand and deal with those events critically. Ehenreich ends her book by stressing her belief that critical thinking is more important than positive thinking, and Marion Woodman concurs.

Dancing in the Flames discusses or deals with the difficulty that women deal with. Instead of sweeping abandonment, addiction, abuse and depression under the rug, Woodman sees those issues as part of a process. These dark days can be transformative. Instead of ignoring our problems or thinking that they will magically get better, Woodman calls women to work with their dreams and discover their true desires. Embrace the archetypes of Eve, Lilith, Mary, The Black Madonna and Mary Magdalene. What lessons can be learned? What insights gained? Language, symbols, dreams and poetry can be tools to open up the subconscious and allow us to be healed. Only by working through our feelings can we be free of them!

In *The Pregnant Virgin,* Woodman talks about Abandonment being a form of being "uncalled' or not chosen by the father and the mother. She views this as a chance for the woman to create her own destiny. Free of her parent's influence, she can give birth unto herself. That symbol is the symbol of The Pregnant Virgin. Pristinely Ungifted, to use Terry Goodkind's words. A woman must learn to be whole, independent and creative within herself. As a Virgin, she is unaware of her incompleteness. To be sexually active is often to feel dependent upon the other person.

First I read *Emotions Revealed* by Paul Ekman and finally, *Delete: the Virtue of Forgetting in the Digital Age.*

Paul Ekman is an expert on lying. He is the inspiration for the show **Lie To Me** on Fox. He is a psychologist whose focus has been on body language and facial expressions. The study of lying is a natural extension of this since our bodies usually betray us. No matter how convincing our words are, there is always some trace of discomfort in our demeanor. Ekman says you need 3 things to lie. 1) To be able to strategically plan your moves ahead of time. 2) To be able to read the needs of other people and put yourself in their shoes and 3) to manage your emotions like a grown up person. While lying is NOT ethical, it is a sign of intelligence. Social manipulation reflects success.

I have never been a good liar. Why? Well, I think I have always had an intuitive sense of other people's feelings. I read body language before I understood it. Because I didn't understand it, I often disregarded it though. I felt like I shouldn't confront people if I had no solid evidence of their deception. I wanted to believe them. Thinking strategically didn't seem to come naturally to me. Learning how to play chess and effectively analyze social situations took practice.

Unnecessary chaos can come from revealing everything all the time.

I reserve a right to privacy and some issues and so long as that issue doesn't directly affect the person, it is okay. It is a slippery slope into the lies of omission though. Make no mistake, keeping pertinent information from someone is a lie. The question becomes how relevant is the information. If it is relevant then it is unethical NOT to speak up!

The last book, *Delete,* is about memory. Before the digital age, it was much easier to forget about the past. It was easy to loose touch with a friend or lover. Before email and social networking, we could let arguments slip into oblivion. We could rewrite our memories. Victor Mayer Schonberger argues that we need to forget in order to learn, "If human actions are never forgotten, there is little need for people to push themselves to change," he says. I am not sure that I agree, but I do believe he has a point about not being able to see the forest for the trees. If we recall all the tiniest details of our daily lives, it is easy to get distracted and not see the big picture. His quote of Borges is probably more precise. "To think," Borges states, "is to ignore the differences, to generalize, to abstract." Perhaps it is better to think than strictly recall. Our constant change is important to change. Facts matter, but not so much as our interpretation of them. Delete is a plea both for internet privacy and for the luxury of creating our own truths.

Erotica

As a teenager I read romance books. Johanna Lindsey and Connie Mason were some of my favorites. For a long time my idea of sex was wrapped up in the fantasy world of romance authors. A couple of times I got to sneak a peak at forbidden books, including *Lady Chatterly's Lover* by D.H. Lawrence and *Tropic of Capricorn* by Henry Miller. The sex scenes I wrote during this time reflected my lack of experience and romance novel influence.

It wasn't until college that I discovered Anne Rice's *Beauty* series as well as her books *Exit To Eden* and *Belinda*. I devoured the world of S&M, intreagued by the blending of pain and pleasure. Eventually I came upon *The Story of O* and *Justine*. It wasn't long until I noticed Anais Nin's *Delta of Venus* on the shelves at Barnes and Noble. This led me to read all of Nin's works, including all the volumes of her diary.

One of my favorite books was a collection of erotic stories called *Yellow Silk*. I also stumbled upon Blue Moon Publishers, who strictly publishes erotica. I got a chance to read some of their reprints of some old French Erotic Novellas. And, out of curiosity, I picked up letters to Penthouse as well. Being open minded, I was not shocked by anything I read. I found the variety of human sexual experience to be beautiful and fascinating.

Having deiced to write my own erotica, I found myself wrestling with a particular problem: vocabulary. It seemed the romance genre was prone to flowery language including words like manhood and womanhood. More serious and hard core erotica used pornographic words like cock and pussy. I felt there had to be an alternative or a happy medium. Was there something less clinical than penis and vagina, less flowery than shaft and womanhood but less dirty than cock and pussy? I researched and found a book dedicated exclusively to all the infinite words and phrases used to describe sex.

Though there were some creative phrases in the book, I was still at a loss. Interestingly, as erotica became more mainstream, more and more women began embracing the pornographic language. Sylvia Day and her contemporaries come to mind. Even romance authors have began to give up the flowery language in favor of more realistic and contemporary love scenes.

Then E.L James came along and made S&M hugely popular. I read *50 Shades of Gray* and wondered what the fuss was. 1) It was poorly written and 2) the sex scenes were mild compared to other things I'd read. Needless to say, I was not impressed. However, I did embrace the nonfiction book *Diary of Submissive* that came out around the same time. Sophie Morgan's honest and insightful book about stumbling into the role of submissive was educational as well as titillating.

While Erotica is predominately found in literature, over the years erotica has found its way to the silver screen. Stag films have been around since the film industry began and porn flourished in the 60s and 70s. But it has only been recently that women have begun turning a male-dominated industry into their own. Some of my favorite erotic films are *Wild Orchid, Wild Orchid 2 Shades of Blue, The Red Shoe Diaries, 9 1/2 Weeks, Two Moon Junction, Bitter Moon* and *Secretary.*

Buddhism Faith and Reason

I caught most of the 7th part of the Bill Moyers series *On Faith and Reason.* Pema Chodron was on. She is a Buddhist Nun who grew up Catholic. When her husband divorced her she turned to Buddhism. For 20 years or more she has been a teacher. They call her a Bodhisattva Warrior.

She says that Reason is an open mind and Faith is an open heart. Chodron explained the idea of suffering and how it is different from pain. We cannot eliminate pain, but we can end our own suffering. She spoke of Shempa or getting hooked on our anger and need for control. One of the things that really resonated with her was the idea that nothing was wrong with our negativity. It was all a part of our human experience. The key was to take responsibility for your suffering and change your perceptions. She discussed the idea of groundlessness. Feeling out of control, like the ground has fallen away is frightening, but this often unpleasant feeling leads to the most profound experiences and awakenings.

At the end Moyers asked about God and Faith. Chodron explained how God is more of an open question to her rather than a fixed notion. There is no proof one way or the other. Instead, of a fear based or security deity, she sees a sense of wonder and mystery. Perhaps the best quote from her Master Rinoche was, "All of you are perfect, but you could use a little improvement."

As the program ended I wondered how I'd reconcile Faith and Reason. Moyers had interviewed a variety of people with a variety of perspectives on a variety of topics. From Philosophy to Theocracy and Christianity to Science and Myth to Islamic Fundamentalism Movement—he covered it all pretty much. Ending with Buddhism was an interesting choice. I think that perhaps Moyers sees Buddhism as the answer. Or at least Buddhism allows for us to hold two conflicting beliefs. The paradox of Faith and Reason is something that a Buddhist is able to do without feeling torn. It isn't such a controversy to the Eastern mind.

In keeping with paradoxical statements I came up with a couple of my own. *"Be reasonable about Faith."* And, *"Have faith in your power to Reason."*

In the end, both are vital. You must learn to think critically about religion and philosophy. Never accept something blindly, especially if it doesn't feel right to you. Questions are an important tool for spiritual growth. However, after you've exhausted all avenues of exploration, sometimes there is nothing left to do but believe. Some truths can only be known intuitively. And that's fine. I can't imagine a world without wonder. If we were given proof or disproof of everything then we would cease to grow and learn. I think that if we work hard in life then we are rewarded with answers in the afterlife. The only pay off for faith in this life is spiritual growth. Well, not the only one, but a big one. Once you surrender your fears and have faith then you reach a place of relative peace inside.

Faith is necessary in order to obtain harmony. Reason is necessary to maintain balance. It goes back to what I said about human beings, about what makes us superior. It is not our intellect alone that makes us superior. It is our ability to understand our emotions that makes us superior. Reason is intellect and faith is very much tied to our emotions. We do not think faith, we feel it. Our emotions are connected to the spiritual realm and so is our faith. Still, we have a need to understand exactly what we have faith in and why

Finding Oz

Finding Oz: How L Frank Baum Discovered the Great American Story by Evan J Schwartz came out in 2009. A groundbreaking new look at a cultural icon—THE WIZARD OF OZ.

Schwartz reveals how Baum's early interest in theatre, tall tales, and entertaining an audience led the restless young man through a string of doomed careers, including actor, playwright, castor oil salesman, and shop owner (trading in knickknacks and toys). In spite of pressure to support his family including his mother-in-law was the radical women's rights activist Matilda Gage. Baum maintained a passion for fantasy and sought pleasure in every venture he undertook, often by way of his talent for yarn-spinning. Falling on hard times again and again, Baum had little to keep him going besides love for his growing family and for storytelling;

For example, Dorothy was inspired by Baum's niece Dorothy Louise Gage who died at 5mos old. The Yellow Brick Road was inspired by the Yellow Bricks in the Dutch city of Peekskill, New York where he was sent away to military school. The Wizard of Oz was inspired by the great Oil Tycoon Rockefeller.
The O in Oz is a sacred symbol and the symbol of Z is all about how life and Zigzag. Baum failed at a great many endeavors before becoming a successful writer. Theosophy enters Oz via his mother-in-law Matilda. *Isis Unveiled* was influential in his world view.

The silver shoes like the silver cord that connects us to the astral plane.

Baum moved to Aberdeen in the Dakotas during the Westward expansion of America. It was full of tornadoes and was bleak, not unlike Kansas. The Winkie's color was Yellow and that represented the American West in Baum's mind. Were the Winkies to be patterned after Native Americans?

Unfortunately, Baum wrote an editorial in the newspaper condemning Native Americans. He thought they possessed false bravery like the cowardly lion. Baum's mother in law Matilda was outraged by her son in laws prejudice and inhumane view of the Native Americans.

Baum created a store called Baum's Bazaar that sold China Dolls and other knick knacks from around the world. P.T. Barnum was also a partial inspiration for The Wizard of Oz because he once said, "There's a sucker born every minute." Baum thought of P.T. Barnum as creating hoaxes or being a humbug.

Baum and family moved to Chicago after his store failed. The gleaming city was his inspiration for The Emerald City. He was amazed by the World's Fair there. For awhile he sold China in Chicago before writing his famous book.

Münchner Kindl was the inspiration for the Munchkins in L. Frank Baum's *The Wonderful Wizard of Oz*. Münchner Kindl means

"Munich child" in the Bavarian dialect of German and is the name of the symbol on the coat of arms of the city Munich.

To find out these things and many more, I recommend the book *Finding Oz*.

For Peace and Justice: Pacifism in America, 1914-1941 By Charles Chatfield, 1971

Historic Peace Churches are the Quakers and the Mennonites. The duty of the nonresistance was sharply defined. The bible records that Jesus forbade revenge or resistance—that he commanded that evil should NOT be returned. The sword should be put up. Jesus taught his disciples to love and pray for their enemies. If the promise of the New Testaments is to be taken seriously, then our duty seems plain. One must not submit to or participate in the violence of this world.

Two famous peace loving Quakers were Robert Barclay and William Penn. Anthony Benezet opposed both war and slavery.

The Principle of total peace and no war has been debated by the Principal of Security and support for the nation and the human lives involved in war.

Kirby Page said, "War is not an ideal. It has an ideal. War is not a spirit. It is waged in a certain spirit. War is always a method and it is a method that must be discussed."

Friend Service Committee provided war relief. The delivered food with a card on it saying something like, "To the Children of Germany: A greeting of friendship from America from the Quakers who have, for 250 years, maintained their service and love and did not give into war or hatred."

Many people who refused to fight in WWI were treated badly—especially if it wasn't for religious reasons. Those who refused to fight were made to work for their community and had to pay the Red Cross. However, they were often looked down upon and bad mouthed—especially in Ohio and Iowa.

"Peace is within reach for the first time in history. Instantaneous communication between the responsible heads of government and simultaneous disruption of information to the peoples of all nations are now possible. International Relations can be watched and guided from day to day. Machines exist for the peaceful settlement of disputes. There is ready at hand an organized peace movement, capable and connected." ~Florence Breua Boekel.

The Peace Year Book listed 109 international organizations, including the professional societies, but not including groups promoting relief and friendship between only two nations. Most had their headquarters in Switzerland. Many were staffed in England, Belgium, Austria and the US.

A commission of coordination of efforts for peace listed 12 international, 28 international, 37 local peace societies listed in the US. In addition, it found 2 international, 56 national and 51 local groups which were not primarily peace societies, but that promoted internationalism through special committees—mainly churches though. Another 120 bodies were organized for purposes somehow related to peace advocacy, however, the general discontinuity in the ranks of the peace forces induced weakness and ineffectiveness.

The Fight for Peace by H Allen.

Lynn J Frazer, the Senator of North Dakota, wrote: War for any purpose she all be illegal and neither the US or any state territory, association, or person subject to its jurisdiction shall prepare for or declare or engage in war or any other armed conflict, expedition, invasion or undertaking with or without the US. Nor shall any funds be raised, appropriated or expended for such a purpose. Section 2: All provisions of the constitution and of the articles in addendum thereof which are in conflict with this are hereby rendered null and void. Section 3: The congress shall have the power to enact appropriate legislation to give effect to this article.

An early Fellowship of Reconciliation Pamphlet cited the example of "A woman is one in a group who is taking needy girls into her home as servants, giving them education and training."

Allen's book Declaration of Principles. "It its struggle for a new society, the social party seeks to attain its objections by peaceful and orderly means. Reconsidering the increasing resort by a crumbling capitalist order to fascism to preserve its integrity and dominance, the Social Party intends not to be deceived by fascist propaganda nor overwhelmed by fascist force...."

In *Gandhi and the Search for Social Truth*, Richard Gregg picked out 4 mechanisms of nonviolent action. "Courageous nonviolence— to try to prevent or stop a wrong is better than cowardly acquiescence. The inner attitude is more important than the outer act, though it is vitally more important to make one's outer conduct a true reflection and expression of one's state. Fear develops out of an assumption of relative weakness, since all men have the innate possibility of moral strength, to be afraid is really denial of one's moral potential powers and therefore is harmful as violence and anger. At least show faith in one's moral powers. Thus is provides at least a basis for further growth. If one has not special courage or discipline or conviction to resist the wrong of violence without counter violence, then I agree with Gandhi that it is better to be violent than cowardly. But he who has the courage to fight and yet refrains is the true nonviolent resister."

"What government seems to doing is to precede along the lines the lines that are almost ? to make peace possible, and then put their people in holes later when trouble does break out, of trying to reverse the process at the time when it is least possible to do so?" ~D. Allen, 1937

Emergency Peace Campaign 1936-1937. That was the greatest unified effort until Vietnam.

Student Strike 1936. Wayne University pledged 1,000 students for the strike. The largest strike was at Broker in Borough Hall with 5,500 students. The most spectacular strike, according to the New York Times took place at Columbia University. It began with 200 members and 20 musicians and ended up with 3,000 students. There is a 52 page illustrated handbook describing the goals of the crusade and ways of bringing legislature for their realization. On the cover was printed STOP THIS FROM HAPPENING AGAIN! PROTECT YOUR DOLLARS AND SAVE YOUR SONS! KEEP THE US OUT OF WAR AND WORK FOR WORLD PEACE.

During the Peace Movements from 1914 to 1941 the distinguishment between violence and nonviolence as well as between coercion and persuasion was made.

Pacifists resorted to direct action, supporting the strikes and initiating sit-ins, believing modern war was unwarranted and they refused to participate in it. However, they had no one formula for peace and no single tactic for effectively achieving it.

Forbidden Faith

Forbidden Faith: the Gnostic Legacy from the Gospels to the Da Vinci Code by Richard Smoley came out in 2006. The success of books such as Elaine Pagels's *Gnostic Gospels* and Dan Brown's *Da Vinci Code* proves beyond a doubt that there is a tremendous thirst today for finding the hidden truths of Christianity – truths that may have been lost or buried by institutional religion over the last two millennia.

In *Forbidden Faith*, Richard Smoley narrates a popular history of one such truth, the ancient esoteric religion of Gnosticism, which flourished between the first and fourth centuries A.D., but whose legacy remains even today, having survived secretly throughout the ages.

Gnosis, from which the term Gnosticism is taken, means knowledge. It is the equivalent of Enlightenment in Buddhism. Katholikos is the Greek word for Universal. Esoteric is Greek for Further In. Urizen, the Blake poem refers to the Limit or the Horizon.

Gnosticism has influenced many great writers including: Hegel, Blake, Goethe, Schelling, Emerson, Melville, Byron, Shelly, Yeats, Hesse, Heidegger, Conrad, Wallace Stevens, Doris Lessing, Isaac Bashevis Singer, Walker Percy, Jack Kerouac, Thomas Pynchon and Phillip K Dick.

The ancient religions of Manichaeism and Zoroastrianism are really the beginning of the Gnostic ideas. They teach that there is a spark of light or divinity in all of us. The Elohim was a demiurge deity—an angel who created the world. Smoley begins with Gnosticism pre-Christian origins and runs through modern times, including the popular perceived offshoots such as the Albigensian Cathars, the Rosicrucians, the Freemasons, and the Knights Templar all the way to Jung, Blavatsky, the DiVinci Code and *The Matrix*.

Smoley says that the Mormons and the Southern Baptists are closer to Gnosticism than Early Christians. American religion tends to uphold the ideas of freedom, self-reliance and isolation more than European counterparts.

Throughout, Smoley makes the point that the appeal of Gnosticism, whatever its form, stems from a lack of vitality in Christianity, which in turn derives from the fact that "crucial material about the earliest era of Christianity seems to be missing." Smoley reinforces that Gnosticism is, and always has been, here to stay. He paves a wide, clear path to understanding it, accessible even to the weekend seeker. Although Smoley writes in a popular style, he never lacks for scholarship.

Fredrich Hebbel and Romantic Degradation

Christian Friedrich Hebbel (18 March 1813 – 13 December 1863), was a German poet and dramatist. He was born into poverty. His father, who died was he was fourteen, was a stone mason. Friedrich worked as a mason's helper and then worked for the church. His common law wife was Elise Lensing, who was nine years older than him. Although he showed a talent for poetry early on, he went to school to study law. Soon he quit school to write plays. Hebbel's principal tragedies are: *Herodes and Mariamne* (1850) *Julia* (1851) *Michel Angelo* (1851) *Agnès Bernauer* (1855) *Gyges and His Ring* (1856) *Die Nibelungen* (1862).

I stumbled across this wonderful playwright when I was researching the term **Romantic Degradation.** Although I'd read it in Joan Didion's essay "*Slouching Toward Bethlehem,*" I wondered if it had been used anywhere else. As it turns out someone wrote about how Hebbel's plays often demonstrated the use of **Romantic Degradation.** So, I took out a book of his plays from the library to read. Interestingly, his plays connected to another book I had just recently read—*The English Patient* by Michael Ondaatje.

In *The English Patient* Katherine tells story of *Gyges and his Ring* to entertain the group of explorers who'd come together in the Sahara. It comes to be the subtext of Katherine and The English Patient's relationship and their **Romantic Degradation.** Like Gyges, The

English Patient is coveting something that is not his and their affair has severe consequences just like in the tale *Gyges and his Ring*.

Judith, the first play in the book, is based on the biblical story and *Gyges and his Ring* is taken from *Herodotus*. Despite his various classical sources, Hebbel is very modern and placing the conflict between the sexes in his work. He sees things in terms of duality and believes duality to be our highest conception of our existence. He sees duality in nature as well as in humans. His characters share guilt, but not for their wrong-doings. They feel guilty because they are individuals who need to individuate as Jung would say. Hebbel's realism is very much a psychological realism. And he has a great understanding of female psychology, as demonstrated by his strong female characters.

Hebbel had a very intense inner life and that made Hebbel a dominating force of nature. He once said, "What you call my illness is yet the source if my higher life." It is the inner sense of isolation that is the true tragedy in his view. In his letters he says that his experience is a universal one and that he couldn't be cured of it unless the world was cured. His view on life was reflected very much in his tragic-comedy dramas. Tragedy, he felt was an expression of optimism and Comedy was an expression of pessimism.

In the introduction *to Maria Magdalena* it is stated, "For Hebbel, the function of drama is to demonstrate the state of man and the world in relation to the idea—that moral center which rules over and protects all things, both nature and human. This is the idea also central to his theory of tragedy. This is the idea degrees that the order of things must be maintained at any cost. Individuals must often sacrifice themselves for the greater good and this is tragic."

Aside from Goethe, there has been no other German Playwright who was held more depth or was more influential than Hebbel. He is definitely worth picking up.

Going Home: Jesus and Buddha as Brothers

Going Home: Jesus and Buddha as Brothers by Thich Nhat Hanh came out in 1999. It is a very simple teaching "This is like because that is like that." Because the waves are, this wave is like this. Touching yourself, you touch the whole. Touching yourself deeply and touching others deeply you touch the other dimension of reality. A wave is made of other waves after all. It is also made of water.

Dharmalakshana School teaches phenomenon as aspects of reality. Madhyamaka School teaches emptiness. We know that the person is made of non-person elements and vice versa. The non-self is known as Anatta. In Christianity they talk of the true self, while in Buddhism they talk of the no-self.

Emptiness means the emptiness of a separate existence, the emptiness of a permanent entity, emptiness of all concepts. The teaching of emptiness helps you to transcend the notion of birth, death and the notion of coming and going—the notion of being and non-being.

Mindfulness is to be aware of everything you do everyday. Mindfulness is a kind of light that shines upon all your thoughts, all your feelings and all your words. Mindfulness is the Buddha. Mindfulness is the equivalent of the Holy Spirit or the Energy of God.

When you are mindful, you realize that the other person suffers. You see him or her suffering and suddenly you don't want him or her to suffer any more. When you begin to see the suffering in the other person, compassion is born and you no longer consider that person your enemy. You can love your enemy. When we hate someone, we are angry at him or her because we do not understand him or her or their environment. Understanding is the foundation of loving.

Faith has to do with understanding and knowing. Faith is a living thing. It has to grow. The food that helps it to grow is the continued discoveries, the deeper understanding of reality. Faith is nourished by understanding. As you understand better, you faith grows.

Love is a kind of energy. Love can also be described as faith because faith is a source of energy that can sustain us and give us strength.

In the process of love, you learn a lot. You love better, you make fewer mistakes. You are more capable of being happy and making other people happy. That develops your faith in your ability to love. And faith here is not being caught in any idea or thought or dogma. True faith comes from how the path you are taking can bring you to life and love and happiness every single day.

People who don't believe in anything are those who suffer the most. When you don't believe in anything, you become a sort of wandering soul. You don't know where to go or what to do. You don't see any meaning in being alive. Because of that you may try to destroy yourself physically and mentally.

Hungry Ghosts are described as beings whose belly is as big as a drum but whose throats are as tiny as needles. So their capacity to receive food is limited. Even if people have an understanding of love and love to offer, sometimes they are still suspicious and feel they cannot receive it.

We forget that in us there other kinds of energy that can manifest besides hate, anger and despair. If we know how to practice we bring back the energy of insight, of love and of hope in order to embrace the energy of fear, of despair and anger.

Non-duality is the main characteristic of Buddhist Practice. You can embrace your suffering and your negative energies in a very tender way. For the Buddhist knows that everything is changing. There is a saying, "No one can ever step in the same river twice." Rebirth happens to us daily. Rebirth is merely a continuation.

The nature of Enlightenment is the very base of your being and of your practice. If you have, there is not reason for you to get lost. The Bodhicitta is the deepest desire in all of us, the desire to become awakened, to liberate ourselves from suffering and help other living beings. Because you can touch the Buddha in you, you can produce the mind of enlightenment. Once you are filled with the energy of Bodhicitta, you become a Bodhisattva right away.

Love cannot exist without suffering. In fact, suffering is the ground on which love is born. Love is born from suffering Jesus teaches us. True love needs patience. A tree without roots cannot survive as a person without roots cannot survive either. It takes time to put down roots and let love grow.

Jesus is our brother. Love your teacher. Love your students. We need our teacher and we need our students. And with his presence around us, we feel happy. This love is quite tangible, touchable and conceivable. You can feel the love of God full time. You touch one wave, you touch them all. They are all interconnected.

Two people of different religions should marry and be open to other religions. It is important to be tolerant. You can love apples and mangos. You can love French and Chinese cooking.

Gothic: 400 Years of Excess, Horror, Evil and Ruin
By Richard Davenport-Hines, 1998

Davenport-Hines begins with the Goths in Eastern Europe in 410AD when they sacked Rome. In the 1300s, the word Goth came to denote the architecture of that flourished in France, Germany and eventually England. The buildings had sharp angles, jetties, narrow lights, large statues, lace and other cut work, thick walls, clumsy buttresses, towers, sharp pointed arches and doors as well as turrets. The revival of this architecture in later years was an expression of counter-enlightenment.

"Images of power have always been paramount to the meanings of gothic revival, symbolism: the power of nature forces over men, man's power our nature, then power of the autocrat, the mob, the scientist for much of the 20th century, the power of Goblins to torment one's psyche, and in the 1990s the invasive power of health police, religious fundamentalists and child care vigilantes." (2)

Beginning with the savage paintings of Salvatore Rosa, Richard Davenport-Hines then traces the evolution of the gothic imagination. This history covers art, architecture, gardening, literature, photography, filmmaking, music, and clothing design, and takes in artists and creations as various as Byron, Horace Walpole, Goya, Frankenstein, Edgar Allan Poe, Jackson Pollock, David Lynch, The Terminator, and The Cure. It seems as if the darkness has always fascinated us. It isn't just a recent phenomenon.

113

Davenport-Hines launches into a discussion about the symbolism of castles. Landowners wanted to take pride in their heritage instead of tearing down their ancient falling down homes. Arbury Hall, Halgey Hall, Henell Grange and Halsowen Grange were particularly famous fixer-uppers during the 1700s. He goes into great detail about the Duke of Argyll Archibald Campbell, who was the inspiration for Horace Walpole's anti-hero.

The Marquis De Dade and Mathew Lewis were the next to take up gothic tones and themes in their writing. Anne Radcliff, Jane Austen, Lord Byron, Mary Shelly and Emily Bronte soon followed. And although Bram Stoker's Dracula is perhaps the most famous Vampire, James Malcolm Rymer, John Pagets, Sheridan La Fanu and Lord Byron all wrote about Vampires as well.

Gothic Literature started in England, moved to Germany and then back to England over the course of time. Eventually America caught the Gothic fever and came up with their own version of the genre. Charles Brockden Brown was perhaps the first, followed by Hawthorne, Poe, James and Faulkner who all wrote stories that could be considered Gothic. The Gothic genre was quickly picked up by the burgeoning film industry and soon Ghosts, Witches, Vampires and Monster were given a new life on the silver screen during the early 1900s.

Though Gothic Literature never completely died, it saw a slow resurgence throughout the 1960s and 1970s. Anne Rice wrote *Interview with a Vampire* and the New Goths emerged from Punk music. *Souxsie and the Banshees, Bauhaus* and *The Cure* ushered in a music genre.David Lynch and Tim Burton took the film version of Gothicism a new level. Then, by the 1990s, being Goth became a fashion statement and subculture all its own.

He explains that, "Body mutilation of the 1990s registers dissent from god's arrangement for humankind; it expresses our self-disgust and death wish. It recognizes that demoralization is one of the most effective modes of seduction. It declares that adult acts of self-reinvention are ultimate acts of freedom, certainly as enriching and liberating as searching for an inner self through anxious introspections, or seeking a heavily mediated identity based on childish experience and childish perception." (5)

Davenport-Hines covers his history pretty thoroughly; however, there isn't much on the modern Goth. Even still, I would recommend this history to anyone who wants to know more about today's trends and where they came from.

Gothic Tales

"Deep into that darkness peering long, I stood there, wondering, fearing, doubting, dreaming dreams that no mortal ever dared to dream before," wrote Edgar Allan Poe in his famous poem **"The Raven."** I thought that particular quote apt as it encompasses themes from the novel *The White Forest* as well as from the movie The Raven.

The White Forest came out in 2012. It is a Gothic tale set in Victorian England. The main character, Jane Silverlake, has an unusual gift. She can hear the soul of man made objects. Later she comes to realize that she is not of this earth. She is the Red Goddess. She is a bridge to the Empyrean or the great Aether. The Aether represents the opposite of creation. It is the unmade. It is silence. And so there is a tension between Nature and Technology as well as light and dark in the novel. McOmber even mentions Poe in passion as a reference to the occult and metaphysics.

The movie The Raven came out in 2012 as well. It stars John Cusack as the Poet Poe. Though lavish as a period piece, it lacks an equally lavish plot. It echoes the pilot of the TV show Castle. A serial killer starts killing off people just as described in his favorite author's books. Castle gets to keep solving mysteries and falls in love, where Poe sacrifices himself for the woman he already loves. Although a bit of a downer, it was an interesting take on the author's actual death.

Poe died not just tragically, but mysteriously as well. It was said that he died of Pneumonia on October of 1948. Some think perhaps the real cause of death was foul play though. There was no autopsy so no one knows for sure. He was ranting, shaking and delirious when he awoke in the hospital after being found unconscious outside a saloon. Originally the diagnosis was "congestion of the brain." Though his symptoms matched alcohol and drug withdrawal, he was supposed to have been clean and sober for six months prior to his death. That led some to suspect a case of Rabies—at least in retrospect. Dr. Benitez at the University of Maryland came to that conclusion some 147 years after Poe's death—in 1996 I think.

Continuing on the Gothic theme, I watched *Vamps*. It is a 2012 Comedy-Horror from the writer of *Clueless*. It stars Alicia Silverstone and Kristin Ritter. Like *Clueless*, *Vamps* is based on a classic novel. *Clueless* took its basic structure and plot from Jane Austen's *Emma*. *Vamps* is loosely centered on *Dracula* but Bram Stoker. Vlad Tempish is now reformed and attending AA-like meetings. Dr. Van Helsing is short bald guy who has a son named Joey. Joey just happens to fall for a Vampire named Stacy. There is even an assistant named Renfield. However, no one goes to Transylvania and the only person who goes to her true death is the stem Ciccerus. She is a sort of Queen of the Damned, borrowing more from Anne Rice than Stoker. It is really more Clueless than Dracula, but it was still amusing. It was silly, but smart as far as historical and pop culture references were concerned.

Grain Brain

Grain Brain by David Pearlmutter came out in 2013. In his book he states that most brain diseases are caused by diet and food choices. Chronic headaches, insomnia, anxiety, depression, epilepsy, schizophrenia, ADHD, irritable bowel syndrome, and arthritis are all influenced by the grain-brain connection. He is up front about the fact that the book is NOT about celiac disease, which is a rare autoimmune disease

Alzheimers is now being considered a 3rd type of diabetes. Insulin escorts glucose into cells, stimulates growth and promotes fat formation, but it also encourages inflammation. Type One Diabetes is an Autoimmune Disease and only accounts for 5% of cases. Type Two Diabetes is reversible through diet, etc. Type Three Diabetes could be considered Alzheimers.

The brain can suffer when we eat too many carbs. We've been told for too many years that a low-fat and high carb diet is healthy, but it isn't. The myth is that cholesterol is bad. When, in fact, low cholesterol is associated with poor concentration. Coronary Heart Disease has more to do with inflammation than high cholesterol. Insulin resistance also plays a part in heart disease.

Cytokines which are present when there is inflammation in the body are present in Alzheimers patients as well. Reducing the oxidation in the blood will reduce the inflammation. Vitamins A, C and E are very important in this process. Oxidized low density lipoproteins are what are bad, not the cholesterol itself.

Gluten is Latin for Glue. Gluten is what holds flour together and make bread rise. Baked goods, pizza dough, margarine and cheese all have gluten in them. Even cosmetics have gluten as an ingredient in them. Celiac is Greek for Abdominal.

Wheat is addictive and triggers the opiate response in our bodies. It raises our blood sugar, and, in turn, our insulin levels. Whole wheat bread will raise our blood sugar more than candy!

54% of breast milk is fatty. Fats help bones assimilate calcium and fats help your clear out the toxins in your liver. We need fats in our diet. Cholesterol is a precursor for Estrogen and Vitamin D. Vitamin D is important in battling inflammation! Fat is not a waste product, but an organ like our skin. It is important.

Leptin is a sleep hormone that also controls our thyroid function. Those who are Leptin resistant have high blood pressure, are overweight and suffer from chronic fatigue.

Damage in the intestine affects the brain. If we have intestinal issues that will affect our absorption of zinc, tryptophan and B vitamins. Serotonin relies on these nutrients, so it is no wonder we are depressed when our bodies prevent us from getting these nutrients. Zinc improves any anti-depressant that we take!

Headaches are often associated with food and diet. Big headache relief can come with changing our diet. 23% of those with Inflammatory Bowel Disease also have frequent headaches. So it would make sense that a gluten free diet would help both the headaches and the IBD.

Great Global Warming Debate

Global Warming is about Global Politics. It should be about community and communion. It should be about connection, not the conservative agenda. Since the future is un-seeable by scientific methods, the immediate needs of civilization take president over any predictions. Curious as to why there is such a huge debate over climate change and population growth, I decided to investigate further. This week I've read opposing view points on Environmentalism.

The first book was *Climate Confusion* by Roy W Spencer. The second is *Betrayal of Science and Reason* by Paul and Anne Ehlrich. These two books helped me understand why there is a debate in the first place.

Any discussion of global warming seems ironic since it has been unseasonably cool the past couple of weeks. Temperatures hover in the 50s instead of the 60s and 70s. It feels as if the seasons have shifted. It was 90 degrees in October and 50 degrees in May. Perhaps we were in September weather in October, just as we are now in April weather in May. Does that make sense?

Anyway, the battle is between so-called Global Warming skeptics or the Brownlash and the traditional Environmentalists. Rachel Carson's books *Silent Spring* on the use of DDT and other toxic pesticides began the debate back in the 1970s. Since then a host of

121

other books have appeared.

Betrayal came out first, being published in 1996. It attempts to answer various attacks on the authors' earlier works. This book does site plenty of articles and papers, both as support and points to refute. It contained a lot of good information, but it wasn't organized as well as it could have been. It was rhetorically weaker than its counterpoint *Climate Confusion*, yet its logic was still stronger. *Betrayal* was the best at backing up their beliefs, but *Climate* was better at battering other people's beliefs.

Climate Confusion was written with a biting sense of humor. Spencer thinks he is funny, but he isn't. That aspect alone was enough to make me reject his position. I read on though, trying to understand. Spencer argues that everything influences the weather and that human beings haven't been a very large part of it at all. He doesn't place much faith in Paleo-climatology. Nor does he place much faith in people who are NOT experts. Stars, politicians and Journalists should all be ignored since none of them are climatologists like him. Spencer is quick to point out that science is about facts and not about truth. The facts can be bent to fit other people's truths. Not to mention the fact that scientists are merely human and subject to bias. Spencer believes that correlation is not causation where CO2 levels are concerned. He taunts that "real" scientists are forced to admit that they simply don't know. Spencer then attacks the church for supporting environmentalism by saying that we must worship the creator and not the creation. To be fair, he dismisses Pagans all together. Pagans and New Agers are painted as flakey and full of faulty logic.

The bottom line for Spencer is that he supports Capitalism, the free market and wealth. He says, "The lack of wealth in poor countries is actually a far greater risk than man-made global warming." It is impossible NOT pollute in this day and age.

Spencer belittles Environmentalists by claiming that they all think that we should go back to living in caves and teepees. He calls that idea dumb and then proposes some less dumb ideas. Nuclear power, hydrogen power, solar and wind power as well as bio-fuels. He ends by saying that people shouldn't label their religious beliefs as science nor should the state support any pagan religion. He concludes that DDT being banned is causing needless malaria related deaths in Africa and that we should feel guilty for allowing Environmentalism to cause such a holocaust. There were no end notes or citations or appendixes. The book was less than 200 pages.

Ehlrich calls Spencer's philosophy *"Cowboy Economics."* People believe if they own property that they have a right to trash it. They believe that people are all basically conservative in nature. No one wants to change their ways. Instead of altering our habits, we choose to deny and rationalize our bad behavior. Many of the claims both for and against man's involvement in climate change comes from uninformed people who only half understand the complex mechanism at work. So-called experts are making some ridiculous propositions.

The consensus of the scientific community is that the earth and its resources are finite. There is a problem with over farming and over fishing—as well as over-urbanizing in general. The toxicfication of the land, air and water threatens the ecosystems—not just isolated areas. Global Warming will eventually destabilize our life support systems, over population and over-consumption contributes to the declining resources. Both developed and underdeveloped countries can be a part of the solution. Environmentalism will not cost precious jobs no destabilize the economy as the conservatives so fear.

My conclusion? Caring for the earth is not about being a liberal or a conservative. It is about common sense! We clean our houses and do repairs because it is important for our safety and our health. The earth is everyone's home no matter what religion or political view they hold. As a part of a global family, we need to contribute to the upkeep of our home. Going "green" as it is now called isn't cheap or easy, but it is the only way human beings are going to survive. Spiritually speaking, there is nothing wrong with feeling connected to the earth. We are a part of the eco-system. We not exist in a vacuum isolated from the plants and animals around us. Appreciating and conserving nature isn't necessarily worshiping it. True, orthodox Christianity doesn't provide a platform for promoting reverence for our home. For the most part, Christians, like the Jews before them, saw nature as a cruel punishment rather than a gift. Nature was feared and therefore subject to domination. It was a power struggle. Modern technology has yielded great advantages in

124

protecting us from the cruelty of weather, but it hasn't given us total control.

As I've said elsewhere, nature is not controllable. Our emotions aren't controllable, as they are tied to our most basic existence. The key is to understand and coexist with nature. It should be respected, but not feared. We need to be able to see humans as part of a larger picture. We are neither more nor less important than any other part of the eco-system. There is a unity, a connection, between humans and the environment and it has nothing to do with religion. Scientifically speaking, we must have symbiotic relationship with the earth. To view ourselves as God over our dominion and kingdom of earth is a grave mistake.

There should be no debate, but there is one anyway. Blinded by fear, greed and laziness, many are reluctant to change. Courage is needed to create a new global community!

Heavenly Fire

"He performs great signs so that even he makes the fire come down out of heaven to the earth in the presence of men." comes from Revelations 13:13. I quote this verse because it relates to to the novel **Heavenly Fire** by Cassandra Clare. It is the conclusion of the Mortal Instruments Series. The novel has Clary chasing after her brother Sebastian, who is turning Shadowhunters. He uses the Dark Cup (Grail). Clary and Jace travel to the realm of demons to vanquish Sebastian forever.

Sebastian is much like the false prophet that Revelations speaks of. He is the Anti-Christ that those with Angelic powers must battle. Interestingly, the Revelations verse goes on to talk about the mark of the beast. The mark is a brand to show those who have become Satan's slave. However, elsewhere, The Beast also denotes Rome and other political nations. That nation was a reference to an ancient nation and yet it could just as easily be about the US or, hell, even Russia or China. The six "evil" empires of the past were Syria, Egypt, Babylon, Persia, Greece and Rome. The bible is very layered with symbolic meaning and specific references that most readers no longer get unless they are biblical scholars.

High Priestess of Steampunk

I read the 2009 book *Boneshaker* by Cherie Priest in 2012. I was hooked after that. I recently had discovered the genre of Steampunk and read that Priest was one of the best and most popular authors of Steampunk. Her *Clockwork Century* series is really the template for the genre, much like Tolkien is the template for high fantasy. Priest combines alternative history with zombies! What is not to love?

After *Boneshaker* came *Clementine, Dreadnaught, Ganymede, The Inexplicables* and *Fiddlehead.* She not only focuses on the destruction of early Seattle, but also explores the politics of the Civil War. It is a smart and enjoyable series to read. Each book focuses on a new protagonist, but intertwine with the rest of the characters in some way. Some of the characters are more likable than others, but each book progresses the world a bit more, so each novel is definitely worth reading.

After I finished her Clockwork Series, I went back and read her earlier Eden Moore Series. *Flesh Not Feather, Four and Twenty Blackbirds* and *Wings To The Kingdom* were all good. Though I generally don't read much in the horror genre, I enjoyed her Southern Gothic Tales. They reminded me of Faulkner and Flannery O'Connor. I was pulled into Eden's creepy world and was drawn on by wanting to more about her past.

Then I moved onto her two vampire detective novels *Bloodshot* and *Hellbent*. Though Raylene Pendle is great fun and I like the urban fantasy genre, these two novel weren't as good as her others. Still, I enjoyed reading them. The plot is quick moving like a movie, but you don't get a lot of background on vampires in her world.

Fathom and *Dreadful Skin* were both interesting as well. *Fathom* was full of mythology and gods and, of course, saving the world. Two teenage girls in Florida stumble upon a horrible murder and get wrapped up in a supernatural story. *Dreadful Skin* was about a werewolf. It was an interesting twist on the age old story with guns and nuns in addition to the shape-shifter. The narrative is told by three people in three different parts and takes place during the post civil war days. Though not my favorite Priest book, it was definitely worth reading.

After reading all of Priest's work and reading Gail Carriger's Parasol Protectorate series, I decided to use Cherie and Gail in my own supernatural tale entitled *The Lost Hotel*. They became the two best friends who stumble into a parallel universe traveling hotel. In order to get back to their universe they need to collect all the items that have left the hotel over the years and return them back to their proper place. Among the places they travel is a Steampunk alternative universe!

I also wrote the Steampunk smash up *Prospector Pirates* and the early American werewolf story *A Fortunate Curse*. Though Cherie and Gail didn't make it directly in those stories, their books were certainly an inspiration to delve to the Steampunk and Werewolf Genres. I thank Cherie Priest for paving the way for authors like me!

Holy Harry Potter

The Harry Potter Series is about death. It is also about the struggle for immortality and the eventual acceptance of mortality even among the magically endowed. In the seventh books of the series, the particular legend of the Holy Grail is paralleled within the tale of the Deathly Hallows.

The Sorcerer's Stone or *The Philosopher's Stone* appears to be the only book that really sticks to the narrow perimeters of the witchcraft and magical world, although a closer look would prove otherwise. The stone that will grant eternal life, which Voldemort so desperately seeks, is a stone from the world of alchemy. The other symbol of immortality and purity is the Unicorn. The Unicorn was mentioned by name in the bible and, in later years, came to represent the purity of Christ.

In *The Chamber of Secrets* Rowling shifts her focus to a slightly more politically charged atmosphere while she explores the ideas of pure bloods, half bloods and mud bloods. The element of the Phoenix is first introduced here as a symbol of resurrection and rebirth. It is not a Christian metaphor, but an ancient Egyptian one. She also adds in the element of the snake, a symbol of the danger of knowledge. After all, the serpent tempted Adam and Eve and led to them being cast out of the Garden of Eden. The serpent tempted them to eat from the Tree of Knowledge, suggesting that the Serpent was not particularly evil, but a symbol of knowledge. The basilisk is monster that is controlled by the sly and power hungry founder of Hogwarts, Slytherin. It is later controlled by Tom Riddle, the future Lord Voldemort.

The Prisoner of Azkaban takes a slightly different turn as it explores the territory of depression. The Dementors are symbols of the horror of depression. The book gives more back-story and then proceeds to play with the idea of time and fate. Rowling introduces us to the subject of divinity and prophecy, which plays a crucial role in subsequent books.

The Goblet of Fire is the first book in which the Holy Grail makes an appearance. The Grail is often represented as a large cup from which Jesus Christ drank from at the last supper and the cup that later caught his blood as he died on the cross. In the Goblet of Fire the Goblet represents first a magical cup in which students place their names. The cup itself decides who is worthy to compete in the TriWizard Tournament. This tournament echoes the sort of tournaments that the Knights of the Round Table faced in the legends of King Arthur and Camelot. Later the cup turns into a port key that transports Harry and Cedric right into Lord Voldemort's clutches. Voldemort uses the key to summon Harry for his rebirth. Harry's blood is the final ingredient that is needed to bring Lord Voldemort back to life. His fetus looking body is tossed into a boiling cauldron. The Grail was also described as a sort of magic cauldron, particularly by the legends passed down the Celts. The death of Cedric follows the Grail legends, as the cup of Christ is as much a curse as it is a blessing. The Grail King was cursed with a barren land while he held an immortal life, showing that eternal life came at a steep price.

The Order of the Phoenix follows the rise of Voldemort and explores the idea of political corruption in more depth. The presence of Dolores Umbridge echoes the idea of the Grail Dolores Spear. At the end of the novel, it is revealed that Lord Voldemort heard of a prophecy and by his own ignorance made it come true. Prophecies play a large part in the Christian bible, particularly the prophecy made about the coming Messiah. The Old Testament references the coming Messiah no less than thirty-eight times. Everyone feared the end of the world was coming soon and that they would be wiped out for their sins as they had been before. Although Rowling does not preach about the sins of the world, it is clear that Lord Voldemort is the embodiment of fear and darkness in the world. It is Harry's love, like Christ's love, that will save everyone. He is less of savior in the traditional sense then he is an ordinary hero. He is more of a Gnostic hero in that he does what anyone else could and possibly would do in his place. He is not a military leader or fearsome leader, but he is brave and compassionate. He is a Christ figure in that he possesses, as we all do, a sort of Christ-consciousness or Bodhisattva mind-set.

In *The Half-Blood Prince*, we gain yet more back-story and insight into the characters, particularly Tom Riddle and Severus Snape. In this book the idea of the Horcrux's are introduced. Voldemort tears his soul each time he commits a murder and discovers how to store these pieces of soul that he might remain immortal. Harry both gains insight into how to destroy the seemingly indestructible dark lord and gains compassion as well. Dumbledore, weakened by his desire for power, succumbs to death. He leaves Harry to carry on his quest to destroy each of the seven parts of Voldemort's torn soul. Seven is a holy number, being the day that God rested when he created the world and the colors of the rainbow.

The opening of *The Deathly Hallows* gives us some much-needed insight into the life of Dumbledore and how his secrets affect Harry and the outcome of the war. After his death, Dumbledore bequeaths the book to Hermione Granger called *The Tales of Beedle the Bard.* One story is particularly relevant and that is *The Tale of Three Brothers.* It tells the legend of how the elder wand, the invisibility cloak and the resurrection stone came to be. Death had given three objects to three brothers, who had succeeded in subverting him when crossing a river. Dumbledore believed the objects to have been created by three Peverell brothers – Antioch, Cadmus, and Ignotus Peverell.

It is no coincidence that it was three knights that set off to find the Holy Grail. One of them named Perceval.

Lancelot first came to the Grail Castle. King Pellam's daughter enchanted him just as Merope Gaunt enchanted Tom Riddle Sr. Lancelot was presented with a ring from Geneviere as Marvolo Gaunt ended up with the powerful resurrection stone.

Balin and Balan were brave knights and brothers, but officially of the Round Table of Camelot. Balin processed a magical sword similar to the sword of Gryffindor. Balin kills his best friend and brother in a duel much as Dumbledore killed his friend Grindelwald.

The Knight Percival was related by blood to the Grail King known as Pellam. Percival, who was the King's nephew, was naive and foolish.

The theme of life and death ultimately becomes embodied in the quest for a modern holy grail. Harry Potter's quest echoes the ancient tale, which combines pagan and Christian influences. It is a perfect parallel for JK Rowling's modern classic and I think it is a parallel that deserves further study.

Holy High Fructose Corn Syrup

Holy High Fructose Corn Syrup Batman! According to Michael Pollen in *The Omnivore's Dilemma,* High Fructose Corn Sryrup has become holy to the food industry. Since 1980 it has found its way into everything from Soda Pop to Ketchup. It is a cheap substitute for sugar and other sweeteners. Capitalists have created an addiction to high processed foods and high fructose Corn Syrup in particular. Living in Ohio this is easy to see.

Corn fields dominate the landscape here in Ohio. The drive from Mansfield down to Columbus is incredibly long and boring because the scenery consists solely of cornfields. Cornfields surrounded Shelby. Ohio was once filled with lush forests, but most of it has been cleared for farm land. And, increasingly, that farmland is owned by corporations or farmers with huge amounts of land. The small farmer with a variety of animals and crops is fast disappearing.

I had plenty of time to contemplate agriculture and all of the problems our current culture has caused on my drive to Columbus. Truthfully, we eat less corn than many Americans. I fix it as a side dish maybe once a month if that. We don't eat tortillas, salsa or corn chips or Frito-lays or corn bread. Taco Bell is something we eat less than once a month as well. Jason isn't big on Mexican food and I can't eat anything too spicy. Our main source of corn is High Fructose Corn Syrup.

This is where Batman comes in. No, not to save us from the evils of High Fructose Corn Syrup—although that would be nice. Nor is he going to take my GRE for me. No, the only reason Batman comes up at all is because Jason was trying to watch *The Dark Knight* off the internet this past weekend.

Hot Six Started It All

It was the summer of 2001 and I was waiting to get my car inspected. I sat down in the cramped waiting room. I'd forgotten to bring my own book, so I search from some magazine or something to keep me occupied. That is when I spotted a paperback novel that someone had left behind. It was blue and titled in bold letters *Hot Six* by Janet Evanovich.

I opened it up and started reading the Stephanie Plum adventure. I cracked a smile several times and found myself drawn into the story immediately. I was actually disappointed when the mechanic called me up and told me he was finished. I thanked him, took my keys and left with the book in hand. In the twenty or so minutes I'd been there no one had come to claim the book, so I decided it was mine.

That night I lay in bed, devouring the words on the page, dying to know who did it. I even laughed out loud in a few places. My then-husband turned over to shoot me some dirty looks each time I laughed, but I couldn't help it. I'd never read anything like it before. There was the familiar mixture of romance and mystery, but there was also the surprise element of humor as well. What a novel idea! It was so much fun to read.

I went back and got out her previous books after I finished *Hot Six*. There was *One For The Money, Two For The Dough, Three To Get Deadly, Four To Score* and *High Five*. After I'd consumed those, I eagerly awaited *Seven Up.* I was definitely hooked. Soon, I began looking for her books in the used book stores and started my collection. Currently, I own books one through fourteen. I got a little behind, but I plan on purchasing the fifteen through eighteen one of these days.

Little did I know my friend Sarah had discovered Stephanie Plum and gotten addicted like I had. When I spotted a copy of *To The Nines* in her bathroom back in 2005, I had to say something about it. She agreed the books were fun to read and called them "literary crack," suggesting that they were not particularly substantial material, but highly addictive nonetheless. I laughed at her description and have since used the phrase a number of times to describe the series to several people who'd not yet heard of it!

Every time I read one of the Stephanie Plum books I entertain the idea of becoming a bounty hunter myself. After all, Stephanie is completely inept, but she still manages to get the job done. Of course she has Morelli and Ranger to back her up. I wouldn't have two such gorgeous, strong and smart men looking after me if I went into the business. Even still, it does look like a lot of fun. To know that you have the strength and wits to get the bad guys must be quite satisfying at the end of the day.

The urge to change professions also popped up when I finally got to watch the movie version of Evanovich's *One For The Money.* I'd imagined who'd play each of the crazy characters long before the movie was cast. I never imagined Katherine Hegel as Stephanie, but

I must admit she did a pretty good job with the part. I was thinking Vin Diesel or The Rock for Ranger, but the actor who played, Daniel Sunjata, him fit the bill well enough. Jason O'Mara wasn't perfect as Morelli, but he wasn't terrible either. Debbie Reynolds wasn't who I imagined as Grandma Mazur, but she was still enjoyable to watch. I must admit I thought John Leguizamo would play Vinnie, but the Lost and Mad Men Alum Patrick Fischler nailed it. Leguizamo was wonderful as Jimmy Alpha though. He added a lot to the character. Sherri Shepherd as Lulu was perfect.

I do hope that they make *Two For The Dough* into a movie eventually. I'm not sure if they will, considering that *One For The Money* wasn't as hugely successful as they'd hoped. Even if they recast some of the roles, I'd still watch *Two For The Dough*—that is for sure.

I am also eagerly awaiting *Notorious Nineteen* to come out in November. Meanwhile, I guess I will pick up *Wicked Business: A Lizzie and Diesel* novel by Jane Evanovich. Her new magical mysteries are quite charming.

Hunger Games and Shakespeare

This week as I finished up *The Hunger Games* with *Mockingjay* I felt like I could relate to Katniss and her struggles. The themes of physical hardships, poverty, power, versions of reality, identity and social class continue to run through my life as well.

After I finished *Mockingjay,* I read *The Hunger Games and Philosophy.* Mostly it examined the morality of various characters and the society of Panem. Stoicism and other ideas were also addressed. I kept waiting for an essay on The Hunger Games and Shakespeare, but I never came across one. Collins borrowed not only from a lot of Roman Empire, but from the Shakespeare plays as well. For example, the president Coriolanus Snow: *Coriolanus* is the name of a Shakespeare tragedy about a Roman leader. Like his counterpart, Coriolanus Snow has to deal with unpopularity, riots and eventually assassination.

The mute Lavinia is directly taken from the play *Titus Andronicus.* The minor Capital Characters of Portia, Brutus, Flavius, Cinna and Octavia are all taken from the historical tragedy *Julius Caesar.* Cressida is from *Troilus and Cressida.*

Castor and Pollux are from Greek mythology; however they loosely connect to Theseus and the Minotaur in theme. Theseus was an inspiration for the overall plot of *The Hunger Games.* Oh, and the author of *The Life of Theseus* was Plutarch—another name of a character in *The Hunger Games*. The myth of Theseus represents punishment for past crimes. Children were regularly sacrificed to the Minotaur.

Interestingly, the Labyrinth in this myth is also present in *Harry Potter and the Goblet of Fire.* Harry and Katniss are both heroes like Theseus.

If Only

If Only: How To Turn Regret Into Opportunity by Neal Roese, PhD came out in 2005. In his book Roese introduces the ideas of Counterfactuals. A Counterfactual is a product of what might commonly be called imagination. Counterfactuals shape our emotions. They work upward in wishing for what might have been better and downward in thinking of how it could have been worse. Counterfactuals most often center on how a problem could have been avoided and that is good for future reference and that is good.

Regret can be good for you. What is it that we regret most? 1) Education 2) Career 3) Intimacy 4) Parenting 5) Self-Improvement 6) Leisure 7) Finances 8) Relatives and In-Laws 9) Health 10) Friends 11) Spirituality 12) Community.

Interestingly, people remember details of tasks that are unfinished. However, they quickly forget those tasks that are completed. People also regret the things they didn't do more than the things they did and failed at. Human emotions, says Roese, is a lot like a teenager in a Ferrari. He has limited experiences and unpracticed coordination. It is not an elegant sight to try and watch him drive. Nor is it an elegant sight to see the emotional landscape of the average human adult.

"The more you know about how counterfactual thinking operates, the more you can defend yourself against other's cunning attempts to manipulate your decisions," says Roese.

The construction of personal narrative stories about our lives that progress toward a goal for the greater good is a sure sign of mental health. If you keep a diary or tell other people about your tragic experiences can really help you. It is a fact that people who are successful are better at thinking about counterfactuals or the what if's or if only's than people who aren't successful. On average most counterfactuals center on personal or controllable behavior. It is not about blame or judgment. It is a critical analysis of the situation and that can be very productive.

However, counterfactuals can have a dark side—depression. Mild regret is a short-lived emotion that is useful for spurring new actions. Severe regret is much rarer, but can be a first step toward the slippery slope down to mental illness. Self-Blame can lead to Severe Regret which can, in turn, lead to Depression. Tragic events can bring on a sense of despair in the average person, but that person is normally resilient. Depression happens when the average person doesn't have a normal sense of resilience. Depression involves a chronic state of negative emotions such as sadness, anger and down right despair for months at a time. It is accompanied by a tendency to put one's self down and worthless and unloved.

Counterfactuals can be counterproductive when the focus is on things out of one's abilty to control, when there is a fixation on things that are not likely to happen or when thoughts don't dissipate and you obsess. You can't see the big picture if you only focus on one tiny mistake or detail. Sometimes people will take a riskier path to avoid feeling rejected or avoid feeling regret. This is called anticipated regret and it can do a great deal of damage.

On the other side of depression is the creative side to counterfactuals. Fiction and personal narratives are a lot more dramatic when counterfactuals are added in. Take the movie Sliding Doors with Gwyneth Paltrow for example. It was centered on a whole series of counterfactuals and it made for a good movie. The Star Trek Episode "The City on the Edge of Forever" also made for good television. Close calls like from the movie The Titanic are also entertaining. And there is a whole genre of fiction dedicated to alternative histories. Speculative Fiction now its own genre instead of being a part of Science Fiction.

The truth is people create their own meaning and this is a good thing. We can learn to harness our regrets and realize that we haven't necessarily failed. We can take those mistakes we made and learn from them. While counterfactuals can be useful tools, we must remember to spring back fast, don't dwell, don't overreact, look further for additional reasoning that can be grasped from the situation, don't over-think, do write it down and always keep an eye on that bigger picture.

In The Cut

Yesterday, I wanted to write, but I was too shaken. I was disturbed. By what? The ending of a book. It left me with a bad taste in my mouth. It was a good read all the way up to the last page. Then it all went to hell. Hard to imagine a single book being able to upset someone so much. Oh, I suppose the past week didn't hep much either, but I still blame Suzanne Moore, author of *In The Cut*, for my particular foul mood.

I'm done reading Thomas Moore's *Dark Nights of the Soul,* which was very good and comforting. Then I moved onto Suzanna Moore's 1995 novel *In The Cut.* I'm not sure why I felt so drawn to the world she painted. I identified with her English Professor Character Frances. I guess I liked Meg Ryan's portrayal of Frances as a strong woman. She lives alone in New York City, unafraid. She seemed conservative and withdrawn—yet sensual and sexy. At first she came off as a cold bitch, but then we saw her vulnerable side and at the end of the movie she triumphed over the killer. I thought that that was cool.

Then I read the book's ending. Frances is killed or is dying at least. I was disappointed that she had to die. Suddenly I hated her for becoming a victim. Her death seemed meaningless—pointless. Was she paying for her sexuality—her perceived promiscuity? After all, the killer took a sexual souvenir. And the killer…The book gives no motivation, no explanation and no resolution. Rodriguez is still on the loose for all we know. I, as a reader, gained no closure. Terrible ending.

If she must die, at least give us a reason. What did Rodriguez choose her? Had be been stalking her? I know. You might say, "Well, the ending is realistic." Even if she—Frances, doesn't know the reason, there is one. The writer must fill in the gaps—let the reader in on it. Okay, so it was in first person. How do you establish omnipresence or limited 3rd person in 1st Person Point of View. You could let the character speculate or the killer could confess. Anything but leave us with the main character's pointless death. That just threw my whole day off!

Indiana Jones Books

In 1991, I discovered a new series of books that expanded upon the universe created in the three original **Indiana Jones** movies. Author Rob McGregor, who had written the novelization of *The Last Crusade*, returned to write six more adventures from 1991 to 1992. Martin Cadin wrote two books in 1993 and 1994. Max McCoy then took over and wrote four books from 1995 to 1999. One more book was written by Steve Perry in 2009.

The novels begin with Indiana Jones finishing up his college education. Being a fan of History and Greek Mythology I loved the setting of the *Oracle of Delphi*. I loved that Indiana Jones had a mystical vision that would guide him throughout his career. Anyway, then he went to Stonehenge, another favorite. In the 3rd book he went to the jungles of South America and married Deidre Campbell. She dies shortly after they are married. I loved that Indiana was once married. This meant a lot to me and made a lot of sense for the character. *The Dance of the Seven Veils* is Rob McGregor's favorite book and mine as well.

Though *Indiana Jones and the Genius Deluge* was McGregor's most popular book, it failed to strike a chord in me. I found *Indiana Jones and the Unicorn's Legacy* a bit more interesting. *Indiana Jones and the Interior World* seemed the most fantastic of all McGregor's books, but maybe that is why it fascinated me. *The Interior World* connected to two of my favorite cartoons growing up—*The*

Mysterious Cities of Gold and *Spartakus and the Sun Beneath the Sea.*

I lost interest in the series when Martin Cadin took over. He just didn't seem to have the right tone or feel for the Indiana Jones world. I do not own either of his books. Then Max McCoy took over and I found myself enjoying the series again. McCoy failed to capture the magic of the original six that McGregor wrote, but he was able to keep my interest and entertain me nevertheless.

I didn't read *Indiana Jones and the Philosopher's Stone* until after Harry Potter came out, so I couldn't help but compare the two. Perhaps the coolest part of that book was the reference to the real live Voynich Manuscript. The manuscript was written sometime in the early 15th century. It is written in a language that no one can translate, so its contents remain a mystery.

Indiana Jones and the Dinosaur Eggs felt like Indiana had crossed over into Jurassic Park territory, which didn't really grab me. *Indiana Jones and the Hollow Earth* seemed to be treading on ground that was a bit too familiar. I am not sure why he wrote a book that echoed McGregor's, but it wasn't different enough for me to latch onto. There was something about *Indiana Jones and the Secret of the Sphinx* that I really liked though. That is probably my favorite out of all the McCoy books. I think that it was a return to the mysticism in Indiana Jones that I appreciate.

The new movie *Indiana Jones and the Kingdom of the Crystal Skull* came out in 2008. The Crystal Skull motif had been briefly visited in

McCoy's novels. Ironically, McGregor had written novel about the Crystal Skull previous to his employment writing about Indiana Jones. Perhaps they should have hired him to write the script. I liked the plot, but felt the writing was flimsier overall. After a 19 year hiatus, it just didn't have the same feel as the original three. I liked it, but it still felt like it underperformed.

The McGregor's books follow a fairly coherent timeline that doesn't contradict the brief descriptions of Indy's past given by the first three films. While I certainly tuned in to watch *The Young Indiana Jones Chronicles*, which ran from 1992 to 1995, I found them difficult to reconcile with the books. If you tried to write out a timeline for Indy's life with all the various parts of the franchise, the TV show stretches the suspension of disbelief too far for fans. Meeting all those historical figures in addition to all the mystical adventures is just too much.

So even though I liked *The Young Indiana Jones Chronicles*, I tend to focus on the books for Indiana's history. It is fair to say that both the movies and the books influence my own writing. Back in 1989 I attempted to write an Indiana Jones sequel of my own called *California Jones and the Lost Testaments.* It involved Indiana's adopted daughter searching for the lost book of the bible. Later I moved away from fan fiction and created my own world with *The Purple Rose* and then Peruvian inspired fantasy **Tuykame**.

Intimate Terrorism

Intimate Terrorism: The Deterioration of Erotic Life by Michael Vincent Miller came out in 1995, but I didn't read it until 2011. Miller believes that men and women are trapped in an adolescent view of what intimate loving relationships should be and then make constant 'terrorist' attacks on each other when inevitably they don't get what they think they should. He draws illustrative examples from literature from John Cheever, Willa Cather, F. Scott Fitzgerald, and D.H. Lawrence and from movies like Annie Hall, Fatal Attraction and from much-publicized relationships such as that of Woody Allen-Mia Farrow and its breakup.

He says that when two people begin to fail at making each other feel powerful through appreciating and affirming one another they may seek to gain power for the sake of protection at the other's expense. This leads to intimate terrorism.

Lover's touch each other in tender places, but so do intimate terrorists. Lovers do so for the sake of pleasure, but intimate terrorists do so for the sake of power. Terror can come in the form of saintliness, rationality, compliancy, ambivalence, emotional openness, and endless explanations, lying and telling the truth. There can be silence, infidelity, coldness in bed and indifference to each other's concerns. There can also be jealousy, criticism and infantilizing.

In marriage and other intimate relations, such faith comes to an end. When two people are consumed with their own anxieties are no longer able to experience each other as a whole, then the problems set in. Lovers can idealize each other at the beginning only to project negative qualities on each other at the end.

"There is no terror like that of being known," said Ralph Waldo Emerson and he was right. The intimate terrorist can do a great deal more damage than that of a stranger. In order to save the marriage to two people involved must be able to overcome hatred and the disagreements that cause that hatred.

Keep in mind that it is not absolute power that corrupts a marriage, but powerlessness that corrupts a marriage. When one person feels powerless then things are going to deteriorate quickly. The power balance must restored or the marriage must end. In any case, Miller urges couples to create "breathing space" first and foremost.

He's so pessimistic in tone he doesn't leave much hope, but he does do a thorough job of exploring the topic in depth. It is definitely worth a read.

Into The Looking Glass By Sarah Clarke Stuart

From Alternate Universes to ZFT, this book covers it all! Sarah Clarke Stuart demonstrates a deep understanding of *Fringe* in her book *Into The Looking Glass*. She shows that as each season progresses things get curiouser and curiouser. Despite the increasing complexity Stuart manages to methodically dissect Fringedom in a manor worthy of Walter Bishop himself. Trying to deconstruct the Science Fiction world of JJ Abrams and company is as overwhelming as Massive Dynamic itself, but Stuart beautifully balances her approach. She covers everything from character profiles to the science behind fringe science. Along the way she touches on not only Fringe's relevance in popular culture, but its importance in tackling current issues and providing spiritual insight as well.

Fringe is full of subtext and Sarah Clarke Stuart does a wonderful job in explaining the literary references throughout. Though its focus isn't solely literature, as was her previous book *Literary Lost* was, literature does plays a central role in decoding the various layers of meaning. She points out how Dr. Walter Bishop's role can be illuminated by such classics as *The Mysterious Case of Dr. Jekyll and Mr. Hyde*, *Frankenstein* and *The Island of Doctor Moreau*. She also discusses the influences of such classic dystopias as found in *Brave New World* by Aldous Huxley, *Cat's Cradle* by Kurt Vonnegut, *Oynx and Crake* by Margaret Atwood, *1984* by George Orwell, and *Do Androids Dream of Electronic Sheep* by Phillip K

Dick. Not to mention the influence of *Slaughterhouse-5*, *The End of Eternity* and *Alice through the Looking Glass* on the Fringe Universe.

Philosophy also finds its way into the Fringe mix as it did in JJ Abram's previous show *Lost*. Stuart skillfully navigates her way through the themes of Duality, Balance, Fate Vs Free Will, Creation and Destruction, Passion Vs Reason, Doppelgangers and Time Travel. Along the way *Fringe* has found inspiration in JJ Abram's *Star Trek, Stargate SG-1, Dr. Who, Donnie Darko* and *Blade Runner*. Stuart weaves a rich tapestry of references to further the readers and viewers grasp of the infinite possibilities of *Fringe's* intertextuality and transmedia effects.

I recommend *Into The Looking Glass* for any fan of *Fringe*. It is great addition to anyone's library rather they are avid readers of literature or just curious about all the connections in the intelligent and interesting television show that is *Fringe*.

Irish Spirit Wheel

The Celtic Way of Seeing: Meditations on the Irish Spirit Wheel by Frank MacEowen looked like it could connect to this Irish and Pagan themed diary, and it has. MacEowen talks about the idea of *da shelladha* (two sights), *bru dariche* (dream seeker) and *taibsear* (vision seer). These ancient ideas are parallel to modern ideas of psychic powers, mythic memory and synchronicity. MacEowen stresses the idea that there is power in words and that story telling has always had a spiritual quality attached to it. A Celtic storyteller heals the word with words.

The spirit wheel or Mandela is a place to begin meditation. It encompasses the four airts or wind directions. The West symbolizes knowledge. The North symbolizes battle and struggle. The East symbolizes prosperity. The South symbolizes the divine song and poetry. The Center pulls us into the divine ruler, sovereignty and the Great Goddess herself. We must connect the eye to the heart and learn to cultivate a life of awareness and balance through our mediations.

MacEowen explains that the North calls us to leave no stone unturned. It allows us to examine our shadow shelves. We can do battle with our obsessions, addictions and projections, thus finding a way to end our suffering. If we end our suffering, we can then put and end to the conflicts and wars outside of us as well.

The East calls us to become an offering through hospitality. We can consider ourselves and others as sacred. MacEowen urges us to keep our homes clean and open to others, but not to deplete our energies by taking care of everyone else. Our physical homes are representative of the home we give our souls.

The South calls us to listen carefully. Listen to nature, listen to the storytellers and listen to ourselves for God is in sound. The sound of things like waterfalls can provide a portal between the physical world and the spirit world.

The West calls us to seek out knowledge, counsel, vision and wisdom. We must be able to envision the connection between the soul and nature.

Many things throw us off center. We can suffer from illness, insanity and addiction. When we feel off-balance we can find strength and gentleness within the Spirit Wheel and the Great Goddess.

MacEowen suggests that we begin by asking ourselves some important questions. How does your problem relate to the center of the wheel? How does your problem relate to the idea of destiny or a sense of mastery? How does your problem adhere to an inner sense of housekeeping? How does your problem relate to a forgotten sense of rhythm in your life? What is it that you long for? What deeper knowledge do you need? Are you doing battle with something?

Is Harry Potter Holy or Wholly Evil?

Is Harry Potter Holy or Wholly Evil? Are the novels rubbish or really literature? If you know me at all, you already know what I think. It is nice to be able to debate the issues properly though. I was curious about the controversy surrounding the books, so I decided to read the opposing viewpoints.

First I checked out of the library a book called, *Harry Potter and the Bible* by Richard Abanes. He was on of the first to publish a book against Harry Potter back in 2001. Since it is an earlier book, it addresses only novels 1-3. I'm not sure if the dark turns and complicated twists would have changed his argument either way though.

The premise of Abanes' argument is that witchcraft and the occult are simply wrong. The bible denounces magic, therefore anything to do with magic goes against the Christian religion.

He seems to ignore the fact that Jesus himself practiced a sort of magic. We call those acts miracles, but there really isn't much difference between the two. Miracles are acceptable because they are supposed to be accomplished through God himself. Magic is often used to describe miracles that are performed by someone undesirable or unacceptable. (Someone not sanctioned by the church.)

Abanes alternates between attacking JK Rowling and attack the growing popularity of Wicca and Magick. Although Rowling is member of the Christian church, her interest in magic and her extensive knowledge of the occult are enough label her a heretic. She does not conform to Abanes' conservative beliefs; therefore, she must be a bad Christian. He ignores the Christian symbolism and disregards the Christian themes because they do not adhere to the strict set of morals he lives by.

The second part of Abanes' argument consists of attacking the ethics behind the books. Because Harry, Hermione, and Ron often break the rules, they are condemned as bad examples. Disobedience, no matter what the circumstances, is intolerable. He views the characters as poor role models for children. Not questioning authority is a very orthodox and old-fashioned view of Christianity. It is a very narrow-minded view, which promotes a congregation of followers, not leaders. It promotes a tolerance of corruption and abuse, which is far more dangerous than typical teenage rebellion.

Jesus rebelled against corruption. He broke the rules. Some would argue that he is the acceptation to the rule—that he was special. However, Jesus is supposed to be a role model. In fact, he is THE role model for Christians. Insisting on complete obedience and blind faith is harkening back to the Old Testament God of wrath. Jesus preached against prejudice and violence. He believed in creating change through peaceful ways and he believed in the power of sacrificial love. Should he have tolerated a corrupt and unsympathetic government in the name of Jewish obedience? He could not have become the messiah without causing a stir. If he is no longer physically alive does that mean no one should ever question authority? Does that mean we should accept oppression and just hope that God has mercy on us eventually? Should we believe that we are powerless to change any evil in the world? Belief not backed up by action is not very strong.

Largely, Abanes misinterprets Harry's motives and Rowling's points. He refers to a couple of books that define occultism and witchcraft, but he doesn't effectively use his sources. He points to other people's weak arguments *for* Harry Potter, but is not able to create a solid or strong argument against Harry Potter. He is frustratingly vague and repetitive at best.

His defense of C.S Lewis is far too flimsy and not focused near enough. Lewis wrote a fairly obvious Christian allegory and although it is fantasy, he doesn't often refer to witches and wizards. Tolkien is acceptable because it takes place in an ancient age and is akin to the epic poetry of classic literature. Rowling is more dangerous because she places her books in the modern age alongside our world. Kids may mistake fantasy for fact he argues.

John Granger refutes Abanes' argument in his book "*Looking for God in Harry Potter*." Granger quotes C.S. Lewis in saying that the "Best books instruct while delighting." Harry Potter examines life greatest themes, including life and death and good and evil. They are well-plotted, well-developed and backed by an extensive background in classic literature. Rowling's examination of Good and Evil is in keeping with the Christian Canon despite Abanes' protest otherwise. Not to mention that the books are enjoyable to read.

Rowling even adds a couple of references to The Chronicles of Narnia. Cedric Diggory is a nod to Diggory Kirke. The Red Lion on the Gryffindor Banners are a nod to Aslan. In fact, there are numerous references to Christ and Christian symbols throughout the series. In the *Sorcerers Stone*, there is the elixir of life in reference to Communion and Transformation. The Unicorn is also a symbol of Christ (and used in *The Chronicles of Narnia*.) Later on Rowling uses the Phoenix and the Stag as symbols of Christ. Harry himself could also be considered a Christ-like figure. The Christian symbols become more transparent with each addition to the series. Granger even mentions the presence of King Arthur and the Holy Grail as elements in *The Chamber of Secrets* and *The Goblet of Fire*.

Overall, Granger provides better scholarship and much more open mind where it comes to Harry Potter. Granger is Christian and even considers himself a conservative, yet he endorses the Harry Potter series as a positive thing for kids. He feels that reading about magic and the occult is harmless enough. (The bible doesn't specifically forbid reading about the topic, just practicing it!) It shouldn't push kids into summoning evil spirits or trying to emulate Lord Voldemort. He believes that the average reader can differentiate between fantasy and reality. Personally, I think he stretches some of his pro-Christian arguments, but most of his points are valid and obvious.

The debate will continue on I imagine. There will always be those who fear and condemn anything unorthodox and there will always be those will find a way to work other beliefs into their own. Many people and most Harry Potter fans do not even care about these issues. A book, they say, is just a book and is neither good nor evil. The person reading the book will make of it what they will. Questioning the intentions, beliefs and life of the authors has only a minimal effect in the end. The reader is the one who interprets and integrates the story into their life however they see fit.

My own experience of the Harry Potter series is that they are largely positive and very intelligent. Perhaps Rowling does not fit the current academic standard with her prose or whatever, but they are sure to remain classics no matter what. And while the series has many Christian themes and symbols, to classify the books a strictly Christian literature would be over simplifying them. Rowling is by no means Antichristian, but nor is she strictly orthodox. Her unconventional beliefs make her an outsider, (not to mention the fact she is a woman…) but that does not mean she is not deeply spiritual or completely compassionate.

I was raised Christian and have not abandoned my beliefs, yet I embrace many other paths to enlightenment. Like Rowling, I am an advocate for tolerance, peace and love above all else.

Jesus: The Unauthorized Version

Jesus The Unauthorized Version: Ancient Accounts of the Unknown Christ is Edited and Introduced by Mian Ridge and came out in 2006. It opens with the discovery of the Nag Hammadi library in 1945. Muhammad Ali was a peasant who found the papers. His mother tore some of the pages to burn and other pages were traded for cigarettes, so the world may never know some secrets.

Paul was the first KNOWN Christian writer in 50 A.D. Mark was around from 65-70 AD and John was 110 A.D. Ortho means straight and doxa means thinking. So, orthodox Christianity is all about straight thinking. Heresy means choice. It can also mean sect, faction or merely different. Bishop Irenaeus wrote Against Heresies. He specifically mentioned *The Gospel of Truth* and Valentinus in 136 A.D.

Greek Gnosis means Knowledge. The first Gnostic was Simon Magus possible. The Pleroma of Sophia is mentioned. The Gospel of Thomas is the most exciting find. The first fragment was discovered in 1896 and then another in 1904. The Gospel of Mary and The Gospel of Judas are also exciting finds.

Jesus had four brothers: James, Joseph, Simon and Judas. The church often taught that these brothers came from Joseph's previous marriage or that they were cousins. I guess they did that so Mary could stay a virgin in their eyes, but she wasn't.

Mary's parents were Anna and Ioachim. Joseph was rich. He was a contractor and a widower with children. *The Gospel of Phillip* dismisses Jesus' virgin birth. *The Gospel of Phillip* also draws a distinction between people who "get" Jesus' true message and those who don't. Looking for outward messages and signs is a mistake.

Jesus spent time in Egypt. *The Gospel of Luke* talks about Jesus as a 12yr old in the temple. *The Gospel of Mathew* talks of him taming dragons and how lions adored him. In the *Gospel of Thomas* Jesus is portrayed as a sort of supernatural brat. In *Pista Sophia* he astounds elders with his knowledge. In the *Act of Peter* it says Jesus is a shape-shifter. In the *Gospel of Truth* Jesus is a shepherd who shows kindly affection.

Mary Magdalene was from Magdala. She is the one who finds Jesus' tomb empty and mistakes the Lord for a Gardner three days later. In the Gnostic Gospels she dominates the conversation with the disciples. Is she Jesus' beloved and there is jealousy among the disciples. Does this mean she too was a disciple and that she was married to Jesus? Maybe.

Jesus taught many things. In *The Secret book of James, The Apocrypha of James, The Gospel of Thomas, Acts of John, Apocalypse of Peter* and *The Gospel of Phillip* they show Jesus teaching about the nature of human suffering and how we can all achieve a spiritual resurrection.

In *The Apocalypse of Peter,* Jesus laughs on the cross. Some of the Gnostic Gospels condemn the Jews for Jesus' death, others hint that he was replaced by someone else or didn't die.

Knowledge is Power

Knowledge is Power Knowledge is power. I have said this many times. Reading Stieg Larsson's Millennium Trilogy this week's has only reinforced this theme or idea. Lisbeth Salander is what Lynnette Porter would call a "Tarnished Hero." She lives in a morally gray area. By no means is she innocent, but she is sympathetic. She reminded me of a much darker, edgier Kate from Lost.

Not only did her father do her damage, but the government and society did damage as well. The authorities who should have stepped in to help her and her mother turned a blind eye because she was part of a larger secret. Lisbeth and her mother were sacrificed, so Lisbeth had to take matters into her own hands. Lisbeth is an exceptionally smart and strong woman whose life was condemned to violence because of who her father was—a former Russian Spy. Had she a normal life, Lisbeth Salander might have been a journalist, a police officer, a lawyer, a doctor or a scientist. Instead of succeeding in life, she was lucky to have carved out a niche for herself as a hacker.

It was her desire to gather information and investigate that gave her power. Although trained as a boxer and although she carried weapons, this tough chick got ahead by digging up information on people. Her conflicts eventually led to blows, but she survived largely on her ability to wield knowledge as a weapon. Like me, she became a Lie Detector in order to turn her invisibility to her favor. The police wouldn't listen to her and the psychologists never listened to her. Thankfully one Journalist in particular—Blomkvist—did.

Another Journalist, Tom Matlack, brings up an interesting topic in regards to The Millennium Series. "This book minimizes the brutal rape, torture and murder of dozens of women," Matlack's wife said after reading *The Girl with the Dragon Tattoo*, the first book in the series. While it is disturbing that Blomkvist concealed all victims of Martin Vanger, the books can serve as a way to open a dialogue about Sexual Assault and Domestic Violence. Matlak is right about the fact that this subject is taboo even though it is a shockingly common occurrence. Most victims do not ever gain the power to fight back like Lisbeth Sander. Sadly, despite all of the advances that women have made towards equality, there is still a power imbalance. Society needs to change before this power imbalance can ever change. If you haven't read my link to Matlack's article you should. It is thought-provoking.

In any case, the best weapon in any woman's arsenal is knowledge—knowledge about the people around you, the knowledge about what abuse looks like and knowledge of all the resources at your disposal. Be persistent and ask lots of questions I learned. You have the right to know the truth. Never be afraid to shine the light on people, places and things in the shadows. Knowledge is definitely power!

Libertarianism

Libertarianism is a term I was not familiar with until a few years ago. Oh, I might have read about it before in regards to to the French Revolution or something, but I didn't realize that it was a present day political group here in the US. References to Libertarianism on facebook made me curious, so I looked it up. My friend are definitely of this school of thought.

So what is Libertarianism? In one word—Freedom. However, there are a lot of ideas within the philosophy on how to achieve that goal. Generally, those who support freedom support a constitution in place, but are against Authoritarianism. Coercion, Imperialism and Racism are also rejected. Self-Management, Self-Ownership and Self-Sufficiency are embraced.

Like any philosophy, there is a spectrum of thought within the school. Some Libertarians believe that freedom can only be achieved in a Free Market Capitalist society while others believe that Socialism provides freedom from the unfair wage system.

This is where my friends and I disagree. They does not like that idea of a government coming and taking their stuff away from him. They earned his car and the roof over his head. Why should some lazy ass down the street be given his stuff that they worked so hard to get? Socialism means some big government telling them what to do and that goes against his right to life, liberty and the pursuit of happiness.

I see their point, but Socialism doesn't have to be about a Centralized Government telling us what to do. The Communism of the Cold War has poisoned a lot of people against the very words Communism and Socialism. The corruption and atheism of the Soviet Union leaves a bitter taste in most patriots' mouths. But there are alternatives.

Social Anarchism is one such alternative. Anarchism advocates a government free society. Well, a stateless society anyway. Non-Hierarchical Free Associations can be put in place, but for the most part people are left to govern themselves. The most common form of Anarchy is Individual. It is perhaps the most logical extension of the philosophy, but it is not the only extension. Social Anarchism is dependent upon people helping each other out. They are not bound by law to do so, but they know it is for the good of all. Social Anarchism hinges on Mutualism and Mutualism respects property rights. So you can keep your property while helping others in whatever way you want. It fits in with Libertarianism and with Socialism. The two can overlap.

Lizzie Silver of Sherwood Forest

Lizzie Silver of Sherwood Forest by Marilyn Singer was another tale that inspired my imagination. Lizzie of Sherwood Forest is a funny, touching sequel to *Tarantulas on the Brain*. Ten year-old Lizzie Silver can't accept that her latest obsession, Robin Hood, is make-believe or that her friend is going to music school. Lizzie hatches a plot to get into music school with her friend so she won't have to be apart from her.

I read this book maybe a year or so after it came out. It was published in 1986, but I think I discovered it the summer of 1987. I'd heard of Robin Hood before, but something about Lizzie's fascination made me fascinated as well. I longed to go to a Renaissance Festival and pretend I was having adventures back in Robin Hood's time.

I remember getting back this strange picture from the drug store when I developed my role of film that summer. It was a picture of a man and women dressed in a tunic and gown from a Renaissance Fair. Their faces were dark and I couldn't see who they were, but I guessed that it most likely a picture from someone else's role of film. As much as I wanted to go, I surely didn't remember going. But it made me curious who went and where they went though.

I researched Robin Hood after that and discovered that he most likely existed, but just not quite like the legends. Still, the idea of living in the forest with my bow and arrow sounded fun. I was able to get a hold of an old bow and buy some arrows made for target practice. Unfortunately, I didn't have anywhere to practice. I shot my bow in arrow in my backyard sometimes, but I risked losing it on neighbor's roofs and in trees. Occasionally I would shoot it straight up and see how far it went and where it would land when I got tired of chasing it through my neighbor's yards. I couldn't afford to take archery lessons like I wanted to, but it was still fun to play around with. I couldn't afford horseback riding lessons either, but I was able to go riding a couple of times as a teenager.

The author of *Lizzie Silver of Sherwood Forest*, Marilyn Singer was born in the Bronx (New York City) on October 3, 1948 and lived most of her early life in N. Massapequa (Long Island), NY. She attended Queens College, City University of New York, and for her junior year, Reading University, England. She holds a B.A. in English from Queens and an M.A. in Communications from New York University.

She another wonderful children's book called *The Golden Heart of Winter* in 1992, which corresponded with my novella *Ohio Brown and the Quest for the Golden Heart*.

Long For This World

Long for This World: the Strange Science of Immortality by Jonathan Weiner came out in 2010. Weiner begins with *The Epic of Gilgamesh*. Gilgamesh is promised immortality if he can keep his eyes open for one whole week. He fails. He is given another chance at immortality if he can find the sacred weed. A snake steals the weed and he fails once again. The closest to immortality we can find on this earth is the Hydra Plant. If it is damaged then it can repair itself. If a part of it is cut off then it can re-grow that part.

"I have immortal longings in me." ~Cleopatra

So what keeps alive and what causes us to age and eventually die? It is all about metabolism, anabolism and catabolism. Cells are built and then our body tears them down and devours them. Oxidants cause our cells to rust and degrade via free radicals. Then our cells have harmful debris and trash around them. The slow build up of extra junk in our cells causes us to slowly age. If we could keep our cells cleaning up then we wouldn't age.

"To be a philosopher is to learn how to die." ~Montiange

There are seven deadly things that cause us to die from the inside out. 1) Many molecules get entangled and stiff. This binding causes us to lose elasticity. 2) The mitochondrial fail with age 3) Junk collects inside our cells 4) More junk collects in between our cells 5)

170

Cells get old and quit doing their jobs 6) Cells die and poison collects around them 6) Mutations of cells occur and we get cancer tumors.

"The Gods themselves die out, but poetry is even stronger than bronze. It survives everything." ~Theophile Gauiter

What can we do to combat these things? We have SENS: Strategies for the Engineering of Negligible Senescence. Then there is TOR: Target of Rapamycin and WILT: Whole Body Interdiction of Lengthening of Telomeres.

"Write as if you are dying." Anne Dillard

It is a fascinating topic that I hope to hear more about in the future. Although I did learn a lot from this book, I found it a bit too vague and disorganized. Hopefully his next book will have more information as well as a better focus. Despite its flaws, I still recommend *Long For This World*.

Love Synapse

Love Maps or Love Synapse? How much of our personality and love life is ruled by *psychology* and how much by *biology*? Anthropologist Helen Fisher thinks she has a pretty good idea. I read her book, *Why Him? Why Her?* today. I was skeptical at first, but her book turned out to provide some interesting insights. And despite the effort to label people and put down a template over relationships, Fisher acknowledges that her model if far from complete. She explores love's synapses, but allows room for the idea of love maps.

Here's what I learned in summary. People tend to fall in love with other people of the same ethnic and socioeconomic background usually. They often share similar levels of intelligence, education and attractiveness. They may also hold the same or similar religious views, political views, social values and sense of humor. Birds of a feather do flock together, but opposites sometimes do attract.

Fisher breaks personalities down into four basic types. Interestingly, these types sound a lot like descriptions of various zodiac signs—earth, water, air and fire.

We have Explores who are curious, creative, adventurous, sexual, impulsive and self-reliant. They like to travel, are passionate and full of Dopamine! The thrill seeking and novelty aspect of the Explorer is linked biologically to the chemical Dopamine. The dark side of the Explorer is that they can be bored, restless, disorganized and don't often self-analyze. If you talk with an Explorer, they will want to know what you do.

Explorers are compatible with other Explorers. However, they can connect with Negotiators as well. Explorers and Directors make a good match too. Although, the Explorer is opposite of the Builder and doesn't often connect to them, a match between an Explorer and a Builder may work if they balance each other out. Keep in mind that Explores often look for playmates rather than soulmates!

A Builder is calm, persistent, loyal, traditional, cooperative, social and managerial. Builders are drawn to other builders. Builders and Directors don't generally work well together. Builders and Negotiators are not naturally drawn to one another, but they can work together sometimes. The Builder is looking for a helpmate and is driven by Serotonin.

Directors are analytical, decisive, focused, inventive, competitive, and strategic minded. Directors match well with Negotiators. This is the one time where opposites do attract. They are complementary to one another and problem solve together quite well. Their thinking meshes. Directors will always want to know what you think and are attracted to mindmates. Directors can be women, but they are more often men and driven by testosterone.

Negotiators are imaginative, verbal, intuitive, idealistic, agreeable, and introspective and love to know what other people are feeling. Oxytocin is responsible for their Empathy Abilities and Estrogen is what drives them. Negotiators are known for their verbal abilities

173

and using their mirroring neurons in social situations.

Anyway, Fisher explains that falling in love has to do with timing. It is often when we are the most vulnerable that love finds us. When we are in between things—like jobs, relationships or homes we are more likely to fall in love. Living and working in close proximity to a prospective match helps. We are often familiar with those whom we fall in love with, but being too familiar can sometimes prohibit romance from blooming. Looks, shape, voice, rhythm, and odor all factor into our choices. Once a person is sized up, then the courtship begins. She says that men often overestimate a woman's sexual interest in him, while women underestimate a man's willingness to commit. Casual sex can lead to love and kissing is very important.

Kissing raises the levels of Oxytocin in the bloodstream. It lowers the levels of Cortisol. Men pass Testosterone to women via saliva, thus making her more inclined to have sex with him!

In closing, she gives some advice to the various personality types. To Negotiators she says: stick up for yourself, don't placate, avoid a verbal deluge, keep a healthy skepticism so as not to be gullible, don't over analyze, never multitask on a date and act confident even if you are not. Fisher warns other types that above all, Negotiators admire warmth and want to know your feelings.

So all of that deals with Love Synapse, but what is a Love Map? A Love Map is the term given to all of our prior experiences. The term describes the psychology of whom we choose. Typically, it takes into account what kind of relationship we had with our parents and

174

our early experiences with romance. Our Love Maps are unique and are an entirely different entry!

Lust in Translation

Lust in Translation: Infidelity from Tokyo to Tennessee by Pamela Drukerman came out in 2008. Former foreign correspondent for the *Wall Street Journal* now living in Paris, Druckerman offers an anecdotal exploration of the international etiquette of adultery. Druckerman's work is quirky, digressive and media quotable.

Adultery provokes more outrage in America than anywhere else. In America people often rank cheating as worse than Polygamy or Human Cloning. Americans tend to feel a need to confess their sins, thus causing themselves and everyone around them pain. Only in America do people feel the need to have "the talk" to declare themselves exclusive. We seem to believe that our men will want only us and never get aroused looking at another woman—ever! A fulfilling marriage is not just idea in America is an entitlement apparently. So, men and women find it easy to justify affairs by complaining that their marriages are unfulfilling and that they are unhappy.

When businessmen and presidents, such as Bill Clinton, have affairs, Americans tend to be very judgmental. It is as if lying to their spouses somehow makes them untrustworthy all around. People felt they couldn't trust Bill Clinton after his affair with Monica Lewinski. But should we really judge someone entirely by one mistake they made? Do their follies in their private lives really affect their ability to run a country or do business or be a good doctor?

The Kinsey report from 1948 and 1953 declared that 50% of men and 26% of women had cheated or had an affair before the age of 40. However, when surveyed in 1991 it was reported that only 21% of men and 12% of women were having affairs in America. From 1991 to 2001 articles were written about how women were cheating more and more. Yet, this was also the time that the attitude toward cheating grew increasingly stricter in America.

America has a sort of Marriage-Industrial complex. Marriage, Affairs and Divorce and Self-Help books about these topics are big money makers. There are websites and forums devoted to people who want support while going through the process of discovering and recovering from an affair. They use all kinds of abbreviations in chats like D-Day for Discovery Day and R for recovery and XOP for Ex-Other Person and TOW for The Other Woman. America's cure for adultery seems to be confession. It is all about keeping up constant communication with your partner and having full disclosure. But is that really healthy? Not all countries think so.

So how do Americans ranks among other countries as far as cheating goes? One survey questioned men who were married or co-habituating with a woman about having sexual other sexual partners just in the 12 months prior to the questionnaire. Here are the results:

Africa: Nigeria: 5%, Haiti 25%, Ivory Coast 36%, Cameroon 36%, Togo 37% . **South América:** Bolivia 8.6%, Peru 13.5%, Brazil 12% Others: Italy 3.5%, America 4%, Switzerland 3% and Australia 2.5%

By comparison women didn't cheat near as much. For example 36% of men cheated in the Ivory Coast, but only 1.9% of women cheated. In Togo 37% of men cheated, while only .5% of women cheated. Very unequal in most places.

Although French Men tend to cheat about the same as American men, the French are much more discreet and laid back about the whole thing. There used to be the idea that if men were going to rendezvous, they would do it between 5pm and 7pm. But that is no longer the case. Monogamy is much desired in France as it is elsewhere, but when affairs to happen those who do the cheating do not torture themselves and rack themselves with guilt. Though most of France is Catholic, religion does not play as huge a role in their lives as it does American's lives. They do not worry about sin. Instead, they simply try and be discreet and spare the other person's feelings.

In Russia it is nearly obligatory to cheat! One psychologist recommends affairs as a way of strengthening the marriage. In 1996 it was said that ½ of all men cheat and ¼ of all women cheat. But perhaps men don't cheat as much as they say they do. During the time of the Soviet Union sex was practically non-existent. Even gynecologists weren't allowed to read books having to do with sex. It was all banned. Once things changed in 1991, Russians seemed to become obsessed with both sex and money. And when there are affairs, Russians will bluntly tell their significant other about it. They are harsh in their honesty sometimes. Women find that men die young and so dating married men is about the only way they can date it seems.

In Japan there are no double beds for sale. They sell only single futons. If a husband and wife want to be together they have to push their futons together. Apparently cuddling is not common in Japan. If everyone is having sex in Russia, then no one is having sex in Japan. Traditionally a woman becomes a wife. Once she has a child, she will then sleep in the same bed as that child. The husband will sleep on his own futon, but move a big Flat Screen TV into the room to keep himself company.

Men don't tend to bring work or sex home in Japan. They often visit bars and massage parlors where they are tended to by hostesses. They pay for conversation, snacks, karaoke and sitting. It is very rare that Japanese men pay for intercourse though. They often will pay for oral or anal sex, but not regular intercourse. Women are more likely to have boyfriends to talk to and cuddle with. It is also women who are more likely to initiate a divorce in Japan.

In South Africa it is a very different story. Impotence to them means only being able to go one or two times a night! You wouldn't think non-monogamous sex would be so rampant with the AIDS virus devastating the population, but it is. 1 in 5 adults in South Africa had HIV in 2003. 1 in 4 pregnant women in South Africa showed up at Clinics with HIV in 2000. In South Africa it is thought that 22% of men have HIV and in Swaziland 39% of men have HIV. Still, they are willing to risk death for a few minutes of sex. In Uganda word of mouth was able to change risky behavior and keep HIV from spreading so much, but not in South Africa and Swaziland.

In Indonesia there is a large Muslim population. They used to promote Polygamy. Many men would take second and third wives, but only with the permission of the first wife. However, Polygamy was outlawed by General Subarto from 1967 to 1998. Today it is rare, but not unheard of.

Cheating and affairs appear to be part of human nature, but how we deal with them differs from culture to culture. Each country has a set of unwritten rules and scripts that are run when it happens. Who's to say which approach is right? But perhaps it is worth consideration that our way in America is not the ONLY way.

Madeline L'Engle

Madeline L'Engle is one of my favorite children's authors. I first read *A Wrinkle in Time* in 6th grade maybe. It was published in 1962 and my mother remembered reading it. In any case, I got a copy of it for my 13th Birthday that I do know for sure That year I went on to read the other books in the series, *A Wind in The Door, A Swiftly Tilting Planet, Many Waters* and *An Acceptable Time.*

I enjoyed *A Wrinkle in Time* because it dealt with a geeky girl like myself and time travel. I identified with Meg and was intrigued by her little brother Charles Wallace. Now, as an adult I also admire that it was one of the few really smart science fiction books out there at the time and that it also featured a female protagonist. Though it has strong Christian themes, it also holds science in high regards, which is something of an oddity even now.

Anyway, I did see the movie version which came out a few years ago and thought it rather cheesy. Given the technology of today, I am not sure why it turned out so awful. The unknown actors and lack of a sense of style hurt it too. Even still, I remain a fan of the book! And it thrilled me to see the writer's of ***Lost*** were fans as well, seeing as how they gave it to Sawyer to read on the beach during an episode.

A Wind In The Door (1973) is an equally interesting book, if not more so. The title is taken from a line in Le Morte d'Arthur. For some reason the Debbie Gibson song *"Silence Speaks A Thousand Words"* reminded me of Charles Wallace in this book. So, Charles Wallace is being destroyed from the inside, on a cellular level, by the evil Echthroi (which is the Greek word for "enemy") They are the un-naming. Now that I think about it, the Echthroi seem to have influence both Michael Ende's idea of the Nothing in *The Neverending Story* and George Lucas's idea of the the Force being inside Anakin at a cellular level in *The Phantom Menace*. The idea of possession and evil taking a scientific direction is thought-provoking indeed.

A Swiftly Tilting Planet (1978) was even better I thought. The book's title is an allusion to the poem "Morning Song of Senlin" by Conrad Aiken. The book deals with Runes, Ancient Welsh travelers and Native Americans. What is not to like? I like that L'Engle views Nuclear Disaster as a modern evil born of science and that she tied it to something mystical as well. The Rune repeated in the book is of particular interest and influence a poem of two of mine early on.

> At Tara in this fateful hour, I place all Heaven with its power,
> And the sun with its brightness,
> And the snow with its whiteness,
> And the fire with all the strength it hath,
> And the lightning with its rapid wrath,
> And the wind with its swiftness along its path,
> And the sea with its deepness,

And the rocks with their steepness,

And the Earth with its starkness

All these I place

By God's almighty help and grace   Between myself and

the powers of darkness

Many Waters (1986) has always held a special place in my heart for some reason. The title is taken from the Song of Solomon 8:7: *"Many waters cannot quench love, neither can the floods drown it. If a man were to give all his wealth for love, it would be utterly scorned."* It deals with the twins Sandy and Dennys. For once they are the ones who accidentally stumble through time and into a biblical adventure. They meet the mythical creatures known as Seraphim and the Nephilim and help Noah's family. The twins must mature, and yet at the same time, come to embrace faith as well science.

An Acceptable Time (1989) was perhaps my favorite in the series. The book's title is taken from Psalm 69:13, *"But as for me, my prayer is to You, O Lord, at an acceptable time."* It follows Meg and Calvin's daughter Polly O'Keeffe. Polly, who is visiting her grandparents, meets druids Karralys and Anaral and a warrior named Tav, all of whom lived in the area some three thousand years ago. She soon learns that she is not the first person from her time to meet the Murrys' Pre-Colombian neighbors

I read *The Arm of the Star Fish, Dragons in the Water* and *A House Like A Lotus* because Polly frequently referenced her adventures in those books in *An Acceptable Time*. *An Acceptable Time* takes place about six months after Polly's trip to Greece and Cyprus in *A House Like a Lotus*.

The Murry-O'Keefe books have further connections with other L'Engle titles. The Austin family books have three major crossover characters in common with the O'Keefe books, two of whom are introduced in *The Arm of the Starfish*. Canon Tallis meets the Austins in *The Young Unicorns*, which takes place a few months after *Starfish*. Adam Eddington meets Vicky Austin the following summer in *A Ring of Endless Light*, and Meg and Charles Wallace are mentioned in *The Moon by Night*. The Austin family series is associated with Chronos instead of Kairos.

While I enjoyed all her other titles, **The Time Quartet or Quintet** is the only series of hers that I actually own. I suppose I just never connected with the other characters in the other books as strongly as I did with the Murry family. In any case, I highly recommend reading at least one thing that Madeline L'Engle wrote. It is a must.

Magical Reading

Beyond Another Door by Sonia Levitin, 1977. *Beyond Another Door* is about Daria Peterson was usually a level-headed teenager. But a dish she won at a local carnival began to shimmer with a life force of its own, and then suddenly, the face of her dead grandmother appeared. No one believed her, of course. Not her best friend Kelly, or her mother, who was her exact opposite. And as her grandmother revealed things about her mother's past, about love and loss, Daria began to see her mother in a different light. And with the knowledge came a growing fear of the supernatural and her own growing psychic abilities...

Sonia Levitin was born in Berlin, August 18, 1934, is an award-winning novelist and author of over forty novels and picture books for young adults and children, as well as published essays on various topics for adults. Although I've only read one of her books, she written many, including: *The Journey to America* and *Silver Days*, a series about a family of German Jewish refugees who flee the horrors of the Holocaust, and *The Cure*, a story about a boy in the future sent back in time

I remember sitting in a lawn chair at my Uncle's Steve's house the July of 1987. I was wearing a tank top with a blouse over it. Only the blouse was not buttoned—it was merely tied in a knot at the bottom. I read *Beyond Another Door* while family members talked at the gathering. I remember thinking about the Shelby Fourth of July Festival and being glad I won that Coke cup for 10 cents. I still have that cup! Anyway, I connected with character of Daria and wished that I'd discover my own psychic abilities though that Coke cup I'd won.

Cat's Magic by Margaret Greaves, 1980. *Cat's Magic* is about Orphaned Louise Genevieve Higgs goes to stay with her Aunt in the country. She saves a kitten from drowning and gets to travel through time as a reward from the Egyptian Cat Goddess, Bast. She runs into her great, great Aunt Flora in the past.

I always had an interest in Egyptian Mythology, so I was pleased to be introduced to another Goddess. I was also tickled to find out that I too had a great, great Aunt Flora. Now if only I could meet Bast and travel through time!

The Ivory Lyre by Shirley Rousseau Murphy, 1987. *The Ivory Lyre* is about Dragonbards Tebriel and Kiri who are instrumental in inciting an uprising against the Dark and in locating the magical ivory lyre with the help of four shape-shifting dragons.

Shirley Rousseau Murphy grew up in southern California, riding and showing the horses her father trained. She attended the San Francisco Art institute. Shortly after graduation, she married and worked as an interior designer while her husband attended USC.

I remember going to work with my Grandma the fall of 1989 for some reason. She was a home health-aide and working at an elderly women's house for the evening. I went with her and took *The Ivory Lyre* with me to read. I sat on the couch in the dimly lit house and was quickly drawn into the maze of tunnels and passages inside the castle in the book. The images in that book would later come back to me as I wrote my own fantasy story *Tuykame*.

Mind Wide Open

Mind Wide Open: Your Brain an the Neuroscience Everyday Life by Steven Johnson came out in 2004. As Publisher Weekly says, "It's the rare popular science book that not only gives the reader a glimpse at an emerging field, but also offers a guide for incorporating its new insights into one's own worldview."

Johnson begins by reviewing Freud's idea of **Mind Sight**. *"He that has eyes to see and ears to hear may conceive himself that no mortal can keep secret. If his lips are silence, he chatters with his fingertips, betrayal oozes at of him at every pore."* In other words, our bodies will betray us. We can hone in on these body language skills so that appears as if we can read minds—hence, the term Mind Sight. Mind reading is another word for empathy. Most of us posses empathy to some degree, however, Autism prevents some from accessing these innate tools. Autistic people must go to school to learn how to read people—to learn Mind Sight.

Interestingly, some scientists now believe that memories effectively get re-written every time that they are activated thanks to a process called reconsolidation. The cortex can forget things, but the Amygdala stores memory for us. Thus, we subconsciously correlate things and memories can be triggered. For example sunny days can be more anxious than overcast ones for some people because 9/11 happened on a sunny day. Our brains have been designed to allow the fear system to take control in threatening situations while preventing the reign of our conscious, deliberate selves. Long term stress may, in fact, do damage to the hippocampus—the region that deals specifically with memory and emotion.

Johnson goes on to discuss ADD and ADHD. He mentions Tor Norrentranders book *The User Illusion* in reference to how little stimuli actually catches our attention. He talks about how there is a law of 7. We can only chunk information in groups of 7 or less. Scientists are studying how to combat the malfunctions of attention—including computer programs and the idea of learning how to switch modes when necessary.

Oxytocin is a hormone released by the body. It creates emotional attachments between mother and child during breastfeeding and also between lovers after orgasm. Lactating mothers handle stress better than their non-lactating counterparts due to this hormone. Human can be addicted to love, but reptiles don't appear to have oxytytocin as they abandon their children at birth and move indiscriminately from mate to mate. Scientists have discovered reptiles lack the neo-cortex, which is the seat of higher language and regulates emotional response.

There are receptors in the brain for drugs—particularly Endogenous Opiates. Our brains recognize chemicals in marijuana, nicotine, mushrooms and even chocolate as natural. Drugs substitute or fool our brains into thinking these chemicals are produced by our own bodies instead of coming from an outside source.

Psychiatric drugs work on this same principle. Those who are depressed suffer from "rejection sensitivity." They avoid situations where they could be hurt or rejected. Prozac and other SSRI's help with this particular problem. Bad news is not taken so hard and rolls off us easier when we have more serotonin in our systems.

Interestingly we tend to remember sad memories with more clarity than happy ones. Happy memories become fuzzy over time. Why? Because our brains just don't underline the positive and negative memories the same. We are hard-wired to remember events that some how deviate from our expectations.

Chronically low dopamine levels can induce cravings for food, drugs and other things. Doing thrill seeking activities or taking drugs can help us to fulfill those needs left by the low dopamine levels.

Robert Cloninger came up with the "Unified Bio-Social Theory of Personality." Serotonin=Harm Avoidance. Dopamine=Novelty Seeking. Norephinerine=Reward Dependence. You can be a stay at home hedonist or a fearless reward seeker or an independent seeker searching for new experiences despite danger.

Repression, we find, does not result in a drive dissipating into nothingness. But rather, it creates a kind of potential energy confined to the unconscious. These drives will seek ways to escape and be released, so it is important to deal with things rather than repress them in the long run. Build enough pressure and you will have an explosion of uncontrolled hysteria, anxiety and even madness.

190

Mentally we are a self divided. We consist of two different types of memories. We have procedural memories like how to ride a bike and declarative memories which allow us to remember that bike crash in 7th grade. Our brains have a natural selection all their own.

Readers shy about slapping electrodes on their own temples can get a vicarious scientific thrill as Johnson tries out empathy tests, neurofeedback, and fMRI scans. *Mind Wide Open* both satisfies curiosity and provokes more questions, leaving readers wondering about their own gray matter. I highly recommend reading it.

Mistakes Were Made (But Not By Me)

"*Mistakes Were Made, But Not By Me*" is the title of a book I read this week. It was a study of how we are hard wired to protect our ego at all costs. This means that it is in our nature to deny and self-justify our actions. This inclination is connected to the issues of embarrassment, humiliation, guilt and shame. Those topics were explored further in the book *I Thought It Was Just Me*. Both of these books touched upon many of the issues and topics I've read about previously. Including, "*A Mind of Its Own, Unspeak, The Lucifer Effect*, and "*Counterfactual.* Not to mention, "*One Nation Under Therapy*" and *Generation Me*.

I Thought It Was Just Me discussed shame. What it comes down to is that we tend to avoid any situation that makes us feel ashamed or stupid. When faced with our mistakes we often justify the reasons behind our decisions in order to avoid responsibility for our actions and to maintain a false sense of self-worth. Shame and blame end up covering up the truth. It takes courage to admit your mistakes, take responsibility, and move on. If we take the high road and do not blame others, we often wallow in self-shame instead. Neither response is healthy. Shame, unlike guilt, is not productive. Shame, on the other hand, only serves to chip away at our sense of self. Guilt is "I *did* something bad," and shame is "I *am* something bad." There is no way to really grow from shame. Guilt is a moderate feeling and should provide motivation for change.

Both books call for a change. Learning to grow up, let go and gather courage is what is needed. Learning to approach your problems and the problems of others with compassion and empathy is the only way to escape the vicious circle of shame and self-justification. It may not come easy, but life is much more painfully and difficult if it never comes at all.

Understanding where someone else is coming from creates compassion. It may not erase the past or the pain inflicted, but it does make it easier to move on. Shrugging off conflict as the result of an interaction with a bad person does not help at all. Judging the other person merely traps us in to a self-justification of victimhood. I know that some people are exercising some *Cognitive Dissonance* and suffer from *Displaced Anger.*

As Oliver Wendell Holmes once said, "Trying to educate a bigot is like shinning light into a pupil—it constricts." People would rather stay deaf, dumb and blind than face their problems and mistakes. Self-denial and self-justification are most obvious in sexism and racism, but they also rear their ugly heads in much more simple and sinister ways in our everyday life. Our daily interactions are sprinkled with fabrications and falsified memories. The truth is difficult to come by and even more difficult to recognize when we see it. It is easier to believe that we smart, sophisticated and sly than face our shame at feeling silly, stupid and so easily hurt. Tough people are typically trading in lies. A truly courageous person isn't afraid to be vulnerable, wrong or just plain open!

Nietzsche

The 23rd Psalm and Nietzsche clash in today's exploration. Essentially serves as a request for God to be a provider and protector. It is often heard at funerals because of the line about "walking through the shadow of the valley of death." The Psalm is meant to be comfort. Even in the darkest times, we are not alone. Although I never like the image of God as a shepherd herding sheep, I do like the idea that we are never alone. The Psalm can still comfort you even if you believe that God is inside you—in all of us. When we die it is only our body that does so—our souls pass onward.

I once saw a shirt that read "Nietzsche says God is dead—God Says Nietzsche is dead." I smiled because the shirt had a point. However, I think it was meant to be an attack on Nietzsche's anti-Christian stance. Despite his many faults, Nietzsche still remains influential, if not ever-popular.

This week I picked up *Thus Spoke Zarathustra* and *The Basic Writings of Nietzsche*. At times I found his writing interesting and beautifully poetic, at other times I wanted to through the book across the room! Nietzsche says something brilliant and insightful on one page and then goes off on a hateful rant the next. He is blatantly sexist and often resentful of not only Christians, but Jews as well. The editor explains in his introduction that Nietzsche is a difficult writer to peg. He can be interpreted in many different ways and has been seen in many different lights. Dining on a feast of Nietzsche's scraps are: Existentialists, Chauvinists, Cosmopolitans, Anti-Semites, Philo-Semites, Francophiles, Wagnerites, Brahmsians, Nature Worshipers, Freud's Followers and Freud's Critics! Whatever category you impose on Nietzsche, it is undeniable he has influenced modern literature. Among those who name him as influential are; Sartre, Camus, Thomas Mann, Rainer Marie Rilke, Shaw, Yeats, Joyce and Eugene O'Neill.

I've read about Nietzsche for years, but had never actually read much of his work. I was introduced to the name in class. We were required to read *The Birth of Tragedy*. Although helpful in understanding the themes we studied, Nietzsche wasn't an easy read.

It surprised me that Marina Ferrer in *The L Word* mentioned *Thus Spoke Zarathustra*. Although the text has certain aesthetic beauty to it, it is a dense text with sexist undertones. As an intellectual woman she should not have found the text so stimulating. I suppose one can be a lesbian and not a feminist, but it seems contradictory. Perhaps once can be a feminist and appreciate Nietzsche anyway.

There were things I liked about *Thus Spoke Zarathustra*. He believes we shouldn't focus on guilt. He is an advocate for appreciating the body and sexual desire. Of course, he goes on to mock love and compassion, which is disturbing. He believes that we should rise up and above our beast-like selves. We should evolve into a sort of over-man or superman. I like the idea of becoming a better human being, and in turn, a better human race. I just think he is wrong about needing to be hardened intellectuals to do so.

The death of God is about the lack of tough love. He claims that God died of pity because he felt sorry for his creations. Humans are a despicable lot who are nothing but a disappointment to their heavenly father.

I am not sure one can write Nietzsche off as an atheist. He mentions the soul a number of times, pointing toward some sort of spirituality. He has an affinity toward Greek Mythology, but I am not sure he is exactly pagan either. He doesn't believe in Jesus as our savior, that much is clear. Although Nietzsche advocates the same sort of mind set that Buddhism does, he rejects the cornerstone of Buddhist faith—compassion. I agree that in order to grow one must have a spiritual death and rebirth. Nietzsche says, "You must wish to consume yourself in your own flame; how could you wish to become new unless you had first become ashes." (64)

Interestingly, Zarathustra addresses his disciples or followers as sheep. He addresses his audience as his herd. This is an insult, I believe. He believes that Christians are nothing but a bunch of mindless sheep. His tone is bitter, negative and mocking. There are many moments of biting sarcasm that read as very serious. It would be easy to believe that he is supporting something that he actually despises.

While I agree that people need to learn to think for themselves and not just follow the leader, I disagree with the rejection of love, comfort and an afterlife. Nietzsche is only half right. Courage to rise above your former self and a strong work ethic is important, however, without love and happiness life is still meaningless. To not give our suffering meaning and to not give ourselves hope is a path to depression and self-destruction.

You know what I think? I think Fredrich Nietzsche was a sensitive soul, beaten down by religion and society. I wouldn't be surprised if he was abused. Perhaps even from a member of the church. Sexism is the norm in society during his day, but his prejudice seems to stem from some sort of personal experience as well. He could have witnessed his father abuse of his mother or even been abused by his mother. He may also have felt that any show of emotion, especially love, meant showing weakness. That sort of thinking is not uncommon for someone whose been abused. Nietzsche was intelligent, but suffered from depression or manic-depression. Certainly, he succumbed to insanity at the end of his life. Syphilis is thought to be the cause. I can't help but wonder if he didn't catch it from a prostitute that he mistreated as some sort of karma. One can only wonder how his views would have changed if he'd lived today instead of over 100 years ago! Would medication or therapy dulled his senses and silenced his soul? Or maybe made his head clearer? Could Nietzsche have been better without being so bitter? We may never know. At least he did provide some food for thought and a call to action!

On Desire

Desire is the topic today. I just finished reading *On Desire* by William B Irvine and found it very interesting and thought-provoking indeed.

Many people do not the desires that drive their decisions. Much of internal process is subconscious, which means there isn't much logic or rational thought behind our actions. And as Irvine points out, even when we are aware of desires, it doesn't always mean that we can control them. The best we can do is learn to live with our desires by mastering them. Mastering them does not mean eliminating them all together, but learning what to act on and what NOT to act on. Christians pray for relief, Catholics confess their sinful thoughts or deeds and Buddhists meditate and seek the middle path between hedonism and aestheticism. There needs to be a balance then between pleasure and perfection.

Two particular desires tend to create problems for everyone—the desire to be accepted in society and the desire to seek sexual pleasure. Irvine mentions that Nietzsche thought outsiders to society were "godly beasts" or "philosophers." David Weeks prefers to view outsiders as eccentric. The eccentric, by definition, is someone who lives outside of society. They are often financial failures, but happy nonetheless. Not only are they nonconformists, but they are curious, creative, intelligent, idealistic and opinionated. They are also obsessive and passionate. Eccentrics posses a childish delight with things that many people envy. Their obsessions tend to bring them joy rather than misery because they can be intense without being consumed.

As far as sex goes, one can practice free love until such an intimate act becomes as commonplace as a handshake or one can become celibate. Again, most people practice the middle way, but there is something to be said for those who choose the extremes. Those who practice celibacy say that it allows love to be free of possessiveness helps one to focus on helping others. Sex tends to lend itself to people trying to take advantage of one another. Irvine compares celibate love to the love a parent feels for a child. It is supposed to be about selflessness.

I've always been drawn to Thoreau and other such eccentrics and I suppose my views on desire and love are particularly unconventional. I don't believe sex should be as freely given as a handshake, yet I do not believe being celibate is the only source of liberation from selfishness. Ideally one could desire others without being possessive or selfish. Sex should be somewhat selective, but not necessarily exclusive. Love making is sacred, but that doesn't mean you can't love more than one person at a time. You can love many people just as a parent can love many children. Sex shouldn't mess up a perfectly good friendship, but instead enhance it. If you truly love someone then you can give them the freedom to love and help others. Your fears shouldn't prevent your loved one from loving and supporting other people. Certainly when one enters into a relationship one would not demand that you give up all your family and friends! That would be selfish of them. I know it is a bit different where it comes to sexual relationships, but perhaps it shouldn't be. Unconditional love is what we should strive for. Relationships may have their boundaries, but love itself does not. Desire has no boundaries either, even if society does.

On Truth

On Truth by Harry G Frankfurt came out in 2006. Having outlined a theory of bullshit and falsehood, Harry G. Frankfurt turns to what lies beyond them: the truth, a concept not as obvious as some might expect.

Bullshit, he says, come from those "who are attempting by what they say to manipulate the opinions and the attitudes of those to whom they speak." This follow-up, which is an equally thin volume, is incisive and insightful. It is another extended essay on a topic closely related to the first.

He states that we cannot live without the truth. "When I was a child, I often felt oppressed by the chaotic jumble of implausible notions and beliefs I felt various adults were attempting to force on me. My own dedication to truth originated, so far as I am able to recall, in the liberating conviction that once I grasped the truth, I would no longer be distracted or disturbed by anyone's (including my own) speculations, hunches or hopes."

Our culture's devotion to bullshit may seem much stronger than our apparently halfhearted attachment to truth. But that can be dangerous. Lies isolate the liar. Loneliness is unutterable. So when we lie we have no real intimacy and we feel very much alone in the world.

The mindless groping toward the truth may work well enough for awhile. Inevitably, however, it will lead us to finally blunder into trouble. We do not know enough to avoid or to overcome the obstacles and dangers that we are bound to encounter. Indeed, we are doomed to remain entirely unaware of them until it is too late and we've already been defeated. So we often need help finding our truths.

Facts belong to the objective reality. The truth is NOT facts. Truth is in our sense of identity. It is in our sense of self and our perception of said facts.

If we devalued the truth then society would be making a huge mistake. The truth must remain important Frankfurt concludes. "A society that is recklessly and persistently remiss in [supporting and encouraging truth] is bound to decline."

Harry G. Frankfurt is a professor of philosophy emeritus at Princeton University. His books include *The Reasons of Love*; *Necessity, Volition, and Love*; and *The Importance of What We Care About*. He lives in Princeton, New Jersey.

Origins of Oz

As a child I loved reading about the Land of Oz Although unique in that it was the first truly American Fairy Tale, there appears to be more to it. I took an interest in New Age thought around 1990. When I read about Edgar Cayce something struck me. Perhaps there was a connection between Cayce and Oz?

Cayce spoke of the Lost Tribes of Israel. Hebrew people migrated to America during the time of the Assyrian Exile, which was around 722 BC. These immigrants mixed with those descended from the people of Mu or Lemuria. Specifically, Cayce said that the Inca's were the successors of those of OZ or OG in the Peruvian land and successors of Mu in the southern portions of that now called California and Mexico and southern New Mexico. The mention of migration from Lemuria and Atlantis connected to something else well.

I often wondered if the writers of *The Mysterious Cities of Gold* hadn't taken their myth of the *Mysterious Cities of Gold* directly from Cayce himself. In the cartoon Atlantis and Lemuria fought a great battle and used nuclear weapons to destroy one another. Before their ultimate destruction, the Emperor of Heba or Lemuria had seven cities of gold placed around the world.

These Cities of Gold coincide with Cayce's idea of a migration of the people of Mu and the so-called Lost Tribes of Israel. If these advanced people sailed to the Yucatan Peninsula and parts of Peru then they could have very well influenced the Maya and the Incas.

Atlantis and Lemuria was a favorite topic of Madam Blatsvksy and of her Theosophy. It was known that L Frank Baum had a knowledge and interest in Theosophy. Was his invention of Oz a coincidence or did he really view himself as a historian of some long forgotten island?

Dorothy gets carried away in cyclone—not a tornado. Cyclones are generally over the Pacific Ocean. Later, in *Ozma of Oz*, Dorothy is on a steam ship bound for Australia with her Uncle. When she is shipwrecked, she washes up on an island which holds Oz. The island, like Australia holds deserts, mountains and farms land. Dorothy encounters the land of Ev and then crosses the deadly desert before returning to Oz.

In *Dorothy and The Wizard* in Oz, Dorothy is in San Francisco when the earthquake hits. She falls down a crevice—presumably the San Andres Fault—and travels into an underground kingdom. Eventually her travels lead her to Oz, which is presumably located in the Pacific.

We see that Oz is a magical country from the beginning, but we know little of its history. Throughout his fourteen books, Baum gives a bit of back story here and bit there. We discover that Queen

Lurline and her band of fairies enchanted the land, making it difficult to visit and impossible to figure out the exact location of the island. They make it so that no one ages and no one dies in their land. People can be chopped into little pieces but they are unable to killed per se. It is a paradise on earth filled with magic. Wizards and witches were once quite common in Oz, but Ozma eventually outlawed the practice of magic except by The Wizard and Glinda.

For the most part, people from the outside world know nothing of Oz. The Wizard was the first outsider to arrive in his balloon. Then later on Dorothy arrived in her house. Dorothy returns several times before bringing her Aunt Em and Uncle Henry to live in Oz with her. Cap'n Bill, Trot, Betsy Bobbin and Button Bright are also visit and eventually live in Oz.

Interestingly Oz is a subtext to the TV show *Lost*. There are many parallels. Both Oz and the Island of *Lost* are located in the Pacific and notoriously difficult to find. However, people from the outside world have managed to stumble upon it at one time or another. Both islands appear to be magical, though the Island of *Lost* attempts to explain some of its mysterious phenomenon via electromagnetic force. The writer's specifically alluded to Oz via Ben Linus's alias Henry Gale.

One might wonder if both the Island on *Lost* and Oz were, in fact, part of the ancient Lemuria or Mu. But nobody has ever really explored the connections of these magical islands to the Ancient Lost Civilizations in depth before.

Atlantis was first mentioned by Plato in Ancient times. Lemuria came into the picture in the 1864 with Zoologist Phillip Sclater and then later James Churchill. Madam Blatsvksy elaborated on Churchill and other's writings about the fabled lost city beginning in 1882. Since then Geologists have "debunked" such theories with plate tectonics. And perhaps Atlantis and Lemuria were not huge continents, but it is possible that they existed as small islands once in time. Various sites have surfaced showing evidence that cities or parts of cities were submerged over the years.

Rather Atlantis and Lemuria really existed or not, I do believe that Lemuria in particular influenced L Frank Baum in the shaping of his fairy tale land Oz. Oz, in turn, has influenced many, including the writer's of the TV show *Lost*.

Out of the Woods

Out of the Woods: Tales of Resilient Teens was written by Hauser, Allen and Golden in 2008. Seventy deeply troubled teenagers spend weeks, months, even years on a locked psychiatric ward. They were not just failing in school, not just using drugs. They were out of control—in trouble with the law, unpredictable, dangerous and violent or suicidal. Their futures were at risk. How did they turn their lives around?

The doctors found that early childhood experiences are important. Resilience once was thought to be someone who was invulnerable, invincible and a super kid. The authors redefine resilience as someone who is able to lead a fairly normal life after depression and abuse. What are the risk factors for kids in trouble? Poverty, racism, divorce, illness, early parent loss and abuse. What protects kids from getting into trouble? Wealth, beauty, intelligence, optimism and faith. While isolation can create problems for teens, learning how to connect with others can save them.

Many of the teens complained that no one loved them, not unconditionally anyway. But they had to go beyond realizing that feeling to move on. Being able to reflect upon their lives and their feelings critically was important. They had to come to feel they had agency in their lives—or that they mattered and had power in their lives. Many of the teens felt like their behavior was detached from themselves. They didn't feel their actions had meaning. Meaning needed to ome into place for them to change their ways.

When the teens were in therapy the doctors noticed something important. Everyone has a narrative they tell about their lives and themselves. If the narrative was coherent then they had a better chance of understanding their problems and fixing them. A breakdown in coherence meant that the teen was in a very unhealthy place and therapy wasn't going to be helpful. Glib generalizations and glazing over the negative thoughts, feelings and actions made it hard to help them. Why was this? Well, the less feeling a person can tolerate the harder it is to keep an emotionally intense narrative organized.

The teens that were resilient had a thirst for agency and they were very much self-aware. They learned from their mistakes and could be optimistic about their futures. They were able to redefine their understanding of things and change their perspectives. Resilient kids and teens don't focus on escape. Rather, they utilize survival skills. They were able "surf" their anger instead of letting their anger control them. However, the doctors realized that a teen's emptiness inside was far more dangerous than their rage. These teens suffered an appalling number of losses, abuses, inconsistencies, rejections and abandonments. Still, they were willing to keep looking for love and try new relationships. They didn't shut off or shut down.

It was no surprise that storytelling abilities turned out to be an important skill in being resilient. The first step, no matter where you

are, is to learn to see in the dark. Only then can you find your way
out of the woods.

Parallel Worlds

Parallel Worlds by Michio Kaku came out in 2005. In his preface his discusses everything from Galileo Galilee to Copernicus to Kepler to Newton to Hubble to Einstein and beyond. Then Kaku begins at the beginning, literally. He speaks of Chinese mythology and how earth was created from an egg and how in Greek mythology the earth was created from chaos. In Egypt we have Ra and the floating Egg. In Polynesia the cosmic egg takes the form of a coconut shell. The Mayans believed that the Universe lives, dies and is reborn.

From the idea of a baby universe that looks like an egg he moves onto M-Theory and String Theory. He gives a detailed analogy saying that musical notation is like mathematics, violin strings are like superstrings, notes are like subatomic particles, the laws of harmony are like physics, the universe is like a symphony of strings, the mind of god is music resonating through space and the composer is a giant question mark.

The Universe is not infinitely old, although it is billions of years old. 13.7 to be exact. If you traveled faster than the speed of light the light would appear motionless and frozen. There is a genesis to the universe, hence, the Big Bang Theory. Hundreds of people have collected data that points to the event known as the big bang. The

Big Bang probably didn't make a sound in empty space, but it was a small explosion of energy.

From there Kaku goes on to talk about the beginning of Quantum Physics. He speaks of Hubble and how he discovered that the universe is still expanding. He talks about Omega and how the average density of the Universe is -1. Lambda is dark energy and empty space at 0. Omega plus Lambda =1 and a flat universe. Omega 1 means the universe is curved like a circle.

Phases of the universe have been determined. The Planek Era is 10 (-43) was nothingness. A tiny bubble expands. In 10 (-43) Gut Era symmetry was breaking and there was gravitational shock waves. The temperature was 10 (32). The End of Inflation was 10 (-34). The temperature dropped to 10 (27). The forces split into two. Nudei form was 4.3 minutes and that was when Hydrogen fused to Helium. Then Atoms were born at 380,000 years. The temperature dropped to 3,000 degrees Kelvin. Photons traveled freely and the white sky turns black. Stars condense at 1 Billion years and the temperature drops to 18 degrees. Quasars and galaxies form. The De Sitter expansion was at 6.5 billion years. Antigravity drives this expansion. Today at 13.7 billions years the temperature has dropped to 2.7 degrees.

Blackholes are the next subject he goes over. Are they wormholes or Einstein-Rosen bridges? Or would you be instantly crushed to death and slip into nothingness? Some people think that blackholes would allow you to time travel. Hawking say s that time travel is not impossible, but it is unlikely and impractical. Kaku also mentions *The Hitchhiker's Guide to the Galaxy* and Philip K Dick's *The Man in the High Castle*.

All energy occurs in discrete packets called Quanta. The W&Z are the weak forces. There are gravitons, bosons and gluons. Matter is represented by point particles, but probability obeys the wave equation. Before an object exists it exists in all possible states. It is our observation of it that makes it form into a definite state. So is reality objective or subjective then?

Erin Schrödinger came up with the Cat Problem. There is a cat in a box and there is a syringe full of poison. While the box is close the cat is both alive and dead. It isn't until you open the box that you bring into reality one possibility or the other. Once you open the box then you determine rather the cat remains alive or if it is killed by the poison.

Is it possible that the other universes are a sort of trial and error for this one? Maybe, but each universe has its own matching laws and principles. Everything had to be just right in this world in order for it to work. The earth had to be just the right distance from the sun and have just the right atmosphere to support life, etc. Does this mean that there are no coincidences? There are too many variables in order for them to just be "happy accidents."

What about gravity? Can there be such a thing as super-gravity? Does gravity leak into higher dimensions? Are there galaxies behind galaxies? There are Gravity Wave Detectors now that help us determine such things.

If there was a beginning to the universe will there be an end? Will there be a Big Crunch at the end? Will the universe grind to a halt or collapse upon itself? Matter doesn't die. It just transforms, so perhaps death can be defined as the final cessation of all information processing. Can we escape the death of our world or our universe by escaping into another universe? Theoretically we could create baby universes along with warp drive.

What lies beyond the multiverse? As Thomas H Huxley once said, "The question of all questions for humanity, the problem which lies behind all others and is more interesting than any of them, is that of determination and man's place in nature and his relation to the cosmos." We live in a participatory universe. We may not know if our clones will have souls, but we do know that the choice is ours to find or create purpose in our lives. It is, in fact, our destiny to do so.

Patterns of Tragicomedy in Bernard Shaw
By CD Sidhi, Bahari Publishers, 1978

The evolution of tragedy and comedy merged into a new species called the Tragi-Comedy. Happy Endings in historical tragicomedy can be found as far back as he 17th Century.

1) Alternations between tragic and comedic elements
2) Mixing of Social Classes in Dramatic Personae
3) The Unrestricted choice of Subject Mater.
4) Mingling of the lofty and conversational styles
5) Happy Ending and Explicit Didacticism

An example of Modern Tragicomedy is Ibsen's play *Wild Duck*. *Faust* is a tragedy as well as a comedy in spite of the Happy Ending. *Hamlet, Troilous and Cressida* are comedies as well as tragedies despite the slaughter in their endings.

Shaw's philosophy of an evolving universe does not admit the possibility of tragedy, which deal with an individual's trivial failures in personal ends.

The only evil for Shaw is the evil of defective social institutions which are being man-made and can be remedied by better thinking. The serious horrors are those which seem entirely respectable and normal to normal people. Comedy is the manufacturing of misunderstanding.

Ibsen's heroes are miserable and yet not hopeless, for hey are mostly criticism of false intellectual positions which, being intellectual are remediable by better thinking.

From Complete Prefaces (page 200) The Curtain no longer comes down on the a hero slain or married. It comes down when the audience has seen enough of life presented to it to draw the moral and must either leave the theater or miss the train.

Like life itself, the ending of the modern tragicomedy is unresolved, or at best, ironic. The modern playwright is a ruthless reveler of hidden truth and a mighty destroyer of idiots. These plays will make audiences uncomfortable.

A Shavian tragicomedy is primarily the story of destiny of a a nation. It deals with the social, political or religious progress of a country, of the human race itself, at a particular moment in history. The real hero of a Shavian tragicomedy is either the nation or the human race. All seven plays listed are essentially morality plays or allegories dramatizing a particular philosophy of social-political reconstruction. In other words, they are dramatizations of an idea— The Shavian idea of World Betterment.

The Shavian Hell is a soul in torment. He or she tries to redeem themselves through the new gospel. The Hero's mission is to gradually grow up and find salvation through the shattering of false illusions, break free of disillusionment, go through heartbreak and then understand life's purpose.

One side of the hero's quest is for world bettering and the other side is against it or in opposition to it.

Conflicts include: genius vs mediocrity, realistic imagination vs romantic imagination, visionary vs disillusioned idealist, do-er vs taker, the educated vs the self-educated.

The Shavian hero is not based on Antigone but Prometheus—the redeemer of mankind. The Heroes often parallel Christ or Christ-like figures.

In term's of Shaw's life-force is this conflict between the working for the evolutionary will of the universe by the Superman and the self-indulgent or happiness seeking of the less evolved man.

In writing Wagner's Siegfried Shaw says, "The most inevitable dramatic conception then, of the the 19th Century, is that of a perfectly naive hero that is upsetting religion, law and order in all directions and establishing in their place the unfettered action of humanity doing exactly what it likes and producing order instead of confusion there by because it like to do what is necessary for the good of the race."

Shaw rejects the Aristotle view of tragedy that invokes pity. A lot of people are not happy unless someone else is miserable. Shaw doesn't want to pity anyone. He doesn't want people to have a reason to fear. He doesn't want the play to end in death. Death is just a beginning. The only purpose of death in a play is to "awaken" the audience.

Creative Evolution (pg 137-138) The Future is what we make it. We can change it, outgrow our childish or barbaric ways and become evolved. God is creative energy, which is ever evolving. There is no problem of evil. Evil is willed away. The Creative Evolution theory of of history is the reconciliation of opposing views. It believes in a steady moral progression.

Differences between absolutists and Shavian Tragedy. The absolutists are Sartre's play *Huit Clos*, Becket's play *Waiting For Godot* and Albee's *Who's Afraid of Virginia Woolf*. Their view holds that the world lacks any positive energy. It is overseen by a Savage God who appears to be making puppets out of us. But Shaw's view is all about World Betterment. There is meaning and moral design. Shaw's characters may be trapped in their disillusion like the absurdists, but that is not the end of the story.

Tragicomedies employ the new element of abundant discussion that unravels conflict through said discussion.

In Act 1 you have the Exposition to set up the tone. In Act 2 and 3 there is the conflict and climax. There may be a reverse in action after the Climax. There may be an episode that doesn't seem to belong until later. Then it will come back into the play at the end.

John Bull's Other Island dealt with Keegan and Karma. There was an illusion to reincarnation.

Major Barbara envisioned a socialist future and a Creative Evolution Heaven.

Heartbreak House dealt with what was wrong with England. It was social commentary with more attention to dramatic form.

St Joan gained major critical attention with its use of History of the Doctor's Dilemma.

Peculiar

It has been a peculiar week, more so because I've read the sequel to *Miss Peregrine's Home For Peculiar Children* than anything. The week itself has only been peculiar in the usual way that my life varies. When I sat down to write I thought perhaps the title of the second book, *Hollow City,* might be a good theme for my diary entry, however, this week has felt less Hollow than last week, so Peculiar somehow felt more fitting.

Anyway, *Miss Peregrine's Home For Peculiar Children* was published in 2011. I read it in 2012, I think. The dark fantasy was interesting. Ransom Riggs, the author, was inspired by real vintage photos. These bizarre pictures from the 1800s led him to piece together a narrative about these children with strange abilities. The main character, Jacob, follows clues left behind by his dead grandfather and discovers that these Peculiar Children ho tell him about the monsters—or Hollows—that killed his grandfather.

The sequel picks up here the first one left off. Jacob travels with these Peculiar children to London, along the way they meet up with some very strange creatures indeed. I'm about half way through, so I don't know what happens to the children on their journey, but I look forward to finding out!

People of the Lie

People of the Lie: The Hope for Healing Human Evil by M Scott
Peck was written in 1983 originally but was reprinted in 1998. Peck
examines the nature of evil in the context of his psychological
practice.

Forever fleeing the light of self-exposure and the voice of their own
conscience, they are the most frightened of human beings. They live
their lives in sheer terror. They need not be consigned to any hell for
they are already in it. C.S. Lewis wrote that God does not punish us,
rather we punish ourselves. Those who are in hell are their by their
own choice.

Evil is what kills the spirit he says. Evil is often associated with
death and killing. Necrophilia is the desire to control someone and
who is easier to control then someone who is already dead? Evil can
also be considered those who are diagnosed as sociopathic or
psychopathic.

The central defect of the evil is not the sin itself, but the refusal to
acknowledge it. Hence people of the lie—people who are being lied
to, lying and being lied about. Evils deeds do not an evil person
make. There are those who commit crimes but are blessed by guilt.

On characteristic of the evil is scapegoating and projecting. They
may see much evil in the world, but never their own. They try to
destroy the evil in the world unaware that they are really trying to

destroy the evil inside themselves. They would rather sacrifice others than themselves. Peck believes there is a subtle difference between the evil and the general sociopath.

Trying to escape suffering is the root cause of the evil in the world Peck thinks. People are evil in order to avoid self-criticism and imperfection. It is a form of narcissism. Eric Fromm called it a "malignant narcissism" in fact. They will not submit and never surrender. Instead, they will always try to control others.

Evils seems to run in families. However, Eric Fromm believes that people aren't born evil, but rather it is a process of becoming. Born in the thrall of our parents and their evil, we are often the product of nurture as much as nature.

Fear is the most painful of emotions and is avoided at all costs by the evil. The evil live their lives in fear. Perhaps that is why people often use evil to fend off evil. Gargoyles, for example, were a symbol of evil to ward off even greater evils out there.

Satan, Peck says, is the father of lies. Demons are lies. Satan and demons have not power over us except when we believe in his lies. Evil can be seen as immature and can create their own "pretty hate machines" to protect themselves.

Pesher

A pesherist is particularly concerned with the accuracy of language. Assumption is dangerous, therefore a great care must be taken to interpret as precisely as possible. Errors are often made and so much has been lost in translation. Going back to the root words is painstaking, but a necessary task. Once a word (i.e. Sheep) is used as a symbol, then it should continue to be taken as symbolic in each of its further uses in a particular text. Words often have more than one meaning, and in many cases they can mean more than one thing in any given text. There are, then, layers of a text. There is a literal layer and the symbolic layer of language that often coexist in the same text. For the pesherist the subtext is not about implied interpretation, but a set of symbols that are part of specific system. It is a sort of secret speech that relies on a concrete set of rules to decode it. The post-modern consideration of perception and possibility is ignored or denied.

This pesher technique is used by scholar Barbara Thiering in her book *Jesus and the Riddle of the Dead Sea Scrolls* (1992). Her theory relies on idea that Jesus was closely connected to the Essenes and that the Essenes were responsible for writing the Dead Sea Scrolls. Many scholars dismiss her basic premise based on the established dates given for the composition of the Dead Sea Scrolls. They play the composition before Jesus was born, before the central argument of John the Baptist being the "righteous teacher" and Jesus being the "wicked priest" is dismissed.

I'm not sure even carbon dating is accurate enough to confirm the possibility of the Dead Sea Scroll/Jesus connection. There is still a window of 50-100 years that is iffy. That is enough of a window for error. As it is, scholars debate the exact year of Jesus' birth. The gospels don't match up to history exactly, so it is unknown. The bet they can guess is within a 10-20 year time frame. Most opt to go with the later date, despite its inconsistency with the whole taxation and birth in Bethlehem story.

Barbara Thiering places a sort of transparent map over the bible of people and places. She argues that most of the action happened in what is known as "New Jerusalem" or the Qumran. All of the cities, temples and locations correspond to their twin in "New Jerusalem." It is understandably confusing if the locations are all moved. This part of her theory is the weakest to me.

However, she does arrive at some of the same conclusions as other scholars. The virgin birth in Bethlehem and the crucifixion are more myth than fact. It is interesting that the Dead Sea Scrolls provide the same sort of evidence of the life of Jesus as do the Nag Hammadi Gospels. The Dead Sea Scrolls appear to be part one and the Gnostic Gospels of Nag Hammadi appear to be part two of the same story! Alone these non-canonical texts are puzzling, but as a part of a trinity with the canonical Bible they create a tapestry of truth.

Jesus, without a doubt is enigmatic figure. The Orthodox Christian religion portrays him as a mystical incarnation of God, a spiritual being that was completely pure and unspoiled by humanity. This historical figure became a deity, or living God, not much unlike the Egyptian Pharaohs of old. Thiering, instead, portrays Jesus as a political minded man, a person of power and passionate religious background. Other scholars paint Jesus as more of an outsider. He is often seen as a reluctant priest-king who challenged authority. Increasingly, he is being demystified, but his purpose and passion and political alliances remain under debate. Personal perception, not the pesher method, plays the largest role in redefining the past and Jesus' part in it.

Pieces of Light

Pieces of Light: How the Science of Memory Illuminates the Stories We Tell About Our Pasts by Charles Fennyhough came out in 2012. Can you remember the first time you did something? Not all of us do remember. The truth memories are not solid possessions like in Harry Potter.

There are several types of memories. There is Semantic Memory for Facts and Episodic Memory for Events. Declarative Memory is memory accessible to consciousness while Implicit Memory is unconscious memory. Memory is also is divided into short term or working memory and long term or stored memories. Memory is a form of knowledge with a disputed status that servers the self as much as it serves the truth.

Memories in which the remember-er appears as an objective observer are common. They are called observer memories. These are distinguished from typical first person point of view field memories.

Not everyone knows when they are lost. And when they know it, they may not always admit it. Getting lost is a telling kind of amnesia, as it turns out. It has to do with Egocentric Direction vs. Allocentric coding.

Smell is known to bring up feelings and cause involuntary memories. Music also can invoke strong memories in people.

So the reason we forget our early childhoods cannot be because a baby's brain is too immature to do any remembering. Other capacities need to be in place. They have to have the words to describe the memories. Memories also must be tied to the sense of self and they must have the ability to recreate the world in which they live in. Children do often have pre-three memories, but the older they get, the more the likely they are to forget these pre-three events. We do seem to have limited access to our pre-verbal memories.

Remembering anything depends on the process of encoding. People are more likely to remember the meaning of the conversation rather than the actual words or even the style of syntax. We have two kinds of memory 1) I remember that and 2) I DON'T recognize that. We have to know what we don't know.

Toddlers are not amnesiacs. The problem is that they are not sufficiently skilled at organizing their autobiographical knowledge. Memories are not like DVDs that get played back. Memories are constructions made in the present moment of remembering. They are not direct lines to the events themselves.

Parental efforts to manipulate children's memories can be successful. Siblings can will battle over who has the most truthful and accurate memory of their shared past. Some siblings actually recall an event that happened to their brother or sister as happening to them instead. And sometimes they recall a memory and misplace it onto a brother or sister when it happened to them. Memories merge into other memories.

Memories can be believed, non-believed and believed but not remembered. Memories can be disowned or rejected if they are too negative or too painful. People may remember something that happened to them, but consciously not believe it. Other people will believe that something happened to them when it didn't. False memories are easy to believe. They are often more real than real.

So how can one tell what is real and what isn't? Often real memories will be longer, more detailed and contain more references to cognitive process than implanted or false memories. The line between imagination and memory is a fine line. Many people will swear up and down that something they dreamed or thought actually happened, when, in fact, it did not.

There have been cases of those patients with brain damage who cannot convert any new short term memories into long term ones. One woman had herpes simplex attack her brain and left her with a condition similar to the famous HM. Life-logging or video taping everything all day everyday seems to help patients with this type of memory loss though. The opposite of Antro-grade Amnesia is a sort of Deja Vecu. It is a false sense of familiarity with things. A patient constantly believes that he's seen a TV program that is new. He believes the song he hears is a cover of an older song and that he's heard it all before when it really is a new song.

PTSD has been studied a great deal. Emotions can do really strange things to our memories, twisting and distorting them. Painful memories are often a great deal more vivid than our neutral ones. However, only 8% of trauma victims suffer from actual PTSD. They suffer nightmares and intrusive flashbulb like memories. Sometimes these memories can be wrong, but trauma is still the same. Forgetting is not a solution to PTSD though. Filling in the gaps and remembering things correctly is the best solution.

Scientists claim that Google and the internet have affected everyone's collective memory. We no longer rely on our own brains to remember things as it is so easy to look it up all the time. There is debate on had good or bad this particular affect is.

Memory, scientists have found, is not just located in one part of the brain. They have found that many parts of the brain work together to create and recreate memories. From the olfactory bulb to the prefrontal cortex to thalamus to the hippocampus to the Amygdala, memory is a multi-area endeavor.

"Memory has its own special kind of truth," says author Rushdie and perhaps he is right. For often what we remember is not necessarily the facts, but our version of them. Memory is, more than anything, the narrative that we tell ourselves and others about our life. It is a story not some memorization of a sequence of specific dates and events.

Politics and Power

Politics and power are of particular interest this week. They enter into the movies I watched and into my personal life.

First, I watched *The Ghostwriter* from 2010. It is a political thriller based a novel by Robert Harris. Though fictional, it tried to shed light on America's involvement in England's politics. The retired Prime Minister Adam Lang is a thinly veiled portrayal of Tony Blaire and is played by the wonderful Pierce Brosnan. Ewan McGregor plays the Ghostwriter hired to take Lang's painfully dry memoirs and make the readable. In the process, the Ghostwriter comes to uncover the fact that Lang's wife is a CIA agent who reported to a certain Professor Paul Emmett. The CIA used Lang as a sort of puppet for their own personal agenda, particularly where it came to the war on terror and the war in Iraq. It was a good movie I thought.

There was a preview on the DVD for a movie called *Fair Game*, which looked interesting, so I got *Fair Game* from the library next. *Fair Game* is the mostly true account of Valerie Plame. Valerie is a CIA agent dedicated to eliminating the nuclear threats of this world. She is part of the team investing rather Iraq had Weapons of Mass Destruction or not. It was her conclusion that Iraq did not have the capability to put together a Nuclear Program. Her husband, Joe Wilson, was a retired Ambassador to Niger whom was called on to help investigate Niger's connection to Iraq. He concluded that there was no major purchase of Uranium to worry about. The Vice President's adviser Scooter Libby, however, took the CIA's findings and twisted them to his own agenda. Soon it was all over the TV that Iraq had WMDs and that was why we were invading them.

The embarrassing truth was that the American Public was lied to. Facts were twisted around and out right ignored so that we could waste 10 years and trillions of dollars on an ultimately pointless war.

Quantum Thief

In the science-fiction novel The Quantum Thief the main character Jean Le Flambeur is stuck in the Dilemma Prison. His punishment is playing out endless variations of situations with countless copies of himself. This week I found myself in my own Dilemma Prison. Oh, to be able to escape into my own Oubliette!

Anyway, the 2010 novel *The Quantum Thief* was written by a Finnish Scientist named Hannu Rajaniemi. He has a PhD in String Theory. The book is dense and difficult to read at times. The hard-core scientific vocabulary can get in the way, but overall it was a good novel. There were lots of fascinating ideas contained in the pages. I liked the Gnostic elements to the story. The Archons or Engineers of the Soul were interesting. The idea of exomemory isn't that different from the idea of the collective unconscious or the Askashic Records. The addition of the personal Gevcelots or borders was a cool twist though. With technology the way it is the idea of a soul being an up-loadable Gogol may not be far off. Truly Rajaniemi has created a unique blend of science and mysticism that Zukav and others have merely hinted at. The novel feels like a natural progression of thoughts and theories.

Radiant Darkness

I read *Radiant Darkness* by Emily Whitman recently. I tried to reach her to ask her about her title and her inspiration, but she never responded. When I saw her book at the library book sale, I had to buy it. Whitman uses my title to describe the teenage journey of Persephone. The similarities are striking. Did my work inspire her at all or is it merely coincidence?

In any case, her Persephone chooses to go to the underworld. There is no abduction in Whitman's mind. More so, Persephone runs away from her mother for her love of a dark and tragic bad boy. Although Whitman doesn't psychoanalyze, I would guess that her Demeter is demanding, controlling and perhaps even abusive. Be it lack of a male role model or a strained mother-daughter relationship, Persephone is not exactly a damsel in distress. She is troubled and takes on a typical teenage attitude. Although I enjoyed the book, I still couldn't get past our different takes on Persephone.

I understand the allure of all that is dark, but embracing the Radiant Darkness is never completely our choice. Depression and other burdens are inherited. Nature and nurture propel us into our original pain. What we do with it or how we deal with it that is where choice comes into play.

Some people ignore the night and choose to put on a happy face. Others embrace the night and relish the romanticism. Those with masks covering their emotional scars are more likely to up and end it all out of the blue. Those who surrender to their melancholy moods find it easier to eventually move past them. However, it is never wise to flirt with death for too long. Some succumb not only to the angst, but to the anger and hatred as well. Stay too long in the underworld and you'll find no way to return.

A Feast for Crows by George RR Martin also reeks of romanticism. It takes place in a fictional Medieval Europe where seasons last decades. Perhaps it is the most potent pathetic fallacy of all! The Song of Fire and Ice series is loosely based on the War of the Roses and the Albigensian Crusades. Much of it is political intrigue. There are often violent plot twists. It is a world where even the seemingly good can never catch a break.

It is an interesting contrast to The Sword of Truth series by Terry Goodkind. Goodkind's style is less flowery, but there is still a strong romantic thread. The Catholicism in Goodkind's past is present in the series. The idea of a Confessor is perhaps a romanticized version of Catholic Confession. Goodkind also explores the idea of capitalism vs. socialism, as well as racism in his books.

I have yet to determine a specific theme in *A Feast for Crows*. I can say it is like Edgar Allan Poe wrote The Lord of The Rings though. Good and evil aren't as clear as they are in LOTR and certainly there is more sex in the series. Like the Robert Frost poem of the same name, Of Fire and Ice, the series appears to be centered on desire and hatred. It is gritty, but good.

My only problem with Martin is the problem I have with Faulkner. The alternating points of view or shifting stories make it difficult to keep in all straight in my head. Diagrams might help or watching the movie version if they ever made one. If Hemingway is about Subtext, then perhaps so is Goodkind. And Martin, like Faulkner, is about Subversion. I appreciated the breadth and scope of the Song of Fire and Ice Series, even if I can't quite focus on the overall plot!

Scott O'Dell Captivates

When I was 10 years old I read Island of *The Blue Dolphins* (1960) by Scott O'Dell and it captured my imagination. I used to pretend that I was Karana, alone on an island. I fashioned a bow and arrow out of wood lying around my neighborhood. I liked the idea of being self-sufficient and being able to survive on my own. I admired her strength and had fun imagining her adventures as I wandered my own suburban neighborhood.

It wasn't long before I noticed that Scott O'Dell had also written *The King's Fifth* (1966), which my favorite cartoon, *The Mysterious Cities of Gold*, had been loosely based on. In the book *The King's Fifth* Estéban is a black slave and a teenage cartographer of the Spanish Conquistador Army. The story starts when he is imprisoned. Estéban is awaiting trial finding a treasure without submitting the Quinto Real, also known as the King's Fifth. In this journal Estéban describes how he joined a small army band of Spaniards to seek the Seven Golden Cities of Cíbola. Their guide on this dangerous journey was a teenage Native American girl named Zia. Zia is the only one to preserve both her life and freedom. The book also includes Mendoza, a wily adventurer who arrived in the Americas by becoming a navigator on the ship to the New World.

I devoured the book the search for El Dorado and continued onto his Seven Serpents Trilogy. *The Captive* (1979), *The Feathered Serpent*

(1981) and *The Amethyst Ring* (1983) all took place in South America. I learned how to recognize the Mayan numbers from the numbering of the chapters in those books and they enhanced my fascination with the Mayan, Aztec and Incan Cultures. The cartoon and the books led to me doing a great deal of research and longing to visit Mexico and Peru. I jumped at the chance to visit Peru in 2001. However, I have yet to make it to Mexico and the Yucatan Peninsula.

The Severn Serpents trilogy follows Julian Esteban travels to the new world. He is shipwrecked and separated from the crew he arrived with. He is taken in by the Mayans because they think that he the one who was prophesized as returning—that he is the white god known Kukulcán. He is a Captive of the Mayans and a puppet for a powerful priest. Later, in *The Feathered Serpent*, he travels the Aztec city where Hernando Cortez has invaded. In *The Amethyst Ring*, Kukulcán's followers captured Rodrigo Perdoza, a bishop carrying a message to Cortés to detain Julián. Julián wants to be a priest and asks the bishop many times to make him one, but in the end he lets the Mayan priest sacrifice him, and Julián takes the bishop's amethyst ring. He then runs into Francisco Pizarro who is on his way to steal gold from the Inca's in Peru.

I don't know if Scott O'Dell ever traveled to the far-away places he wrote about. I do know that Scott O'Dell was born O'Dell Gabriel Scott but his name was published wrong on a book and he decided to keep the name Scott O'Dell. He was born on Terminal Island in Los

Angeles, California, to parents May Elizabeth Gabriel and Bennett Mason Scott. He attended multiple colleges. After serving in the Air Force during WWII, he became a full time writer. He won many awards during his lifetime and has remained on reading-lists in schools throughout the USA. He made history accessible and interesting to children and young adult, and for that he will not be forgotten.

Secret History of Dreaming by Robert Moss

I found The *Secret History of Dreaming* enlightening. It proposes that our dreams are more real than reality—that they are a deeper reality. Real magic, Moss insists, rides on the sexual energy from dreams. In fact, the first dream ever recorded was in Sumer nearly 5,000 years ago! And it was a powerful sexual dream at that. Writers have always been dreamers and poetry is always the result of some sort of emotional flooding.

Writers can be a sort of *"extemporal being"* as they enter into a state of lucid creative dreaming. "Just as the lucid dreamer is slightly awake, slightly outside the dream while being largely inside it, so the waking author is slightly inside the fiction while being largely outside of it." And Yeats spoke of a *"mingling of minds"* in dreaming creativity. C.S. Lewis dreamed of Aslan before he wrote the Chronicles of Narnia.

Jung believed in synchronicity—meaning through simultaneous occurrences. The physicist Pauli thought perhaps that the term *Correspondentia* was better, signaling a meaningful correspondence or a connection through meaning. And the term *Isomorphy* could relate to the same form reappearing in different structures or materials. In any case, Jung believed that truly psychic dreams were rare. Yet, Jung constantly recorded symbolic signals from his own dreams.

Seven Spells to Farewell

Seven Spells to Farewell by Betty Baker was published in 1982. However, I did not read it until around 1987. It was written for fifth to ninth graders and I was in the fifth grade when I read it. Anyway, in the book, a resourceful girl named Drucilla who goes on a long journey to find the kingdom of Iskany and become a sorceress. She adventures with a talking raven and a performing pig. The book opens with her working in an inn. Dru longs to escape the daily drudgery of domestic life, so she leaves her kitchen job behind in order to fulfill her dreams.

Now, when I went to Whitney Elementary school it was traditional for the fifth and sixth graders to take turns helping out in the school cafeteria. We'd run the dishwasher or help serve food or hand out the milk from cooler. When it was my turn to help out, I began pretending that I was someone like Dru in *Seven Spells to Farewell*. I was stuck with dull kitchen duty, but was destined for something special. Some days I was a sorceress and other days I'd be a princess in disguise, either way I was not meant to stay in the kitchen forever. This flight of fancy lasted into sixth grade, where I wrote in my journal about rather I was a princess in disguise or a sorceress. When I used my blue pencil with silver stars it was easy to pretend I was a sorceress with a magic wand. Once the pencil was all used up, I reverted back to a princess I believe. As an adult I find it less easy to imagine my way out of my kitchen duties.

Anyway, remembering this book fondly, I searched for it as an adult. I purchased it used from the internet several years ago. I lived in Ohio, but my copy is from Arkansas. I've been able to find little information on the author and no image for the book cover. My book is missing the jacket and is merely a faded red cloth cover. I seem to remember a girl standing by a caravan with the pig and raven beside her on the copy I read from my local library back in 1987, but I can't be sure.

I did find a list of other books Betty Baker wrote though. They include: *All By Herself, And Me Coyote, And One Was A Wooden Indian, Arizona, At The Center of The World, Big Push, Beyond Brave, Danby and George, Do Not Annoy The Indian, Dunderhead War, Dupper, Great Desert Race, Ghost Stories of the Old West, Killer of Death, My Sister Says, No Help At All, Partners, Santa Rat, Settlers and Strangers, Shaman's Last Raid, Spirit is Willing, Sun's Promise, The Pig's War, Three Fools and A Horse, Turkey Treasure, Walk The World's Rim* and *Worthington Botts and The Steam Machine.*

Shaw and Joyce: The Last Word in Storytelling
by Martha Fordaki Black, 1995

Both Shaw and Joyce were Irish. Joyce was fascinated by Shaw. Joyce has been a darling to text researchers and scholars because of his rich prose. Shaw's life and opinions overshadowed his plays.

In GBS, apocryphal arrangements the young Dubliner seems to have found man of his own forming attitudes.

Dubliners illustrates the Shavian paradigm of society based on a majority of dead philistines blindly, obediently to the so-called ideas of its institutions of "idealists" with vested interests or insubstantial illusions who pronounced their chosen ideals, although themselves often deluded about incapable of realizing them, and of the solitary budding "realist" who grows by discovering the folly of containing cultural illusions. (Major Critical Essays, London, 1986.)

Exiles influenced the play Candida. Poet Pound despised Shaw. Shaw was a hero to those rebelling against Victorianism though. Joyce's hero was a reflection of himself. James Stephens was a combo of Stephen Daedalus and James Joyce.

Joyce read Shaw's *Quintessence of Ibsen* and it influenced him. And it is evident in Stephen Hero and Portrait. Shaw and Joyce could be called Shavio-Joycean. Shaw concluded that Artistic Independence was preferable to the small beer of domestic happiness.

Both Shaw and Joyce described themselves as "sensitive outsiders"

Shaw said that you might as well divorce mathematics from astronomy if you are going to divorce morality from art. (Michael Holroyd, *The Search For Love*) Art, he argued, should be useful, not merely beautiful. "Every age must look for its sanction to its poets and philosophers." The realities of art alone give and sustain and vivify the force of life.

Shaw and Joyce were critics of social hypocrisy. In his play *Getting Married*, Shaw said that marriage is a useless sacrifice of human beings to an ideal. And the destructiveness of a belief in the purity of hoe life (Major Critical Essays pg 89)

Shaw and Religion
Ed by Charles A Berst, Penn State 1981

"There is to say Be and It Is," is a Shavian saying.

Shaw is indebted to numerous philosophies. He experienced religion in poetic terms. Development religiously was his perception of himself in relation to God.

In *Man and Superman* listed sources thought: Bunyan, Blake, Hogarth, Turner, Goethe, Shelly, Schopenhauer, Wagner, Ibsen, Morris, Tolstoy, Nietzsche. Dickens, Shakespeare, Mozart, Beethoven, Rembrandt, Hegel,and Bergson.

Post Script in *Back to Methuselah.* "The Creative Evolutionist believes firmly in Providence and in what used to be called *The Will of God.* Instead of dwelling morbidly on the quite unedifying and not too interesting interference, Creative Evolution goes back to a very old and pregnant lesson that the beginning was thought and the thought was with the God. The thought was God. Thought being what the Greek's meant by *the word* The Greek Origin of John's word is logos.

"I am not governed by principles, I am inspired by how or why I cannot explain," says GBS. "When I write a play I never invent a plot, he says, I let the play write and shape itself."

Shaw says of Superman in Self Sketches, "The must though learn to stand absolutely thou. Can'st nothing know, responsible to nothing, fearing no power and being within thyself. A little independent universe."

"I was a coward until Marx made a communist of me and gave me faith." 1881-1883

"Like Shelley, I am socialist, atheist and a vegetarian." 1887

"Goethe rescued us, from the horror of aesthetic despair with his eternal feminine that draws us forward and upward, which was the first modern manifesto of the mysterious force in Creative Evolution. That is what made Faust a world classic."

"Such a force there is, however, and it is called the Godhead. And these higher powers are called into existence by the same self-organization of life. Still more wonderfully into rare persons who may by comparisons be called gods, creatures capable of thought whose aims extend far and beyond the satisfaction of their bodily appetites and personal affection, since they perceive that it is only by the establishment of a social order founded on common bonds or moral faith that the world can rise from the mere savagery."

Trinity Gospel
Creative Evolution is the Father
Life Force is the Holy Ghost
and Superman is the Son

Caesar is Superman in the world made flesh. Caesar and St. John are both teachers and they both share the role of transforming the child into an adult.

If religion means codified dogma, prescribed rules for conduct, acceptance of an elaborate institution hierarchy system of of ritual, then Shaw opposed religion. If religion exists to foster the development of ethical and spiritual wholeness in he individual, to let him see clearly the purpose of life on earth, and to ensure that his desires tend toward the moral well being of mankind, then Shaw is deeply concerned with promoting religion.

Shaw's life-force is inside the individual, not outside deities.

Shaw believes that men do evil their he best of intentions, in the name of duty, social responsibility and other abstract ideals. Really bad men are as rare as really good ones.

Creative Evolution is the alternative to Christians and Darwinians.

Back to Methuselah addresses itself to the possibility that if man desired death in the beginning, he should be able to emancipate himself from the natural cycle of life and death by reversing that desire, seizing once again control of mother nature and reducing her to his emanation.

Shaw's Don Juan proclaimed, "He who seeks in contemplative to discover the inner will of he world, in invention to discover the mean of fulfilling that will, and in action to do that will by the so-called means."

Creative Evolution is nothing more than a hypothesis. Faith confronted with the possibility of mediating and reconciling synthesis might lead to the new awareness and rebirth.

Shaw and the Play of Ideas
By Robert F Whitman, 1977

Shaw's hostility to Capitalism as the source of most of civilized man's economic, social and moral ills, is both well known and persuasive throughout his writing....And war in general he viewed as a Marxist fashion—simply as a mechanism whereby Capitalists expand markets and consume goods for their own economic advantage.

As we shall see, Shaw fought through the whole question of whether God is Dead and come out on the otherside with the conclusion that he is indeed alive and still growing. He treats traditional religion as inflexible and intellectually dishonest in their inability to take into account the complexity and evolution of humankind. (pg 23)

If politics and religion and morality and even reason have proved sterile or corrupt, if they have brought us down the wrong road or if they have simply become the tools of selfish men, the solution is not to throw them on the dust heap, but to make them work for humanity. He speaks to us in tones not of despair or lamentation, but of anger and renewed vigor. A man with an idea and a conviction possesses the strength of ten. Shaw never tires of telling us this. He was never one to be caught short of an idea....The road to boredom is paved with good ideas, left there by sincere men who the power to communicate them. Shaw had the opposite problem. (pg 24)

In Don Juan we see the Shavian paradox. "Heaven is the home of the masters of reality. Hell is the home of honor, duty, justice and the rest of the seven deadly sins." It is not the self-indulgence that Shaw despises, but the self-delusion.

His God must not be an existing Omnipotent and Omniscient perfections, but as yet only an ideal towards which Creative Evolution is striving with mankind merely its best attempt so far and very unsatisfactory one at that, liable to be replaced at any moment if at any moment Creative Evolution gives it up as hopeless. (pg 44)

He must face the evil in the world, which apparently reduces the goodness of God to absurdity, as but the survival of errors originally well intended. He must treat life as everlasting, but treat his contemporaries as ephemeral mortals having no life beyond the grave to compensate them for any injustices they may suffer here and now.

"I believe that the universe is being driven by a force we might call the life-force," ~Shaw

Reason as a logical process seemed to him cold and mechanical—the engine, as he put it, rather than the steam. Thought, however, a imagination, as comprehension, as ability to understand ourselves and the world, and our purpose in it, was a creative and ultimately mystical function, the highest activity of which the human animal is capable.

The shelf he would put to the service of the life-force's mighty purpose was his unique gift, his mind.

Shaw was a pacifist, but he acknowledged that "great social changes, if conscious and intentional, are not made until their advocates are sufficiently in earnest to be prepared to kill those who obstruct them.

Even the modified form of anarchy on which modern civilization is based, that is the abandonment of industry, in the name of individual liberty. The upshot of competition for personal gain between private capitalists is a disastrous failure, and , is by mere necessity of the case, giving way to ordered socialism.

Shaw's hatred and hatred is probably not too strong a word—of the rich—on the grounds that they represent useless and unproductive parasites on the community as a whole, was no greater than his hatred for the poor—for what would be the same reason. They were a burden that depressed the common welfare. Shaw hated both, but claimed that he was not misanthropic. He wanted to exterminate both the rich and poor—the conditions not the people.

Shaw believed that Totalitarian Governments were institutions that were acting on realistic rather than idealistic grounds. Pragmatists rather than moralists who felt they had to justify their actions.

Shaw tried to cope within the constellation of theories surrounding the principle of the life-force. Socialism and Creative Evolution, as well as other ideas provided the center of Shaw's thought, are simply different ways of thinking about or coming to terms with some of the central questions about the nature of man.

Socialism or the Fabian Society and beyond. His arrogance and self-publicizing antics, his rudeness and other thing were merely role playing. His personality was truly unknown to everyone except his closest friends.

Argument and dialect, the language of debate and of rhetoric persuasion were adapted in hi dramas. He used his plays as a public forum.

Shaw fought against the institution of the church. He had an irreverence toward it growing up. He had a disregard and contempt for authority. He had little respect for traditional objects of reverence. He had a total skepticism of all religious matters. He had the strong urge to himself to some outside power though. In his 20s, he went about "finding himself."

Schopenhauer distinction between intellect and will. Will guides the growth of the animal and directs all of its activities. Will resembles the life-force and becomes consciousness itself. It creates intelligence.

Schopenhauer worked through Ibsen or Ibsen was influenced by Schopenhauer. "A world will that worked through man, pushing from him from childhood through youth toward maturity, but not in a straight line. Dialectic process, joy in the senses, spirituality beyond and transcendence. It is the unity of the mind, body and soul.

Hegel and the Shavian Dialectic. Hegel has the hero triumph over God and yet in that event the Godhead fulfills itself in something higher. This process of the Godhead transcending itself, the process of transcendence and forms and moral laws it has established as part of its compromise with the world, is, by definition, immoral within the framework of those laws.

Shaw said, "Life itself as a tireless power, which is continuously driving onward and upward into higher and higher life forms of organization, the strengths and the needs of which are continuously superseding the institutions which were made from our former requirements." (pg127)

For both Hegel and Shaw the "hero" is simply a metaphor for the man who rises above what man is or as Shaw put it? "The World is waiting for man to redeem it from the lame and ramped government of the Gods." (pg 128)

Life-Force is not to be associated with the Christian Deity. "The object of the whole evolutionary process is to realize God."

Hegel and the mind is an organ of self-knowledge and self-realization, which is the realization of the spirit.

Don Juan replies that his is a process of a purpose beyond his own, which is to help the Life-Force to "Know itself and its destination."

Hegel says the spiritual self wants to attain the light of consciousness and to come into itself or evolve. Shaw says, "The life force is struggling toward its goal of Godhead by incarnating itself in creatures with knowledge and power enough to control nature and circumstances."

Shaw also wrote, "To me, God does not exist...The current theory that God already exists in perfection involves the belief that God deliberately created something lower than himself. To my mind, unless we conceive of God as engaged in continual struggle to surpass himself, we are conceiving nothing better than an omnipotent snop. (Letters II, 901)

Hegel says God is not an abstract goal. God is self-consciousness. God is not God and cannot be God without creating a world, without knowing himself in the "other." The absolute becomes conscious only in evolution and above all, man.

Shaw says the Kingdom of God is within us. Heaven and Hell is a parable of a dream episode in Man Vs Superman is based on that idea. Hell is the home of unreality, nothingness and non-being. Heaven is process of becoming—of moving from non-being to being purity and absolute self-consciousness.

Thought was God—Creative Evolution. Shaw "To Know God is to Be God."

Not much known of Hegel. He is most elusive and opaque of philosophers that is known better through 2nd hand sources.

Evil eases to be a problem with the "life-force." Evil is necessarily absorbed through the pressure of dialectic or logical reality.

In a world of relative truths, inconsistency can be intellectually honest.

Our morality is impudent hypocrisy our wisdom is administered by inexperience.

Shavian paradoxes in their various form, were not mere topsyturvyism, they had as common element the yoking together of implicitly or explicit contradictions with the purpose of forcing the mind to move, if not ward something as absolute truth—at least toward seeing things more clearly. (pg 168)

Dogma of Toleration. It [the life force] is not omnipotent. "All moral triumphs, like mechanical triumphs are reached by trial and error."

Dramatic truth and dramatic reality are necessary partial and complete, both because of the nature of the medium and the its limitation, conscious or not, of the artist image of reality. Truth should be more of an "as if."

The recognition, however, that the same drive or stimulus that at one stage of human evolution advances the life-force at a later stage prove an obstacle or counter force—contributed to another characteristic feature of a Shavian Drama. The conflict and tension of a play are NOT resolved. Or they lead to a new tension or to a resolution that is, at best, tentative.

"It is often the most self-assured characters in the plays who are drifting, with no sense of purpose, no desire to reach for the is no need to reach and nothing to reach for."

And drifting is death. The uncertain ones seek a way and are at least trying to steer. Shaw wants to be a navigator for his audience.

Marriage is the worlds/life-force will, not our own.

In Don Juan in Hell, Ana and Jack are in the grip of the life-force and its will. The life-force's will is the only will. The will to create new minds in the abode where it can create a better world—in both men and women.

Love is necessary for the life-force. But when it becomes an end in and of itself, it can be an obstacle for life, for which love is a beginning and not end end. (*Man and Superman*) (pg 243)

Hegel system, the passion and energy is necessary to move the Spirit from potential reality in history, necessary confront obstacles and opposition—Possibilities Become Fact.

Every end is a new beginning. Death moves us closer to our evolution to God.

Slant of Light

"A Certain Slant of Light—on winter afternoons—that oppresses like the weight—of cathedral tunes. Heavenly hurt it gives us—we can fine no scar—but internal difference—where the meanings are," wrote Emily Dickinson. The poem talks of light being as oppressive as faith, religion and God can be. Old age and death, Emily decides, is a painful transformation. Still, even death is not purely negative. The agony, it seems, comes from living alone inside one's mind. Heaven is a truth that the living are not privileged enough to know about, thus dying is scary.

A Certain Slant of Light is also the title of a young adult novel by Laura Whitcomb. The book is about a 130 year old ghost or spirit named Helen. Helen is in love with a high school English Teacher, but of course nothing comes of it. Anyway, Helen possesses the body of Jenny so that she can be with James. James possesses the body of Billy. Finally the two ghosts can be together. Only Jenny's parents are super religious and very oppressive. Their control caused Jenny to commit suicide and eventually drives Helen to the same end.

Despite the suicide, sex and drugs the tragic story does have a happy ending. The ghosts go toward the light—of love and of heaven.

Slant of Light Sequel: Under the Light

"Under the Light, yet under the grass and dirt," wrote Emily Dickinson. Her poem is quoted by Laura Whitcomb at the beginning of her 2013 companion to *A Certain Slant of Light,* which is *Under The Light.* Like the poem, the book is about the connection between the dead and the living. I thought it was a good metaphor for my week as well. Like Dickinson, I feel that there is something just beyond my grasp. I know its there, yet I can't see it. Rather it is the other side of mortal life or the other side of this particular part of my life, the elusiveness is the same.

Soul Murder

Soul Murder: The Effects of Childhood Abuse and Deprivation by Leonard Shengold came out in 1989. To abuse or neglect a child, to deprive the child of his or her own identity and ability to experience joy in life, is to commit soul murder. He says that a soul murder is neither a diagnosis nor a condition.

It is a dramatic term for circumstances that eventuate in crime—the deliberate attempt to eradicate or compromise the separate identity of another person. The victims of soul murder remain, in large part, possessed by another—their soul in bondage to someone else. A consummated soul murder is a crime most of committed by psychotic or psychopathic parents who treat the child as an extension of themselves or as an object to satisfy them or their desires.

Child abuse is the abuse of power. And the trauma that results is a sort of too-much-ness that creates sadomasochistic sexualization of future experiences. Soul murdered children often become psychopathic themselves. It is an endless cycle of abuse.

The term was first used in 1903 by Schreber. Soul Murder often includes brainwashing. The victim must register the parent as good even if it is delusional. This split between what the parent should be and what they really are can cause mind splitting, fragmenting and compartmentalizing. The parent will become a sort of Sphinx or Strangler.

Indifference will often mask their murderous rage at having their soul murdered and later killing others themselves.

Rats have come to symbolize child abuse and soul murder. Rats were once used to torture prisoners. Rats are aggressive and are destructive, voracious and omnivorous. The Penis can be symbolized by the rat because it can have teeth and bite so to speak. Rat Children can bite and be bitten or they are abused and can turn around and abuse others.

Metaphors and Symbols can lead to recovered memories of trauma. The memories can lead to insight and that can lead to healing eventually.

As the inside flap says, it is provocatively original in its approach to literature and psychology, unsettling in its vivid portrayal of the darker side of human nature, far-reaching in its conclusions, *Soul Murder* will stand alongside such works as Alice Miller's *The Drama of the Gifted Child* as one of the most important studies of the psyche to appear in decades.

Steampunk

What is Steampunk? Is it a mad scientist inventor in a Victorian setting with airships and metal men? Does it have reactionary politics and an adventure plot? Yes! Jules Verne and H.G. Wells are the Grandfathers of this so-called new sub-genre. It is a mixture of supernatural, science fiction and fantasy. There are sub-genres even within Steampunk, including: Boiler-Punk, Clockwork-Punk, Diesel Punk, Gaslight Romance, Manners Punk, Ray Gun Gothic and Stitch Punk. The genre evolved from Cyberpunk in many ways. Bruce Sterling says, *"Steampunk's key lessons are not about the past. They are about the instability and obsolesce of our own time."*

Steampunk Books

A Clockwork Century Series by Cherie Priest (*My Favorite!*)
Parasol Protectorate by Gail Carriger (*2nd Favorite*)
The Steampunk Trilogy by Paul Di Filippo (*Queen Victoria is Automaton*)
A Clockwork Heart by Dru Pagliassotti (*An Icarus character with Mystery and Romance*)
Steampunk Edited by Ann and Jeff VanderMeer (*Good Collection*)
Leviathan and Behemoth by Scott Westerfield (*Inspirational for my story* **Prospector Pirates**)
The Manual of Detection by Jedediah Berry (*Surreal Fantasy Detective Novel!*)

The Glass Book of Dream Eaters Vol 1 and Vol 2 by Gordon Dahlquist (*Challenging High Style*)

The Difference Engine by William Gibson and Bruce Sterling (*1ˢᵗ Modern Steampunk*)

Pavane by Keith Roberts (1968)

Iron Angel by Alan Campbell (*Interesting Mythology.*)

Crystal Rain by Tobias S Beckell (*Science Fiction Colony Adventure*)

Mainspring by Jay Lake (*God, Angels and Machines! Oh My!*)

The Steampunk Bible by Jeff VanderMeer

The Girl in the Steel Corset by Kady Cross (*The Strange Case of Finley Jayne*)

The Clockwork Wolf by Lynn Viehl (*Female Detective with Supernatural Powers!*)

Steampunk Movies

Le Voyage Dans La Lune by George Melies (French Early 1900s)

20,000 Leagues Under The Sea (*Jules Verne)*

The Time Machine (*HG Wells*)

Wild Wild West (*TV show and Will Smith Movie*)

Blade Runner (*Harrison Ford.*)

Castle in the Sky

Sleepy Hollow (*Hello Johnny Depp!*)

Return To Oz

Tank Girl

Dark City (*Rufus Sewell and Kiefer Sutherland*)

Steamboy (Cartoon)

League of Extraordinary Gentleman

The Brother's Grimm (*Heath Ledger and Matt Damon*)

12 Monkeys (*Brad Pitt!*)

Sky Captain and the World of Tomorrow (*Angelina Jolie!*)

The Golden Compass

Sherlock Holmes (2009) (*Robert Downy Jr, Yeah!*)

Steven Senn's Spirituality

I was about 11 years old when I discovered the book **Spacebread** by Steven Senn about a cat that traveled through space and had all kinds of cool adventures. It was published in 1981, but I didn't read it until 1987 or so. Anyway, it was his adventures that inspired my pretend games of space travel. My mom would be inside the Laundromat doing laundry and I would go out to the old Chevy Nova we had and pretend it was a space ship. I'd shove a tape into the tape deck and pull down the visor and pretend that I had maps and star charts up on a screen. From there I would re-enact many of the scenes from the book where Spacebread uncovers a plot to dominate the planet Ralph while she goes in search of her stolen belt buckle.

That same year I read another novel by Steve Senn called *A Circle in the Sea*. It came out in 1981 as well. In the book a 13-year-old girl with problems adjusting to her new school enters an undersea world through the power of a ring, becomes a dolphin and aids the whales in retaliating against slaughter by whalers. This led me to pretend to turn into a dolphin every time I went swimming that summer. I'd make high pitch noises underwater and close my eyes. I found that I could tell by how loud or soft the noise was how close or far away I was from the wall of the pool. It was not an exact science, but still a lot of fun to try and master. Then my friends and I would try to find each other in the water using the echo-location techniques we'd practiced. It was kind of hit and miss, but it gave us a little bit of a sense of direction. I thought it would be awesome to really be able to transform and see what it was like to be a dolphin.

Anyway, there were other young adult titles by Senn besides *Spacebread* and *A Circle in the Sea* including: *Ralph Fozbek and the Amazing Black Hole Patrol, Loonie Louie Meets the Space Fungus, , Born of Flame, Sand Witch*, and *In the Castle of the Bear*. Oscar Steve Senn has also written some award winning adult short stories, including: "The Blood of Eden," "The Wall," "The Unexpected Guest," and "Squeeby Rolic." I've not read any of these, because my local library didn't own any of them. I didn't realize he'd written others until I began to research him as an adult.

His first book *The Double Disappearance of Walter Fozbek* was adapted for an animated special on the Emmy nominated CBS Storybreak, hosted by Captain Kangaroo himself, Bob Keeshan. The story is about a boy who wakes up in a different universe that is exactly like his own except everything that was Human is now Dinosaur.

I couldn't find much about him. But I do know that Oscar Steve Senn is an executive/designer, illustrator and an author. He was born in Americus, Georgia in 1950 and was raised in Dawson. He went to school at the Ringling School of Art in Sarasota, Florida. He worked for The Florida Times-Union and the Miami Herald newspapers as an illustrator. He also worked as an Art Director in Jacksonville, Florida.

Oscar Steve Senn obviously has a very vivid imagination and is a very talented writer. I couldn't help but feel a sense of spirituality seeping through his words and because of that I always felt a particular affinity toward the two books of his I read. I made sure to get copies of them for my own personal libraries so I could share them with my own kids.

Stuff: Compulsive Hoarding and the Meaning of Things by Randy O Frost and Gail Stekete

In 1947 two dead bodies were found in a New York Brownstone. What made news was the fact that the house contained 170 tons of junk, including 14 Grand Pianos and a Model T Ford. Hoarding has been around a long time, but it has only recently gained media attention.

What are the characteristics of a hoarder? Many suffer from perfectionism, indecision, powerful beliefs about attachments to objects, being unable to figure out where things go or where to put it. They have a fear that if it is out of sight, it is out of mind.

Hoarding is a subset of OCD. They often shop compulsively, some are even kleptomaniacs. They have a fear of waste and take comfort in objects. Hoarders sometimes keep stuff "just in case they need it later."

But what gives things value? Why do we own what we do?" Plato says that ownership should be banned but Aristotle felt that ownership was essential for a person's moral character. Sir Thomas Aquinas believed we just held stewardship over God's things. Locke felt things belonged only to those who work for them. Hume saw possession as a part of the person. William James believed that me, mine and self consist of what we possess. Erich Fromm felt acquisitions create the core aspect of our character. Karl Abraham felt people kept things to keep a part of themselves and Freud felt keeping things was a part of anal fixation.

What separates normal everyday collectors from hoarders?

Often times there is abuse or some sort of trauma that happened in that person's childhood. Some have a pathological fear of missing out on things or a deep seated fear of failing to remember their past. Others attach collecting things to a need for perfection in their lives. They collect in order to control certain situation and gain self-esteem in creating something that is perfect. And they get very upset when it doesn't go "just right."

Animal Hoarders exist too. That crazy cat lady suffers from OCD and Hoarding as well. Most animal Hoarders are indeed women over 40 who are single, divorced or widowed. They usually suffered from abuse or neglect as a child. They collect animals out of a mission to rescue them or they become overwhelmed by what they feel is their duty. Some can even become exploitative of the animals and ended up charged with animal cruelty—thought that isn't extremely common. These animal Hoarders are often delusional about their problem until they finally take steps to overcome it.

Hoarders don't like to clean or organize their messes because it causes them pain. Sorting out their belongings causes anxiety and depression, so they avoid doing so. They often avoid making decisions or taking action in other areas of their lives as well. They often claim they don't have time to really dig in and do what needs to be done.

Hoarding rubbish is called Syllogmania. This is often in conjunction with Diogenes or Senile Recluse Syndrome. The elderly neglect themselves—having poor personal hygiene and living in squalid conditions.

ADD or ADHD is frequently observed in those with Hoarding issues. They are distracted easily, can't finish projects, lose things, are forgetful and talk excessively. However, Hoarders often describe themselves as "artists" even if they don't actively practice an art.

Doctors have found that the prefrontal region of the brain is responsible for goal directed behavior, planning, organization and decision making. They also found that lower metabolic rates in the cingulate cortex are found in Hoarders. This lower metabolic rate can cause lack of motivation, lack of attention, an inability to identify errors and issues with decision making. Does that damage to that region cause the Hoarder to become what they are or does it simply reflect what they've already become? That they have yet to figure out.

Kids can be Hoarders too. There are several documented cases of kids obsessively collecting, stealing and keeping objects. At such an early age it is the behavior surrounding the objects that garner the most attention. Some kids throw many tantrums and appear to be very particular about their belongings in addition to other issues. Usually the other behavioral problems overshadow the Hoarding itself, but they do exhibit many of the same thoughts, feelings and behaviors of adult Hoarders.

Overall, those who Hoard believe that without their things they don't exist—that they are nothing. They readily confuse HAVING with BEING. Their things are an extension of themselves and those people who throw away their stuff are seen as a threat. Hoarders feel violated when their stuff is messed with even if it a health hazard to them.

There are many self-help books out there for those need some assistance in dealing with Hoarding. There are also plenty of trained psychologists and therapy groups to help, should the Hoarder want to reach out. Usually it takes a lot of love and understanding from the loved ones of Hoarders to get them past their need to Hoard though.

Summerhouse, Later

Are we drawn to literature that speaks to us directly? Can we know someone through what they read? Is literary biography accurate enough to even bother with?

I am reading *Summerhouse, Later* by Judith Hermann. The collections of short stories are existential in nature. They are thoroughly modern in the character's search for meaning and for love. It is a bleak portrayal, but yet not without hope. It is sad, but not pessimistic. The stories are realistic, yet poetic. They are beautiful like Wim Wender's *Wings of Desire*. I am happy to have discovered them.

"Sonja" in particular stirred something within me. The main character is an artist who has a girlfriend, but takes an interest in another woman who seems younger. He gets pulled into her world. It is a strange relationship that is subtle, sublime and somehow satisfying despite the lack of passion. He is ambivalent toward Sonja, both annoyed and intrigued. He wants to push her away at first, but doesn't. His girlfriend Verna accuses him of cheating, though he has not even touched Sonja. When Verna is away all summer he spends time with Sonja. The relationship is platonic. The thought of having sex with her is somehow incestuous, yet he finds that he still loves her. This creates a sense of fear, guilt and anger. He allows Sonja into his heart anyway and into his bed. They do not have sex, but there is an emotional intimacy between them. The narrator panics and pushes Sonja away eventually. He thought perhaps that he would be relieved, but he discovers that he misses her instead. She moves away and he never sees her again.

Anyway, happiness is the moment before, so says Judith Hermann. Before what you ask? Before the realization that you are happy, before the consciousness perhaps. Ignorance is bliss right? Sometimes. Sometimes happiness comes at an unexpected moment. We all pursue happiness, but true happiness is nearly always elusive and just out of grasp. We pursue an intellectual ideal rather than our heart's desire. Happiness cannot be thought up or created as an ideal. No, happiness is in the small stuff, the Zen like state of mindfulness. The details are where it is at because the big picture is full of struggle and suffering. So, while you ache and accept your place in life, there are moments of bliss. Once we become aware of that bliss, then the fear sets in. We become attached to our happiness and try too hard to maintain that high. Life isn't one big high though. It is a series of ups and a down. The secret is to let go and go wherever it takes you. The joy found in the moment can never be permanent. The only security you have is the life will surely present you with another up. If nothing ever stays the same then you can't possibly depressed all the time. It is probably *that* rational realization that kept me sane the past few years. After a long dark night, I've found my way to the dawn. At last I feel good about things.

Sweet Valley High

Ana and I watched Season 1 Disc 3 of *Sweet Valley High* on DVD. I remembered catching the show a couple of times on a Saturday or a Sunday, but I never knew its regular time slot. It aired from 1994—1997. Watching the DVD I couldn't believe how big and colorful the fashions were. The show was a bit cheesy, but enjoyable enough. It brought back memories of reading the book series.

My Aunt Kelly first introduced them to me to the Sweet Valley High world around 1989 or so. I remember seeing one of the first few books of the series lying around her house. I asked if I could read it, which I did. From then on I began reading the entire series. I usually just check them out of the library, but occasionally I bought a used copy at a yard sale or used book store.

It didn't take long to catch up on the books written from 1984 to 1989. Each year after that they'd put out another book or two and I read that as well. I read about the first 100 books before getting bored with them. There are roughly 181 books in the Sweet Valley High series today, not counting the most recent reinventions like Sweet Valley University and Sweet Valley Confidential. Although I got rid of most of my Sweet Valley Books, I do still own four of them. *Kidnapped*, *Secrets* and *On the Edge* along with *Double Jeopardy* Super Edition.

My friend Elizabeth Keene and I shared the love of Sweet Valley High and would often trade books and discuss them. We both loved Elizabeth Wakefield. I liked her because she was a writer like me and Elizabeth liked her because she shared the same name. Elizabeth continued reading the series long after I stopped though, so she has read more of them than I have over the years. I never really got into Sweet Valley Twins book either like she did.

The inspiration for Richard's sister in my 1992 story *In Too Deep* was Regina Marrow from the book *(#40) On the Edge*. She tried cocaine once and tragically died of an allergic reaction. Also, I would often imagine my hunky boyfriend as Nicholas because I liked the character of Nicholas Marrow.

Though light and easy reading, they were inspirational. For a girl of 12 years to 14 years old they weren't bad reading. They were full of mystery and drama without being overly dark or depressing. I recommend picking up the books if you are young or want to feel young again. They are great fun to read!

Theosophy

Theosophy means "God Wisdom." It is a New Age movement attributed to the late great **Madame Blavatsky.** God is said to be revealed through mystical insight, in other words, Gnosticism. Much of the occult is really offshoots of oppressed Gnostic Christianity. (Although Paganism does play a large role too.)

Theosophy has influenced George Lucas—at least according to a Wikipedia article. The article also lists L. Frank Baum who wrote the Oz series. Thus, it is also an influence on the television show Lost.

Madam Blavatsky wrote about Hyperboreans, Atlantis and Lemuria. Shirley McLaine's vision in *The Camino* is very much in line with Madam Blavatsky's own vision. Among other things, Blavatsky wrote about The Great White Brotherhood, Higher Selves and Reincarnation. She claimed to have a look at an ancient Tibetan book called the Book of Dzyan.

The Batterer: A Psychological Profile

The Batterer: A Psychological Profile by Donald G Dutton, PhD with Susan K Golant came out in 1995. The book examines the abusive relationship in detail and gives insight into how and why the abuse happens.

The abusive man is addicted to brutality to keep his shaky self-concept intact. The only time he feels powerful and when he is engaged in acts of violence or control. Abusers fear abandonment and fear being engulfed by the relationship at the same time. They can have a duel personality like Dr. Jekyll and Mr. Hyde. Friends don't see the violence. Only close family.

Abusers shame and humiliate their partner verbally as well as physically. They degrade them and blame them. The abuser will seek to make their victim dependent on them. And they will show jealousy and rage when the victim asserts any independency.

Alcohol often plays a role. The batter self-medicates his anxiety and depression by drinking and that often fuels his rage. Post-Traumatic stress can cause a person to lash out at their partner and begin abusing them as well. Post-Traumatic stress is characterized by crying, sadness, trouble breathing, panic attacks, nightmare, dizziness and sometimes even black outs.

Abuse often stems from the abusers childhood experiences. They feel rage because they too were victimized and they feel helpless. Instead of seeking help, they become an abuser. Often they view women within the Madonna/Whore complex. Woman can be saintly or dirty and nothing in between. They will put their woman up on a pedestal only to knock her down-repeatedly.

The relationship may not start out as abusive, but there are often precursors. For example, one of the people in the relationship may be clingy while the other is distant. An then anger follows unmet attachment needs. Men sometimes feel angry when their partner isn't happy. They will wonder why their partner can't make them happy.

Abusers are neither psychotic nor neurotic. Instead, abusers suffer from Borderline Personality Disorder. Borderline Personality disorder is characterized by apathy, anxiety, anger, wavering energy levels and self-destructive behavior. They will have a preoccupation with secrecy and maintaining emotional support. They are deeply afraid of loss and fear isolation. They have conflicting emotions toward others—fluctuating from love to rage and then to guilt. Borderlines are quick to blame their partners when things go wrong in intimate relationships. Men are more likely to strike out against others if they have Borderline Personality Disorder. Women, on the other hand, are more likely to be self-destructive.

Socially speaking most abusers are blue-collar workers, though it can be anyone. They will often have a father who shamed them and a mother who was ambivalent toward them. To the abuser intimacy means trying to accomplish the impossible—gluing together their shaky ego. When the relationship fails his very sense of self will be threatened. The projection and blame he casts onto his partner is his self-defense.

How can the batterer be helped? The two biggest obstacles are getting the man to acknowledge the violence and be accountable for it. If these hurdles aren't cleared, then nothing else will have any effect.

This is an excellent book for anyone who wishes to understand abuse. I highly recommend it.

The Divided Self

The Divided Self by R.D. Laing came out in 1960. What was his message? His message was that maybe mad people are not as 'mad' as they seem; maybe they are just 'divided selves'. Whilst simple, this was revolutionary. For centuries, society (we) had excluded, ignored, imprisoned, laughed at, and been afraid of these 'mad' people.

Laing discusses how the schizophrenic lives under the glare of the black sun. Everything withers under this black sun, which operates like an evil eye. They are preoccupied with being seen or visible. Sometimes they have fantasies of invisibility. They feel like they can appear and disappear like they are still an infant playing peek-a-boo.

The schizophrenic may objectify or depersonalize. They feel as if they are on the fringe of being. They may even go so far as to feel as if they are a nobody and literally have no body. Speaking of madness Yeats once said, "Things fall apart, the centre cannot hold. Mere Anarchy is loosed upon the world."

Madness can be like psychic cancer—an overgrowth of something inside. It is a false sense of having one's oxygen cut off. Reality is broken down into pieces and the person is fragmented or shattered. They may feel empty or dead inside while others may feel charged with hatred, fear and envy.

The mad may have mystical experiences. They may suffer delusions and demonstrate odd behavior. They feel like their selves have been lost, robbed, stolen or even murdered. The reasoning is that if they are dead then they can't be killed. They cut themselves off from others and their heaven turns into a hell.

Sometimes the schizophrenic will have erratic and bizarre speech patterns. Most of it is not important and a deliberate misleading away from the self. The self is a pearl at the bottom of the sea and the psychiatrist must dive in to find it. The schizophrenic doesn't trust anyone, so treating them is particularly difficult.

The Elegant Universe

The Elegant Universe by Brian Greene came out in 1999. The book is broken into five parts. Part I: The Edge of Knowledge. Part II: The Dilemma of Space, Time, and the Quanta. Part III: The Cosmic Symphony. Part IV: String Theory and the Fabric of Spacetime. Part V: Unification in the Twenty-First Century.

Greene begins by breaking down the elements. He explains how we have the atom, the electron and Protons and Neutrons and then we have the Quark. Then he moves onto String Theory.

Just as the strings on a violin or piano have resonant frequencies at which they prefer to vibrate—patterns that our ears sense as various musical notes and their higher harmonies—the same holds true for the loops in string theory. But we will see that rather than producing musical notes each preferred patterns of vibration of a string in string theory appears as a particle whose mass and force are determined by the string's oscillatory pattern. The Electron is a string vibrating one way; the Up Quark is string vibrating another way and so on.

The Theory of Everything or T.O.E. is an effort by Steven Weinberg to pull together all the separate theories into one theory that covers everything. The Electro-Magnetic field that Michael Faraday and James Clerk Maxwell theorized on was the beginning of The Theory of Everything.

Light is an electromagnetic vibration perceived by our eyes. Time is not an absolute. Length varies with extreme speed. That is where Einstein's famous E=MC2 comes in. Energy=Mass at the Speed of Light or C squared. In other words, a little mass goes a long way in producing energy. Greene also addresses Newton's view of gravity which is not compatible to Einstein's Theory of Special Relativity. He also discusses blackholes and the idea of the Event Horizon, which is the point of no return.

Greene also covers the Big Bang Theory. He says that the universe is unfurling like a coil or spreading out like a tidal wave. Then he goes back to talking about Max Planck and the beginning of Quantum Physics. Matter comes in Waves or Particles—Quanta can be both. Richard Feynman was the greatest theoretic physicist next to Einstein. Feynman was the one who theorized the Quantum Mechanics wasn't about one path but all possible paths.

After the Big Bang, Gravity, The Special Theory of Relativity and Quantum Physics came the String Theory. What happens when these strings collide? Two can combine into one or they can split off in different directions. This means that the state of the observer depends on the interaction and that the interaction depends on the state of the observer. We not only affect reality, but create it and change it by our very consciousness of it.

There are different types of string theory. Kaluza or Klein which represent dimensions curled up on a grid. Calabi-Yau Space represents the dimensions as multi-holes or multi-donuts. Greene also addresses the theory of worm holes. Let's say you have a U-Shaped universe then you could take a short cut across it.

The last bit of the book is dedicated to the idea of the M-Theory. The M stands for Membrane, but it could also stand for Mother or Mystery or Matrix. M-Theory says there are 11 dimensions of space and time; which include 7 higher dimensions and 4 common dimensions.

You don't need to be a scientist to enjoy this book. It is easily written and easy to understand. I highly recommend it.

The Ethical Slut

The Ethical Slut: A Practical Guide to Polyamory, Open Relationships and Other Adventures by Dossie Easton and Janet W. Hardy first came out in 1997. It was updated and reprinted in 2009. The two authors want to reclaim the word slut to mean something more positive. Slut is generally used to describe a woman who is voracious, indiscriminate and shameful in her sexual encounters. However, a man who acts the same way is known as a stud. To the authors the word slut has come to mean a person of any gender who celebrates sexuality and believes that sex is nice and good for you. Solo sex, sex with the 5th Fleet, heterosexual sex homosexual sex, and bisexual sex are all included under the umbrella of sex is good and nice here.

The term Polyamory was coined in 1990 by Morning Glory Ravenheart Zell. Modern marriage is no longer essential for survival; so many other arrangements have crept up over the years. Kinsey once said that the term nymphomaniac simply meant someone who had more sex than you. In any case, Polyamory is not necessarily promiscuous, amoral, sinful or pathological. Why is being easy considered wrong? Is there some virtue in being difficult?

Easton and Hardy go over the common myths. 1) Long term Monogamous relationships are the only real relationships. And that we will automatically lose interest in other people if we are in love 2) Romantic love is the only real love. 3) Sexual desire is a destructive force. 4) Loving someone makes it okay to control his or her behavior. 5) Jealousy is inevitable and impossible to overcome. 6) Outside involvements reduce the intimacy of the primary relationship. 7) Love conquers all.

Ethical Sluts know that it is important to treat people well. They do their best not to hurt anyone. They value consent and honesty over all else. They recognize the ramifications of their actions and they are respectful of other's feelings. Being an Ethical Slut requires skills like communication, emotional honesty, affection and faithfulness as well.

The best way to describe the attitude of an Ethical Slut is this, "We believe its okay to have sex with anybody you love and we believe in loving everybody!"

Abundance of love and sex is entirely available. Far too often people believe in the starvation economy theory of love—that there is only so much to go around. Just because you love one person doesn't mean you can't love another. Loving more people doesn't take away from the feelings you feel from anyone else.

There are a variety of ways to experience love and sex. There can be long term couples and long term couples who swing with just one other couple in a long term situation. There are swingers who have

Saturday night puppy pile orgies. Swinging often embraces bisexual women, but not bisexual men.

As an Ethical Slut you can be single or in a relationship either one. It can be tricky, but vital to introduce your lovers to one another. People can make commitments to each other in numbers greater than to as well. Remember in a three-some there are three couple. There is A&B, B&C and A&C. Things are often broken down into primary relationships and secondary relationships.

An important thing about sex is that it should be fresh and fun for everyone. Some pointers are to slow things down, make sure you practice clean or honest loving but talk dirty and embrace the use of toys. Find what turns you on and get loud about it. Don't feel ashamed for enjoying yourself.

In any case, boundaries are very important for Ethical Sluts. They need to have clear, strong, flexible and conscious boundaries. Don't dump on others or allow them to dump on you. Don't project your feelings onto them or allow yourself to be projected upon. Don't have revenge sex or treat others as objects as you wouldn't want others to treat you that way either.

Sex shouldn't just be safe. It should be safer. Perhaps have agreements to keep "fluid bonding" with your primary or people you know and use protection for people you don't know as well. You should always get tested and do your best to prevent any sort of infection or STD. Condoms aren't always the most fun, but lube inside and out can help with that.

Childrearing in such a situation can be a good thing. In the author's opinions it has been easier to raise children with more people around. There is security for children in sexually interconnected extended families. Group living has its advantages, such as built in babysitters, etc.

Jealousy can be a problem, but not an impossible one. Jealousy may be an expression of fear. It could be a fear of abandonment or simply feeling left out. It could be a fear of not being good enough, feeling inadequate or just plain feeling awful. Jealousy is often rooted in a sense of grief and loss. But have you really lost anything when your partner comes home from a hot date happy and ready to try new things with you? It is important not to deny jealousy. But it is also important to talk about it and not necessarily act on it.

As Khail Gilbran says, *"Your pain is the breaking of the shell that encloses your understanding."*

It is healthy to embrace conflict, but in doing so they suggest a few things. Begin your complaints with "I" and not "you." Schedule fights. Write it out. Own what's yours and don't blame everybody else. Time is your friend. And know that fairness doesn't mean perfect equality.

Make agreements to divide up your time. Your lovers and your primary both deserve time with you and neither should suffer. Give your consent to allow your lover to be with others and devote time to them as well.

The Single Slut has rights. They have the right to be treated with respect, have feelings heard and responded to, have dates and plans honored even if lover is in a marriage or another relationship, right to have help when needed, have limits and set limits, right to not be blamed for other people's problems, right to not be a dumping ground for someone else's problems and a right to be valued and welcomed. As an Single Ethical Slut you are responsible for making clear agreements, having safer sex, being honest and promoting intimacy.

The life of an Ethical Slut neither demands nor excludes marriage. It is a possibility like anything else. Keep in mind no matter if you embrace monogamy or the life of an Ethical Slut that relationships have an ebb and flow. Break-ups happen to the best of friends and most passionate of relationships. But that is okay.

The words of Edna St. Vincent Millay perhaps say it best:

After all my erstwhile dear
My no longer cherished
Need we say it wasn't love
Just because it perished?

The Fault in Our Stars

"The fault, dear Brutus, is not in our stars, but in ourselves, that we are underlings." Cassius tells Brutus in Shakespeare's play **Julius Caesar**. Cassius is urging his friend into action, telling him that there is no such thing as fate, that we are responsible for our own destinies. While the line suggests Shakespeare was of the opinion that we make our own fortune, the tragic nature of the play suggests otherwise.

John Green took this line, plucked it from the pages of history and made it the title of his young adult novel. *The Fault in Our Stars* in a novel about two star-crossed lovers stricken with cancer. The tragic teens don't make poor choices or incur the wrath of God due to their hubris. Life simply dealt them a bad hand. Green sees the utter meaningless of their early deaths. Instead of buying into finding the Bright Side or create meaning, he takes a more existential approach. He turns the straight up Love Story style tragedy and turns it into a Shavian Tragicomedy. But perhaps the most interesting part of the book is the Italo Calvino like quest for the missing part of the book *The Empire Affliction*.

The God Gene

The God Gene: How Faith is Hardwired into our Genes by Dean Hamer came out in 2004. The God gene hypothesis is based on a combination of behavioral genetic, neurobiological and psychological studies.

The major arguments of the hypothesis are: (1) spirituality can be quantified by psychometric measurements; (2) the underlying tendency to spirituality is partially heritable; (3) part of this heritability can be attributed to the gene VMAT2; 4) this gene acts by altering monoamine levels; and (5) spiritual individuals are favored by natural selection because they are provided with an innate sense of optimism, the latter producing positive effects at either a physical or psychological level.

Essentially Hamer says that we can't answer if there is a God, but we can answer why we believe in God. The idea of self-transcendence as the yardstick for faith or enlightenment was created by Robert Cloninger. Self-transcendence is a sense of at-one-ness. We forget all sense of time, place and identity when we transcend ourselves.

Women are 18% more likely to be spiritual than men. Spirituality comes from within and not from any particular religion. Mysticism is a fascination with transpersonal identification with nature and unexplainable phenomenon.

Monoamines such as serotonin and dopamine are important in our consciousness. Monoamines and mysticism have been linked through the use of LSD, Mushrooms and Psychiatric Medicine. D4DR is associated specifically with self-transcendence, as is the VMAT2. VMAT2 stands for Vesicular Monoamine Transporter. It has its head and tail tucked inside the vesicle and it has 6 coils that are triggered by hormones. It is like a gift being unwrapped and then the signals begin. As in Realty: Location, Location, Location. The Gift wrapping protects the contents from being too quickly degraded or lost. VMAT is vital. If we don't have this gene then we don't have a desire for survival.

Ecstasy releases Serotonin. Prozac is Ecstasy's cousin in the drug world. Paxil and Zoloft are the next closest cousins. With Serotonin it is like "I am at one with God." Cocaine releases dopamine, which makes one feel more like "I AM God." Music and dance can also induce mystical type states. Our temporal lobe is in charge with music appreciation and spirituality as well. Epileptic seizures are similar to electrical storms in the brain, but they too can trigger a sense of spirituality.

We do not know God intellectually, we feel him, and so it makes sense that our sense of spirituality is connected to our emotions.

The Gospel of Judas

Reading The Gospel of Judas and the Shaping of Christianity was written by Elaine Pagels and Karen L King and it came out in 2007. The papyrus codex was found in Egypt near Al Minya. It is estimated to have been written in the 2nd century C.E. This text was left out of the canonical bible. In 180 AD, Irenaeus, the Bishop of Lyons, wrote a document in which he railed against this gospel, indicating the book was already in circulation. The Emperor Constantine united Christianity at the Council of Nicea in Turkey 352 C.E. and decided which books of the bible should be included and which should be excluded.

Judas became known as the betrayer, but perhaps that picture wasn't complete. Dante saw Judas as the incarnation of evil. But maybe he wasn't. Judas records what Jesus revealed to him about "the secrets of the Kingdom." Gospel of Luke blames evil for Jesus' crucifixion. Gospel of John blames not only evil, but Satan himself. The Gospel of Mathew argues that Jesus' death was all a part of God's plan. Judas acted out of greed. Gospel of Luke says Satan was in control. Gospel of John says that Jesus orchestrated in all, even his own betrayal. *The Gospel of Judas* shows that others played a role in it as well.

The Gospel of Mark shows Peter as the designated leader of the group. *The Gospel of Mathew* confirms Peter as the leader. *The Gospel of Peter* shows tension between Peter and Mary Magdalene. *The Gospel of Thomas* shows James the Just—Jesus' brother—the leader. *The Gospel of Mary* shows that Mary is braver than the men as she comforts and encourages them after Jesus' death.

In Galatians 1:9 Paul believes that Jesus' death is a sign of salvation for the chosen people. He attacked Peter for being a hypocrite who acted out of fear. Christians were once a small, obscure group of people. Persecutions were once local and sporadic against them. Constantine adopted Christianity for Rome in 313 A.D. Paul adopted the idea that Christ died for our sins in I Corinthians 15:3. The Gospel of Mark backs up this idea of self-sacrifice.

The Gospel of Judas tells us of a wider universe of the spirit beyond our limited perspective. We must widen our perceptions to know God, fulfill our own spiritual nature. If we are ignorant then we will fall prey to false Gods. It is said that perhaps the other disciples do not worship God, but an Angel who is leading them astray. The False God is responsible for having Jesus killed.

The Gospel of Judas objects to any sacrifice demanding God. Early Christians have made a mistake by worshipping an angry, vengeful God. The Gospels of Judas rejects the notion of resurrection of the body. What is the meaning of Jesus' death then? He has risen from an earthly existence into an infinite God. And being created in God's image doesn't refer to physical image, but our own spiritual nature hidden deep within everyone. God made humans know that they were superior even to the Angels of Chaos. We are not saved by dying martyrs, but by accepting God's forgiveness and standing fast against those who teach error and violence.

By seeking the spirit within them, humans can overcome the rulers of chaos and oblivion. They can see God and enter the heavenly house of God above. Jesus death proves that world's rulers are powerless and wicked. Those who believe in the resurrection were called "fools" in *The Gospel of Phillip*.

The symbolism of Jesus on the cross is similar to Jesus being on the tree of knowledge. He is the fruit of knowledge—of good and evil. And the Eucharist means that Jesus is inside of us. In the Acts of John there is a poem about dancing around the cross. The poem means that those who become aware of their suffering and recognize its universality find release from it. Then they can join the cosmic dance.

The texts does not tell us the fate of Judas, but Judas tells Jesus that he had a vision in which the other apostles stoned him to death.

The Gospel of Mary Magdalene

The Gospel of Mary Magdalene by Karen L King came out in 2004. German Scholar Dr. Carl Reinhardt bought a copy of *The Gospel of Mary Magdalene* in 1896 in Cairo, Egypt at an antiquities market. It was in the language of Coptic, but was originally written in Greek. It was a codex on Papyrus rolled into sheets that were stacked and placed into a leather cover. The Greek fragment of *The Gospel of Mary* was also discovered. It was put in Ryland's Library in Manchester, England in 1917. Then it was published in 1938.

In *The Gospel of Mary Magdalene* there is no hell or eternal punishment mentioned. God is the Good and not a father or male figure. Jesus says that there is no sin or crime against God. The end result is that *The Gospel of Mary* does not teach that people need to suffer in order to gain salvation, nor do people deserve to suffer because they sin.

The Gospel of Mary is different in themes, but the language and style of writing is similar to the canonical gospels. It also reveals the words and life of Jesus, but it disagrees with Paul's version.

The Apostles were Levi, Andrew, Peter and Mary in the Gospel of Mary. Levi is a tax collector and defender of Mary. He was not in the Gospel of John, but was in the Gospel of Phillip. Andrew is the brother of Peter and a follower of John the Baptist. Peter is also Simon and a Cephas Fisherman. He was married and traveled through out Asia. He denies Jesus, but is one of the apostles to see Christ rise.

It is missing six pages and opens in the middle of the scene so the circumstances are unclear. King believes, however, that references to the death of the Savior and the commissioning scene later in the narrative indicate the setting in the first section of the text is a post resurrection appearance of the Savior.

As the narrative opens, the Savior is engaged in dialogue with his disciples, answering their questions on the nature of matter and the nature of sin. At the end of the discussion, the Savior departs leaving the disciples distraught and anxious. According to the story, Mary speaks up with words of comfort and encouragement. Then Peter asks Mary to share with them any special teaching she received from the Savior, "Peter said to Mary, 'Sister, we know that the Savior loved you more than the rest of the women. Tell us the words of the Savior which you remember—which you know (but) we do not, nor have we heard them." Mary responds to Peter's request by recounting a conversation she had with the Savior about visions.

(Mary) said, "I saw the Lord in a vision and I said to him, 'Lord, I saw you today in a vision.'" He answered and said to me: "Blessed are you that you did not waver at the sight of me. For where the mind is, there is the treasure." I said to him, "So now, Lord, does a person who sees a vision see it <through> the soul <or> through the spirit?"

In the conversation, the Savior teaches that the inner self is composed of soul, spirit/mind, and a third mind that is between the two which sees the vision. Then the text breaks off and the next four pages are missing. When the narrative resumes, Mary is no longer recalling her discussion with the Savior. She is instead recounting the revelation given to her in her vision. The revelation describes an ascent of a soul, which as it passes on its way to its final rest, engages in dialogue with four powers that try to stop it.

Her vision does not meet with universal approval. Andrew answered and said to the brethren, "Say what you think concerning what she said. For I do not believe that the Savior said this. For certainly these teachings are of other ideas."

Peter also opposed her in regard to these matters and asked them about the Savior. "Did he then speak secretly with a woman, in preference to us, and not openly? Are we to turn back and all listen to her? Did he prefer her to us?"

However Levi defends Mary Magdalene and quells Peter's attack on her. In the text, Peter appears to be offended by the discovery that Jesus selected Mary above the other disciples to interpret his teachings.

Karen King never calls *The Gospel of Mary* a Gnostic Text. Gnosticism didn't exist as a specific order. It meant a group that committed heresy against the early church. The label means nothing here, so King never uses it. But it does represent many of the principles that have come to be known as Gnostic.

Karen King considers the work to provide, "an intriguing glimpse into a kind of Christianity lost for almost fifteen hundred years...[it] presents a radical interpretation of Jesus' teachings as a path to inner spiritual knowledge; it rejects His suffering and death as the path to eternal life; it exposes the erroneous view that Mary of Magdala was a prostitute for what it is—a piece of theological fiction; it presents the most straightforward and convincing argument in any early Christian writing for the legitimacy of women's leadership; it offers a sharp critique of illegitimate power and a utopian vision of spiritual perfection; it challenges our rather romantic views about the harmony and unanimity of the first Christians; and it asks us to rethink the basis for church authority."

The Gospel of Thomas

Beyond Belief: The Secret Gospel of Thomas by Elaine Pagels came out in 2003. The Gospel According To Thomas was discovered near Nag Hammadi, Egypt, in December 1945, in one of a group of books known as the Nag Hammadi library. It was written in Coptic. Pagels points out that in spite of its being left out of the Catholic canon, being banned and sentenced to burn, many of the mystical elements have proven to reappear perennially in the works of mystics like Jacob Boehme, Teresa of Avila and Saint John of the Cross.

Unlike the canonical Gospels, it is not a narrative account of the life of Jesus; instead, it consists of sayings attributed to Jesus, sometimes stand-alone, sometimes embedded in short dialogues or parables. The text contains a possible allusion to the death of Jesus in logion 65, but doesn't mention crucifixion, resurrection, or final judgment; nor does it mention a messianic understanding of Jesus.

The Gospels conflict in information and versions. John is more spiritual. In the Gospel of Mark Jesus is divine and not merely human. Mathew, Mark, Luke and John discuss the end times, but John and Thomas only discuss the beginning of things. Thomas is Greek for Twin. Was this the first name of Judas? In any case, Mark seems to be the basis for both John and Judas Thomas Gospels.

In The Gospel of Thomas all have the God inside of themselves. It says, "Jesus said if you bring forth what is within you, what you bring forth will save you. If you do not bring forth what is within you, what you do NOT bring forth will destroy you." There is light within a person of light. If it does not shine then there is darkness. This takes after the Jewish Mystical tradition, which Bishop Irenaeus dismissed as heresy.

It was John who created the idea of the Doubting Thomas. Who was John? A follower of Jesus who lived in Ephesus or Antioch 90-100 C.E. John the Gospel writer was a follower of John the Baptist. Christians assume that John is the brother of James and that Jesus loved John. Mathew, Mark and Luke along with Peter were the first to believe in Jesus as the Messiah. Later John and the Apostle Paul believed as well. Thomas misses the last supper because he is not an apostle.

The disciple Luke wrote to Paul of Tarsus. Luke claimed to have a divine vision of Jesus choosing Paul as a special representative for him. Paul called himself Apostle from the Greek Apostolos, which is Greek for Representative.

Gaius, a Christian leader in Rome, charged that the Gospel of John and Revelations were not written by John, but by a denounced heretic. Bishop Irenaeus claimed to be practicing the true religion because he'd been taught by Polycarp, who heard John the Baptist speak. Irenaeus also had a friend, Florinus, who joined Valentinus in the so-called Gnostic sect. Once Bishop Pothinks dies, people looked to Irenaeus for leadership.

At this time many people claimed to have Charismata or the ability to heal, exorcise, prophesize and even raise the dead. Who can tell the Holy Spirit to stop or when it has stopped on its own? Claim of direct revelations can be chaotic, confusing and down right dangerous. That is why Bishop Irenaeus and other felt it was important to declare that the age of miracles was over. The Gospels were no longer to be taken literally.

After this effort to unite Christianity and the Church many "secret" writings surfaced. Egyptian monks recopied the texts from Greek to Coptic and kept them. In 378 C.E. the Bishop of Alexandria demanded that all non-canonical texts be destroyed. St. Pachomius gathered the Books of Athanasius and buried them in a heavy 6ft Jar at Nag Hammadi. They weren't discovered until some 1600 years later.

So how were the canonical texts chosen? Irenaeus created the pillars of four. He chose the four Gospels supposedly written by Jesus' disciples who were eye witnesses to the events. New Testament scholars do not know who wrote the Gospels. They claim that they don't really know who wrote the four Gospels. To this day though, many traditionally minded Christians believe whatever trespasses conical guidelines must be "lies and wickedness" that came from the evil of the human heart or the devil.

The Emperor Constantine took up Irenaeus's vision of a Catholic church. Catholic means united or universe. Constantine believed that you had to believe in the orthodox faith or reject the faith all together. And if you rejected the faith all together you ended up in Hell. Orthodoxy means straight thinking. Heterodoxy means thinking otherwise.

The Council of Nicea was held in June of 325. The Bishops (or Supervisor in Greek) hoped to resolve all conflicts facing Christians at the time. Bishop of Alexandria was the successor of Athanasius and he contested certain texts that Arius threw out. Athanasius was challenged and then forced into exile. Bishop Gregory from Cappadocia took over. In the year 367 C.E. we have the earliest list of the 4 Gospels plus 22 Old Testament books that were to become the bible.

So how do we tell the truth from the lies? Jesus says Seek and Ye Shall Find. It may be a difficult path to sort through all this information on our own, but it is our choice in the end.

The Gothic Flame

The Gothic Flame: Being a History of the Gothic Novel in England:
Its Origins, Efflorescence, Disintegration, and Residuary Influences
by Devendra P. Varma, 1966. Some of the earliest Gothic novels
include: *Mrs. Radcliff, Romance of the Forest, Northanger Abbey,*
The Mysteries of Udolpho, Monk Lewis. Gothic Literature is
characterized by conflict between the imagination and rationalism in
order to explain seemingly supernatural occurrences. There is also
an application of Freudian Psychology with a surrealist dependence
on dreams and the subconscious. We have a natural terror for the
living dead. Gothic Literature can also be a response to the political
and religious insecurities of disturbed times.

The term Gothic was in references to the Germanic Tribe. They
built gloomy castles, somber cathedrals and appeared dark and
barbarous to the Renaissance mind. The Goths brought to mind
frost-bitten kind of strength. The word Gothic came to mean
archaic, uncouth, ugly and down right uncivilized. However, the
term soon came to evolve into meaning something that was wild or
of the ghastly imagination. Eventually it was no longer a synonym
for barbarism, but came to enshrine the highest moral and spiritual
values. Gothic art became sublime.

The castle became the focus of the Gothic novel. Massive doors
swung on rusty hinges and then closed with a clash. There were

dark and eerie galleries, decaying chambers, moldering roofs, tolling bells and stalking phantoms haunting dark ivy covered walls. Shakespeare's *Hamlet* is a good example of an early leaning toward the Gothic.

The Castle of Otranto by Horace Walpole opened the floodgates for the popularity of such gloomy backdrops. The year in which it was published, 1764 reveals a disillusioned public who was exhausted by politics and personal tensions. Romantics were repressed or uneasy, but there was an interest in poetry and Shakespeare at the time. Walpole felt novels, not just plays and poetry, were works of art. There was beauty in the shadows he felt. His concepts about revolting against moral lessons, sentiment, domestic familiarity were original in his time.

The Gothic Quest is, "The connection which the surrealists are anxious to trace between their own paths and principles and ideas and inspiration to have no existence…based upon misapprehensions that are far fetched and fantastical." The quest is often guided by the unconscious and uproots the hero from proper society. This quest has an emotional and intellectual impact on the hero, who is a sensitive barometer to the horror and terrors of the world.

The Gothic Novel is distinguished by three qualities: 1) The Subjectivity of the writer 2) Turning the Picturesque into a Passion and 3) The Supernatural and Horrible shocking the gentle soul.

Mrs. Radcliff made a craft out of terror and melancholy. Her tales were more romantic than horror filled. They alternated between hope and fear, keeping up the suspense and mystery. She utilized the principle of contrast for her Gothic Romances.

The Monk recalls Dr. Faustus. Lewis was inspired by Shelly, Byron and Coleridge. *Frankenstein* was written by Mary Shelly and published in 1818. It is a pseudo-scientific horror story considered a Schaur-Romantik. Charlotte and Emily Bronte also wrote Gothic Romance in the forms of *Jane Eyre* and *Wuthering Heights*. Later *Dracula* by Bram Stoker arrived on the scene.

The Romance aspect of the Gothic Romance insists upon aspiration, yearning and desire as well as mystery and wonder while the Gothic aspect of Gothic Romance focuses on the melancholy and suffering in the world. Nietzsche perhaps best summed it up with his discussion of Apollonian vs. Dionysian. In the end, The Gothic Flame is a reminder that there is always death as well as love.

The Insanity of Normality

The Insanity of Normality by Arno Grun which was published in 1987 was translated from German in 1992. He says in the preface "Whereas people who can longer bare the absence of human values in the real world are considered "crazy" those who have severed themselves from their human roots are certified "normal."

Good and evil are not determined by the intercourse of people with one another, but entirely by man's relations with himself says Jakob Wassermann. To feel one's self accepted by another's love is a basic pre-requisite for human growth.

Society demands obedience and when we can't obey we feel a great deal of self-hatred. And what is self-hatred if not self-betrayal? Many people escape the chaos by focusing on another reality. This withdrawal into themselves often is seen as a symptom of schizophrenia. Schizophrenics remain in their inner worlds because the outer world is too painful, and yet sociopaths will remain in the outer world because their inner world is too painful. Psychic death occurs from this split in reality.

Helplessness will then become an overwhelming threat against which we must arm ourselves. Children find fault in self for not being loved by parents. Child's self develops without awareness of pain and death, yet it can become unwilling devoted to pain and death. Children who experience pain at not being accepted for what they are will NOT always be seduced by power though.

Self-hatred is the origin of destructiveness. Only hatred and destructiveness give criminals a feeling of aliveness. Only through rage and murderousness can they obtain the feeling of wholeness and heightened sense of self.

When people murder someone they are often trying to kill a part of themselves that they have projected onto that person. We can only overcome our attraction to death and destruction if we truly feel another person's pain. Those who glorify death and are devoted to death are not "overcoming" it. They are merely denying their fear of it. Pity the aggressor because they are the ones who are afraid.

Yes, many Nazi's felt guilt. They suffered from stomach cramps, tremors, high blood pressure and were often alcoholics. Many eventually committed suicide.

Sometimes we hate the victims because they make us uncomfortable. We hate the victims because we hate the victim within ourselves.

In the Chapter about Comformity, Rebellion and Violence he discusses how both Conformity and Rebellion are forms of dependency. In prison there are different reasons for the high numbers of inmates who turn to homosexuality. In female prisons homosexuality provides a sense of closeness and security, while in male prisons it is mostly about power.

Women define positive self-esteem traits as particularly male traits, while they describe low-self esteem with negative female traits. Mothers are supposed to be good, but happens when they are not? Men tend to overlook our own mother's shortcomings and vilify other women. Lurking in every rebel is the fear of a mother who might use him or devour him. They may pay lip service to his mother, but hate womanhood in general.

The rebel distances himself from feelings because he fears the love he is seeking. The conformist, on the other hand, hates love because otherwise he'd have to acknowledge that his never loved him. Both the rebel and the conformist are cut off from love and their own helplessness. It is two sides of the same coin. They turn away from what threatens them—which is their need to love and be loved. They wish to be loved for one's self.

One is afraid of acceptance because one fears it will mean losing one's self, for in the deepest recesses of one's soul, one seeks deliverance from the pain of rejection by wishing to merge with the mother (or mother figure) forever.

To accept other people means to see them as they really are without needing to lose one's self in them. It is the unconscious wish to lose one's self that destroys a person. Terrorists have no official power. Revenge against the oppressor helps the victim gain some recognition from that oppressor. The sadist recreates the terror of his early childhood. The victim cannot touch the victimizer. He cannot save him or destroy him either one.

The psychopath has a split between tenderness and concern for his mother and a simultaneous hatred for her. The psychopath Peer Gynt once asked what it meant to be one's self. Did it mean to kill one's self?

Schizophrenics try to arouse compassion by reject to prove everyone hypocritical. *The Divided Self* by R.D. Laing says that the schizophrenic has a fear of him or herself disappearing completely like they had a fear of their mother disappearing as a baby. The mother who basis self-esteem on her attractiveness to males cannot recognize and respect her child's intrinsic value and this can create issues later in life for the child.

Milan Kundera said in The *Book of Laughter and Forgetting,* "The struggle of man against power is the struggle of memory against forgetting."

Being truly responsible for your actions and have genuine humanness are possible, but only if there is an autonomous self that integrates both the internal and external worlds. In this possibility lies the hope for our future.

The Jesus Mystery by Lena Einhorn

The Jesus Mystery by Lena Einhorn: Astonishing Clues to the True Identity of Jesus and Paul by Lena Einhorn was translated by Rodney Bradbury from Swedish. While I disagreed with her general premises, that Jesus became Paul after the crucifixion somehow, she did have a lot of interesting points to ponder.

She discusses the idea of the Q source for the bible. Q stands for Quelle or Source. Scholars believe that the first Gospels were written around 50 B.C. but that this original source material has since disappeared and all we are left with is copies of copies of copies.

The word Messiah appears in the Hebrew Old Testaments some 38 times. The Greeks used the word Khristos. Josephus Flavianum wrote about Roman History and he does include Jesus. While many people take this to mean this as proof of the historical figure, other scholars thing perhaps this was added later by Christians. Each of the four Gospels are written in different styles with different audiences in mind. Mathew is for Jewish Readers. Mark for the Greek Speaking people of the Roman Empire. Luke is the most literary and was written for a Greek audience that was Non-Jewish. John was radically different then all of them and had a more metaphysical tone.

There is some disagreement on when exactly Jesus was born. Were the Gospel written to fit the prophecies? There is no real evidence that Jesus was born in Bethlehem. Luke points to 6 C.E., but King Herod was before 4 B.C.E. So the date Jesus' birth is somewhere between 4 B.C.E. and 6 C.E. His birth is oddly only described in two of the four gospels though. The Gospel of Mark is full of Miracles, but even in Jesus' time people said Miracles were evil magic. But what is magic but Miracles done but someone undesirable or unacceptable?

Einhorn talks about the Essenes and The Dead Sea Scrolls. John the Baptist was likely to have training with the order of the Essenes. Jesus comes to the River Jordan to be baptized by John. Why does Paul never mention John the Baptist? Was John the Baptist also named Theudas?

Jesus was very charismatic. People seemed to either love him or hate him. There were 12 Apostles and 12 Tribes of Israel. Coincidence? Jesus was to be the leader of the new Israel. The Passover meal or The Last Supper was described by Mark briefly. John devotes five whole chapters to it. Paul also describes it.

Why was Jesus arrested? He had not carried out any military attacks on either Jews or Romans. He did launch a few verbal attacks and disagreed with people on a legal basis. It seems as if Jesus provoked his arrest and execution. He prophesized his own death after all. Was it irrational or part of a perfect plan?

Did Jesus have Roman citizenship? It was considered high treason to crucify a Roman citizen. Jesus' final charge was high treason.

Why did Pontius Pilate try to save Jesus when Pilate was often described as cruel? Maybe Jesus was connected to the government somehow?

Jesus refused to drink to numb his sense and dull the pain on the cross. What caused him to die? It would be unusual for someone to die on a cross after a mere 6 hours. Usually the death was a slow and painful four days. Someone gave him a sponge to wipe his face and lips. Did that cause him to pass out or lose consciousness? He was also spared having his legs broken because he died before the others. Aloe and Myrrh were brought to his grave. Those were used to treat wounds, but why bring them if he was dead?

Perhaps Jesus didn't die. Maybe his disciples stole his body from the temporary tomb and the crucifixion was meant to be symbolic. After all, Paul stakes everything on Jesus' crucifixion and death. What happened next if Jesus didn't die? Did he get married and have a family like it is suggested in *Holy Blood, Holy Grail*?

Is it possible that Jesus was arrested in 52 C.E. instead of 30 C.E.? Paul goes to Jerusalem in either 57 or 58 C.E. Paul dies a martyr's death in 66 C.E. Did he travel to Spain first before he died? Could Apollonius of Tyanna be Paul? Apollonius dies in 97 C.E. Apollonius sometimes went by Pol.

The last chapter is by far the weakest. It is the only chapter in which Einhorn tries to connect Paul and Jesus. She says that Jesus and Paul were born and lived in the same area. Both were ambivalent toward their Jewish Heritage. Both were unmarried, which was considered unusual at the time. Paul had the wound of Jesus marked on him and both were Roman Citizens. Both use the same terminology or spoke the same. Does that mean they are the same? I don't think so.

The Jesus Papers

The Jesus Papers: the Greatest Cover up in History by Michael Baigent was published in 2006. The book documents the political context of Jesus' birth, and then goes on to examine the history of the migration of the family of Jesus, the chronicles of his teachings, and his death.

The book opens with the Saint Sulpice at Abbe Sauniere in France. There is a picture of Jesus being carried out of his tomb at night. What ever could this mean? Could Jesus have faked his own death, gotten married and moved to France? Baigent thinks so.

Jesus was brought up to fulfill his role as Messiah. He was a Son of David in the Royal Line and perfect to fit the prophecy. He was trained to fill a role as Messiah for the Zealots, but he did not want to start a war or kill anybody. So, Jesus faked his death and was smuggled out of Jerusalem by Joseph of Arimathea along with Mary Magdalene, his wife. Eventually Jesus and Mary moved to France.

Michael Baigent claims to have seen two papyrus documents, the so-called "Jesus papers," written in Aramaic. They were discovered in the Old City of Jerusalem during the 1960s. Baigent claimed these documents dated to AD 45 and were letters to the Sanhedrin from *bani meshiha* ("the Messiah of the Children of Israel"), defending himself against the allegation that he claimed to be the Son of God.

Baigent claims these two papyrus documents were authenticated by the Israeli archaeologists Yigael Yadin and Naham Avigad, which distressed Pope John XXIII. The Pope asked Baigent's friend to destroy these two papyrus documents, but he refused and said he would release them after 25 years. However, the documents have not been released because of the rift this information would create between Israel and the Vatican, also creating a revivalism of Anti-Semitism.

The mysterious priest and mysterious documents that no one has seen makes me a bit skeptical. However, there have been others who have come to the conclusion that Jesus did NOT die on the cross before he did. Perhaps Baigent didn't have the most solid of proof, but that doesn't mean he didn't latch onto a grain of truth somewhere. I think there is a possibility that Jesus didn't die on the cross and that, in all likelihood, he was indeed married to Mary Magdalene. Was Jesus the Son of God? That is perhaps debatable.

In any case, the book is worth a read even if you don't buy into the hype. There is much to ponder.

The Maiden King

The Maiden King by Marion Woodman and Robert Bly came out in 1998. It is based on the Russian Folk Tale *The Maiden King* or *The Maiden Tsar*. Persian story tellers say *"At one time there was a story and there was no one to tell it."* Or *"At one time there was a story, but there was no one to hear it but God."* Sometimes they even say, *"In a certain land in a certain time."*

There is an intimate connection between dreams and fairy tales. For example, the pin prick and fairy tales can be a shamanistic tool. Siberian Shaman prick their finger with a pin and fall into a sleep. The fairy tale of Sleeping Beauty can be seen as a ritual or rite of passage.

In fairy tales sometimes the tutor is the destroyer of imagination. They expect you to get poison from standing water, and so some women need to develop their masculine side deeply enough so that they can cut off the head of their interior tutor.

In the folk tale there is *"The Kingdom of Difficult to Find."* It is the kingdom of 3x10, which lies beyond the kingdom of 3x9. Women must travel to this Kingdom for women ARE this kingdom. The divine female is represented by the number 3X10.

Baba Yaga, Kali, Demeter and Persephone are all dark mothers. They represent a death that brings you back to your mother's womb.

Baba Yaga eats people, particularly those who think in term of only black in white instead of gray.

The Firebird is energy. It represents artists and people like Janis Joplin, Jimi Hendrix and Jim Morrison. Democrats lose artists because democracies believe that an artist has to be sincere. Garcia Loca says, *"Very often intellect is poetry's enemy because it is too often given to imitation because it lifts the poet to a throne of sharp edges and makes him oblivious of the fact that he mad suddenly be devoured by ants or a great arsenic lobster may fall on his head."* Spanish Bullfighting is also a firebird type event. The Firebird's greatest gift in "Perception of the infinite."

But the secret is out. "There is a Goddess who doesn't love you any more." It is easy for men and women to devour each other, but ingesting one's love for the other gender is a different matter.

The Maiden Tsar has loved Ivan since the foundation of the world, according to the fairy tale. Their love IS the foundation of the world. The appearance of the Maiden Tsar gradually transforms the profound despair caused by materialism into life renewing energy. Ivan's true wealth is not the lasciviousness of the step-mother, but rather in the creative transformation of feminine energy originating in the great mother.

The Maiden Tsar is the Golden Maiden that initates Ivan's journey. At this state, he naturally projects his divinity onto her. The Maiden Tsar is too radiant for him. He can't deal with the loss possibility.

315

When the young man's weak response to the maiden has her retreating in anger, he must go on a quest for self-discovery that leads to Baba Yaga, the fierce yet empowering old woman of Russian folk tradition.

The three horns in the folk tale represent the Triple Goddess. It is virgin, mother, crone or life, death and rebirth. The Unconscious feminine is tied to nature and the laws that govern it. The Firebird represents full flight without any compulsion, which means it is of pure spirit.

The loss of connection to the positive mother or father is the core of emptiness. But Presence is not the opposite of absence. It is what remains hidden in absence.

There is an inner marriage even still. What is the Maiden Tsar thinking when she eats the egg? "Ivan, I think, I shall love you. Yes, I have been angry with you. Yes, I did withdrawal and I am sorry." She is the Felix Culp or the fortunate blunder. In the end, The Maiden Tsar wakes Ivan up to authentic personhood.

The Maiden Tsar shows the male tendency toward impotence in the face of feminine magnificence, the female fear of power and abandonment that leads to rage, the need to get beyond oppositional thinking en route to the Divine. These are issues the book addresses with wisdom and lyricism.

The Metaphysics of Star Trek

The Metaphysics of Star Trek by Richard Hanley came out in 1997. It explores both Philosophy and Metaphysics so it covers both the wisdom and the principle of things after physics.

"That is the exploration that awaits you. Not mapping stars and studying nebulae, but charting the unknown possibilities of existence." ~Q to Jean Luc Picard in *All Good Things*.

The first chapter is about *Logic Vs Emotion*. Spock is a Vulcan. Emotions caused a war on his planet, so his people learned to suppress their emotions. This is where a discussion of Plato and Aristotle comes in. They say that the human condition is a struggle between reason and passion. In one episode Kirk gets split into 2 halves. Part of him is like an animal and acts only on emotion. The other half acts only logically with no emotions.

The second chapter is about what it means to be human. Is Data an Android or human? You can be human in the 1st sense which is physically, the 2nd sense which is psychologically and the 3rd sense which is morally. Star Trek explores the moral sense of humanity.

The next chapter explores *New Life and New Civilizations*. It discusses Artificial life, Intelligent Life and Personhood or what it means to be a Sentient Being. Hanley talks about the sanctity of life and the commandment thou shall not kill. Deana's ability to detect emotions and Spock's mind meld are mentioned. Are the ship's life's sensors something that could be a reality? What is intelligence? How could we possibility ever measure it.

Why is it nearly all the aliens look human and speak English? We assume that the computer probably translates for the crew. And perhaps they carry pocket translators when they are down on the alien planets. Darmok time. Imagine if language was all about symbols on the most basic level. Image would be everything.

The Chapter *Insufficient Data* talks about the computers within the Stark Trek Universe. In Next Generation, Deep Space Nine and Voyager they use Holodecks. Are the Holodeck Creations real or not? And are Androids human or not? Descartes had two tests for personhood. The language test and the action test.

And wouldn't Data run out memory? He would need to have a cache for short term and download to his hard drive for long term. Does Data have a soul? Can a spirit inhabit anything besides a body of flesh and blood? Or are the body and soul mutually exclusive? According to Maddox, Data couldn't be fully self-aware like Picard. He doesn't have emotions because he doesn't have an emotions chip, but he seems to have developed the lower emotions anyway.

In *Temporal Distortions*, Hanley discusses issues of time travel. There were 22 episodes in Next Gen of Time Travel. Plus three in movies and others shows. Anyway, we experience everything in the now. History gives us a reference base to predict future knowledge.

318

God is supposed to see all time happening at once. Does the past die when no longer present? Or do all possibilities exist? Then there is the Grandfather Paradox. You might wipe out your own existence if you traveled back in time.

In the next chapter Hanley explores the idea of parallel universes or the multiverse. He talks about Yesterday's Enterprise, Identities in Crisis, Casual Loops and Loopy Loops. In Time Squared Picard meets himself. Does knowing what will happen effect what happens? How would you effectively deliberate in the face of foreknowledge?

The end of The Next Gen sums it up. *All Good Things Must Come To An End.*

The Myth of Monogamy

The Myth of Monogamy: Fidelity and Infidelity in Animals and People David Barish and Judith Eve Lipton came out in 2001. Margaret Mead said that monogamy is the hardest of human marital arrangements. It is also one of the rarest. It is unusual and difficult despite society telling us it is the normal standard.

Polygamy is the practice of men having more than one woman or wife. Polyandry, on the other hand, is the practice of women having more than one man or husband. Poly simply means many, so many go by the label polygamous. For the sake of biology the authors use the terms EPC, which stands for Extra-Pair Copulation for cheating and IPC or Intra-pair Copulation to refer to married couples or mates.

Many males throughout the animal kingdom seek out various females to mate with. Males have many sperm to spread whereas the female has so few eggs. On a biological level this makes sense. The propagation of the species may depend on the males having many offspring with many mates. A female, once impregnated, has to gestate and give birth, which takes time. The males don't wish to wait to mate with that particular female again later.

Zebras may mate with up to four females in one day. However, after their mate gives birth they can stay faithful.

Unattractive males guard their mates more closely. What is considered attractive? Symmetry is considered attractive. Low or uneven symmetry is considered unattractive across the species. The more attractive a animal or person is, the more likely they will have affairs or EPCs.

But what animals have devoted fathers? Foxes, coyotes, beavers, gibbons and marmosets. What ones lack devoted fathers? Woodchucks, porcupines, squirrels, deer, wildebeests, cougars and bears.

Rape does occur in the animal kingdom. It was observed that several male geese attacked a female goose in the wild. It was violent and did not appear consensual. But there is the question of free will in the animal kingdom. Interestingly, some females, chickens and snakes in particular, can create coitus interuptus. They can shake out unwanted sperm.

Males aren't the only ones who copulate frequently. Females in the animal kingdom can be initiate or be willing to mate frequently as well. Lions may copulate as frequently as every 15 minutes day and night during the female's four day long cycle.

Divorce is closely related to adultery in humans and animals. Yes, animals have their own sort of divorce. There are many reasons for animals to divorce. It may be incompatibility; however it is usually because of an EPC. An animal may have an "affair" to see if there is a better mate for them out there. If they determine the EPC to be a better mate, then they will leave their current mate.

Often times the male of the species will not care for any offspring created by the female's "affair" or EPC. Female birds may lay eggs in other bird's nests if they were not properly mated. This is called "egg dumping."

Moles may seek multiple mates and even be polygamous, but they end up monogamous because their female Ulo won't let them bring their girlfriends home! Female birds can be quite competitive and even kill off their mate's EPCs if they feel threatened.

It is true that long term mates and monogamous unions do raise better offspring. Better matches create better monogamous rates through. No matter what the case fathers tend to do less fathering than mothers do mothering. Unclear paternity offers better protection for the offspring because if a mate knows he isn't the father, he is unlikely to take care of the offspring all together.

Out of 185 societies 39 of them encouraged extra marital liaisons. Many cultures have arranged things so that marriage and sexual exclusion are not necessarily the same thing. Most encourage men to take on multiple wives since that produces the most children. It is rare to find a society where women can take on multiple husbands. Group marriages, however, are even rarer than Polyandry.

Out of 116 societies survived 63 allow husbands to be unfaithful. 13 allowed the wife to be unfaithful and 13 allowed both the husband

and wife to be unfaithful. 27 have a single standard where only one or the other may have an affair, but not both.

Did you know that masturbation is a way for men to get rid of the old sperm that won't be able to impregnate a woman? And that Low PH levels may actually harm sperm? Women often tend to wear shorter skirts and look sexier during the time they are ovulating?

The evidence is overwhelming that many people are not only capable of "making love to" but also loving more than one person at the same time? But we are socially prohibited from doing so. The promotion of monogamy causes jealousy and a great deal of drama where there need not be any.

The myth is that some animals and most humans are hard wired to take a mate for life, which just isn't true. In the end the authors say if you want to be monogamous, go ahead. It is a wonderful ideal to aspire to. It just isn't natural or easy for us humans any more than it is for animals.

The Peace Reader

The Peace Reader by Joseph Fahey and Richard Armstrong:
Europeans did not conquer North America without Violence. Yet
some deliberately sought in these colonial ventures to establish
peace practices. That gave new dimensions to the western peace
traditions.

Customarily Indians viewed as an episodic exercise that offered a
minimum of violence and a maximum of opportunity for the
individual warrior to humiliate an enemy without inflicting physical
harm,. Killing even amongst the bitterest rivals was discouraged and
if a warrior did die, the other victims in the family were entitled to
compensation from the attacking group. War parties seldom
consisted of more than a few of the most fearsome of men who had
perfected the hit-and-run skirmish over set piece battles.

Yet Peace reforms have gone on for 2 reasons. 1) Because they have
denounced war as a collective behavior that corrupts social order,
Christian ethics as well as human wellbeing. 2) They have worked
from the principal to establish alternative means of evolving human
conflicts and developing forms of group harmony so that peace
might persist as a living social dynamic.

Despite these intramural differences, however, the peace movement
moved forward after 1919 upon the shared awareness of the

consuming destructiveness of modern totality of war. Rationally, the issue seemed simple. Industrial people would have peace or they would perish.

William Penn was the first authentic Peace Hero in Anglo-American history. Pennsylvania was far more than a business venture for Penn. It was the only place where prosecuted Quakers could escape and do their thing. It was the only place to work out the New Testament in the New World. With help of the radical Republican theories that Penn absorbed from his contemporizes he made an attempt at the worlds boldest attempt toward planned social harmony. He and his associates fashioned a policy rooted in the vision of peace rooted in Justice.

William Penn went to jail for two years and wrote the essay ***"Essay Toward the Present and Future of Europe."***

Through patience, not weapons, Quakers and Indians carved out a record of peaceful relations that remains unmatched in the meeting migratory peoples.

Mennonites identify themselves as defenders of the Christian saying, *"Our weapons are not the sword and spear, but patience, silence and hope and the word of God."* They would suffer for God, but not kill for him.

There was several dozen state and local societies between 1826 and 1840. But the American Society for National Consolidation lost Momentum in 1840

In early December 1915, forty merchants and clergy form the New York Peace Society. It was the world's first non-religious peace organization. New societies such as the Rhode Island Peace Society quickly came afterward. Then the London Peace Society in 1921 and the Societies Des Amis Dela Morale Chrestienne et de la Paix came next in Paris.

People were discouraged and didn't approve of the Revolutionary and, later, Civil War. People published pamphlets and books.

Organized Peace Seeking rather slipped in strength until a retired New England Sea Captain William Ladd (1778-1841) gave it new life in 1825. Ladd decided that countries shrinking in their peace movements needed to become National in scope and more efficient. He formed The American Peace Society in May of 1828.

A division of the American Peace Society was the New England Resilience Society.

Most Peace reforms tolerated or weakened on the topic of slavery and the violence to slaves after 1850. In May 1861 the delegates to the American Peace Society declared their support of the Union. Joshua Blanchard-Ezra Heywood created the Universal Peace Association Reform UPA. A Feminist, Delva A Lockwood (1830-

1917) severed as the organizations most effective lobbyist. However, most feminists failed to sustain any sort of Peace Organization.

The most promising post-war feminist Peace Effort was September 1870 when Julia Ward Howe (1819 to 1910) until she lost support from both sexes.

David Dudley Field (1800-1892) coordinated an Independent Effort that produced that landmark draft of "An International Code" In 1872.

Alfred Love and UPA leaders sponsored an annual series of Summer Meetings in Mystic, Connecticut after 1893. The Mystic meeting attracted thousands of visitors to the joyous celebration that featured games, Peace displays and the climatic release of 1000 confused doves of Peace!

Leo Tolstoy (1828-1910) was a Russian Literary giant. He wanted to replace the human law of violence with the Christian law of love. In 1887 he spread his message of love to the US and the world.

June 15, 1898 there was a large crowd of Boston Reformers that met to form the Anti-Imperialist League. While differing over imperialism, cosmopolitan Peace workers rallied as one in support of the first Hague Conference called by the Russian Czar Nicholas III in 1890 to consider arm limitation. The first Hague Conference met in early 1899 in an attempt to move the powers to deal with the question of international arms, the rules of war and an international court of justice. America's Peace Works was greatly interested.

The outbreak of the Great War in 1914 undermined their first assumptions and opened the way for the creation of the Modern American Peace Movement. Between 1901 and 1914 new Peace Organizations appeared in the US in a growth spurt unequalled in the history of Peace Reform.

Operational, the most advanced achievement of practical Peace Movement took place in 1907, when over 1200 delegates, including US Cabinet Officers, Senators and Supreme Court Justices from 39 States and 18 nations met at the 4 day National Arbitration and Peace Congress in New York.

It was funded by millionaires—by people like John D Rockefeller and organized by Carnegie. The congress aimed to generate popular support for an advanced American position at the upcoming Hague conference. They also (Carnegie at least) had hopes of a National Peace Society and disarmament.

Over 40,000 people attended the congresses 7 meetings in Carnegie Hall. It was the largest and most respectable peace rally in American History.

School teacher Fannie Fern Andrews formed the American School Peace League in Boston in 1908 to extend international amnesty to

Emory School children. Years later Chicago formed the Chicago Peace Society.

Edwin Ginn was at the 1909 Lake Monhonk Conference action on the proposition for enlarging the Peace Movement. In July 1910 he received $50,000 toward the formation was an International School For Peace. 5 months later the school became the World Peace Foundation or WPF.

In the same month that WPF stared, Carnegie contributed 10 Million in Steel Corporation bonds toward the formation in NYC of the Carnegie Endowment for International Peace or CEIP. Carnegie told Endowment Officers to *"Hasten the absolution of international war, the foulest blot upon civilization."*

Church Peace Union CPU formed in 1914. Members of the Conferences Continuation Committee met and formed the World Alliance for International Friendship in 1915. Also League to Enforce Peace LEP.

Julia Grace and Carrie Chapman Catt promoted 3,000 leading woman to meet in Washington in January of 1915 and formed the Woman's Peace Party or WPP. Also American Union Against Militarism (AUAM)

But Peace activism gained fresh momentum as two vibrant new modes of action liberal interaction. League of Free Nations in 1924.

War Resisters League 1924. National Council for Prevention of War in 1922. National Conference on the Cause and Cure of War in 1924. League of Nations Non-Partisan Association.

1934 Harvard Lawyer named Richard Greg wrote a book called *The Power of Nonviolence.* In it, he spoke of Gandhi.

On April 13, 1934 various socialist and communists joined a rare united effort to produce a massive student strike against war. Nearly 25,000 students left class to protest.

One British Commander called the anti-war movement "A formless affair made up of many groups and many leaders, not one who can be called to be a representative of the whole." Yet another anti-war opposition clearly proliferated.

Clarence Steril in 1939 wrote a book Union Now. Committee on National Legislation (FCN) 1943. Congress of racial equality (CRE) in 1942.

On June 26, 1945 delegates from 55 Nations met in San Francisco to sign the charter of the new United Nations. (UN) Pledging to *Unite Through Our Strength in common pursuit of Justice and Security.* Seven weeks later the atomic bomb devastated Hiroshima and Nagasaki. It helped an the war and brought the US to a new level of being armed. Peace Seekers generally disliked the modest scope of the UN, and yet they valued the UN as an essential step toward the sort of International Cooperation that was all the more vital with the dawn of the atomic age.

Beginning in the mid-1940s there arose a group of anti-communist liberals who supported Truman's Cold War Politics and greater public works through military spending.

Radical Pacifist in CORE and FOR had long been active in resisting racial discrimination through nonviolent action. Yet none of their work galvanized blacks and sympathizing whites like the storm the swept Montgomery, Alabama in 1955 and like Rosa Parks and Dr. Martin Luther King. Turn Toward Peace (TTP)

Anti-War activism expanded in the US during 1965-1970 with such rapidness, diversity and spontaneity that it seemed to prelude the very existence of an organized movement.

These early Peace Promoters prompted nearly 4 million people to take different actions toward opposing the war in Vietnam years later. International Day of Protest in NY on 5th Ave in 1965 and 1966. Hippies spoke of the need for simplicity and community as well as love and peace. And they were bothered by the middle class people of America. Stop the Draft Week October 21 and October 22 in 1967.

38 hour March Against Death began on a Thursday when participants carried placards with the names of every American killed in Vietnam. They marched from the Arlington Cemetery past

the White House to the Capital, where signs were placed in wooden coffins.

National Peace Action Coalition (NPAC) and People's Coalition for Peace and Justice (PCP) came around in 1971. 300,000 people in Washington and 150,000 in San Francisco demanded immediate withdrawal from Vietnam. Nixon had over 12,000 people arrested.

1971 Peace Treaty and US withdrawal terms set down by the NLF.

Many Americans have consistency resolved to govern themselves in ways accountable either to reform Christian sensibility or to some humanitarian consciousness and self-accountability, they are obligated to act in pursuit of some higher good. Over time large numbers have perceived this good as work toward peace and they voluntarily struggled to make it real.

The Physics of Consciousness

The Physics of Consciousness by Evan Harris Walker, PhD, came out in 2000. Walker shows how the operation of bizarre yet actual properties of elementary particles support a new and exciting theory of reality, based on the principles of quantum physics-a theory that answers questions such as *"What is the nature of consciousness, of will?" "What is the source of material reality?"* and *"What is God?"*

Walker begins with Newton's conception of reality and then explores the ideas behind Quantum Physics. Quanta are chunks of energy and light that often moves in waves. He goes on to discuss Heisenberg. *"What Heisenberg discovered was that the limit to our ability to observe the universe determines the boundaries of reality. Physical reality and observability tie together...If you and I cannot observe it, it doesn't exist. Or is it perhaps if it exists, it is because you and I observe it?"*

Niles Bohr said that merely by watching things we change them. Walker goes onto say, *"Matter is not really both particle and wave, but rather discrete packages of energy that dart from place to place in a frenzy of quantum jumps—that ebb and flow in waves of chance. It is a world in which nothing stays long where it should be, but only stays where it could be. And yet none of this is what is there. All of this motion is frozen. All this darting and quantum jumps exist only as potentialities..."*

The mechanics of quantum physics works in a strange way. They way it should work is not the way it does work. It is not set up to describe how things actually are, but in terms of the way we think about these things. Looking deeper into the structure of matter, physicists have found a new set of particles that like to cluster into groups of twos and threes. These particles are called quarks—so named for a word James Joyce invented. There are Quanta, Leptons, Mesons and Baryons. Quarks are named Up, Down, Strange, Charm, Bottom and Top.

Hugh Everett III proposed in his Doctoral Thesis that instead of things going from potentialities to actual events, every one of the possible states actually occurs. He suggested that every time two objects interact that all the possible states take place. This means that every time two electrons, for example, collide somewhere in the universe that the total universe splits into two, three or an infinite number of copies so that there will be at least one universe with each possible outcome.

Walker says that our quest for the fabric of reality has brought us from religion to science. When asked to show us reality, science has caused us to look into a mirror and see what we are. It is the last place that science would have chosen to search, yet now we must look into that image that we see within ourselves. Now we must find out what the observer is and find out what threads consciousness weave in creating the quantum mind.

Consciousness is not thinking. Consciousness, Walker states, is not thinking about one's own consciousness either. It is not self-reflections. Consciousness needs no words and no things to exist. Consciousness is not perception or attention. Consciousness is the experience of ideas, words and thoughts that play on the mind as we read a novel, as we remember the past, or as you now read these words. But consciousness is not thinking. Consciousness is merely the carrier of thought. Consciousness cannot really be defined. It is all things in totality. It is reality. It is the "feel" of things. If you have discovered enlightenment then that is the consciousness of consciousness.

Physicists have one thing in common with psychologists; they have always considered Consciousness outside their domain. The physicist is prone to seeing himself as the high priest of science, but that means dealing with the brain and thoughts—not spirituality. But The Tao of Physics combines both spirituality and science. The central aim of Eastern Mysticism, says The Tao of Physics, is to experience all the phenomenon in the world as manifestations of the same ultimate reality. This reality is seen as the essence of the universe underlying and unifying the multitude of things and events that we observe. The Hindus calls it Brahman, the Buddhists call it Dharmakya or Tathata and the Taoists call it Tao.

How much you write in a diary, it turns out, year later, will only hint at the life that time has rinsed into a sea of forgotten moments. To understand the world, Walker says, we must understand the quantum picture of that world. To understand quantum mechanics, we must know what consciousness is. Thus quantum tunneling must lie at the center of these data switches in the brain. This must be where the spark of life begins to filter into a flame of consciousness. The quantum mind IS our consciousness.

Time does not flow as a stream, but passes by in chunks. The pieces of time that we consciously experience are ordinary, brief—a few hundredths of a second long—single moments in time. It is not everything that happens during this loop that has this spread out time. It is only the piece of information that causes that selection of memory in that moment. Quantum minds measure time in loops. And maybe there in that moment, that loop, you can see something of the fabric of time and reality. At least perhaps you can see the cords, fibers and threads. Perhaps you can see the many colors that dance across the tapestry of reality.

In the end we find that reality is the observer observing. We find that the dancer and the dance are one. The two parts come together as one through consciousness. There is no space between them. There is no matter to die. Our observations created matter. Observation itself is that stuff of space that reaches out past the vast clusters of galaxies. Reality is the fruit of love's embrace Walker concludes.

The Pregnant Virgin

The Pregnant Virgin: A Process of Psychological Transformation by Marion Woodman came out in 1985. I didn't read it until 2010. I picked up her newer book *Dancing in the Flames* and then went back to read her other work after that. *The Pregnant Virgin* is a book is written with a thinking heart, blending art, literature, religion and extensive case material. It is a wonderful read full of insight and interesting ideas.

The Unicorn is an allegory for Christ. It is so pure that it can only be approached by virgins.

Everything moves in cycles. Fear of change is about insecurity. **Torschlusspanik** is German for Panic at the thought that the door between one's self and life's opportunities has shut. Graduation not gone to, marriage not taken place, baby never born and job never materialized sort of thing. The meaninglessness of our suffering often drives us to drink and do drugs. But Rilke says, *"Do not seek the answers, which cannot be given because you should not be able to live them. And the point is to live everything. Live the questions now. Perhaps you will then gradually, without noticing it, live long some distant day into the answer."*

"What is the knowledge of freedom?" Thomas Merton asked. "One must ascend all the steps, but then where there are no more steps one must make the leap. Knowledge of Freedom is the knowledge, the experience of this leap," replied a Buddhist Monk.

Sleeping Beauty is about Abandonment in the Creative Woman. Abandonment is a word from Old English. Bannan means to summon. Abandonment literally means to be uncalled and symbolically it means to be without a destiny. A father is supposed to create a destiny for his daughter, but if he doesn't then the daughter has to make her own destiny. Now she can turn it around and give birth to herself.

Sylvia Plath felt abandoned. Her suicide was the last act of vengeance against the savage God who abandoned her. God has taken her out of life, so killing herself is a way of affirming him. Suicide is a sort of Liebstood or "Death Marriage." It is a way to embrace the Darkside of God and the Negative Mystical Woman.

A girl can be initiated into womanhood without losing her virginity. The Pregnant Virgin gives birth to herself, to the man, to creation, to a new world of radiating light. "Only what is really one's self has the power to heal," says Jung.

The Black Madonna is the awakened positive mother. She is black because she herself has literally and figuratively been through the fire and emerged within an immense capacity for love and understanding. Eve is man's view of a woman as sexual. The Virgin Mary is man's view of a spiritual woman. But the Black Madonna ties the sexual to spiritual. She is a Sophia—a woman of wisdom.

The Sociopath Next Door

The Sociopath Next Door by Martha Stout, PhD, came out in 2005. The Diagnostic and Statistic Manual of Mental Disorders 4 says that a sociopath is diagnosed with Anti-Social Personality Disorder and these are the characteristics: 1) Failure to conform to social norms 2) Deceitfulness and manipulativeness 3) Impulsivity and failure to plan ahead 4) Irritability and aggressiveness 5) Reckless disregard for the safety of self or others 6) Constant Irresponsibility 7) Lack of remorse at having hurt, mistreated or stolen from another person.

Sociopathy is, at its very essence, ice cold, like a dispassionate game of chess. Often sociopaths are charismatic. But they suffer from narcissism. Originally they might have felt confused, alone and abandoned. Eventually they come to be consumed by their own feelings and they are unable to understand what others are feeling. Sociopaths may marry, but not for love. Its like they know the words, but not the music.

Yes, these sociopaths may have been abused as children. They are most likely suffering from attachment disorder though. They suffer from severe emotional frustration as children. Then as adults they end up with Adult Attachment Disorder. They can fluctuate between being needy to being belligerent.

Interestingly sociopathy is rare in Asia where there is a sense of interconnectedness. In the USA where Individualism is strong, sociopathy is more likely to occur. Sociopaths make excellent warriors, assassins, snipers and soldiers.

Stout says we should avoid contact with "the sociopath next door." Sociopaths are incurable and perhaps even suffer from "the selfish gene." Living with them will create an unhealthy sense of shame and may lead to depression and even suicide. They are doomed to lead a failed life because a life with conscience is a failed life.

The Dali Lama commented on the sociopaths that committed the acts of terrorism on 9/11, saying, "Technology is a good thing, but the use of technology in the hands of people who don't have well-developed human lives can be disastrous."

The Spiral Dance

The Spiral Dance: A Rebirth of Ancient Religion of the Great Goddess by Starhawk came out in 1979 and was reprinted in 1989. This bestselling classic is both an unparalleled reference on the practices and philosophies of Witchcraft and a guide to the life-affirming ways in which readers can turn to the Goddess to deepen their sense of personal pride, develop their inner power, and integrate mind, body, and spirit.

In the introduction Starhawk introduces herself. In 1968 she spent the summer hitchhiking and camping along beaches in California. She went to college at UCLA and formed a Coven. Though she was raised Jewish, she embraced Wicca. She learned to appreciate her body and sexual intimacy. Soon she began teaching and training women in the ways of Feminism and Wicca. She majored in film making, but wrote the book The Spiral Dance at age 21. She received many rejection slips and took a yearlong bicycle trip to New York. When she saw the sea, the star and the hawk in a set of tarot cards she became Starhawk and moved back to the West Coast.

The three core principles of the Goddess religion are immanence, interconnection and community. Immanence is the manifestation of the God or Goddess in nature and life and everything. Everything—nature, animals, humans and the cosmos are all connected. And it is important for everyone to work together with nature.

There is no good and evil. There is only an understanding of cycles. There is birth, death and rebirth.

Witchcraft is not to be feared. It is older than Christianity and older than even Buddhism. The Spiral Dance is the dance of life and death, the moon and the sun and the seasons. Unfortunately the Goddess culture gave way to Warrior cultures. The Goddess Worship was driven into the mountains and hills. They were often called the Sidhe, Picts, Pixies or the Fair Folk by those in Scotland and Ireland. The Celtic Druids adapted to the Greek and Roman Gods and Goddesses.

The Goddess is important to women. She inspires us to get in touch with out divine selves. For men it allows them to get in touch with their femininity—that deep and sensitive part of themselves. Do not believe in the Goddess. Know the Goddess. The Goddess is the first of all the earth and the heavens. She waxes, wanes and is full like the moon. While she waxes she is the full maiden, when she if full she is the mother and when she wanes she is the wise crown.

The God of the Pagans is the Horned God. He is they dying God, gentle, tender and comforting. He is also the hunter and untamed sexuality. It is the image of men that women would see if they were liberated from patriarchy. He is the undivided self.

Magic is the art of sensing and shaping the subtle unseen forces that flow through this world—awakening deeper levels of consciousness. We have an unconscious mind that often operates in flashes of

342

pictures and memories. We have a conscious mind that is are rational talking self. The 3rd self is the deeper self or the higher self. That is our inner divinity.

A spell is a symbolic act done in an altered state of conscious in order to cause a desired change. To cast a spell is to project energy. Spells work like psychotherapy in a way. Symbols are not spells though. They are a metaphor for the swirling energy of inside of us and throughout the universe. Spells can change attitudes and even change the physical world. Directed emotions can act like a laser beam.

Witches have a difficult time coming out of the broom closet. Covens are a good way to feel safe and create a community. You need a place that you can call your sacred space. First you cast your circle by pointing your dagger in each direction and changing. East is represented by air and the sword, South by fire and the wand, West by Water and North by earth and the pentacle. The pentagram points can mean sex, power, self, pride and passion or love, power, wisdom, law and knowledge. They may also represent birth, initiation, consummation, repose and death.

The dangers of magic stem from our own defense strategies—not from the shadow self or the Guardian. People run from the shadow self and use drugs or alcohol, which can cause great problems. Say to yourself, "Powers of Evil Be Gone!" Get you to the Outer Darkness! I will have both Power and Love!" Remember other people can manifest your inner conflict, so pay attention to that and try to change yourself instead of lashing out at them.

You can expand your awareness by paying attention to your dreams. Keep a dream journal and talk about your dreams with other people. Learn to take conscious control of your dreams.

Starhawk speaks of the ritual of cleansing. Allow yourself to be taken blindfolded to a river, ocean, lake or pond for a ritual bath. Use herbs, oils, incense and candles and look for a new name. Later an apprentice will come and guide you through a symbolic death and rebirth.

The Wheel of the Year is the Calendar of Pagan or Wiccan Holidays. Yule is the Winter Solstice which is December 20-23. Candlemas is February 2nd. Beltane is May Eve. Litha is the Summer Solstice of June 20-23. Lugnasad is in August. Mabon is the fall Equinox September 20-23 and Samhain which is October 31-November 1.

The Steal: A Cultural History of Shoplifting

The Steal: A Cultural History of Shoplifting by Rachel Shteir came out in 2011. She starts out with the fact that in 2009 there was a dramatic rise in shoplifting. Why? Economic downturn perhaps. But shoplifting has a long history.

There was a pamphlet in 1591 about it. Moll in the novel *Moll Flanders* was a cut purse as they called her. In 1778 someone was caught shoplifting paintings. In the 1880s Jane Leigh Perrot was caught. She was rich and didn't need the money so why did she do it?

The psychologists thought she had kleptomania and couldn't help it. It was an illness.

In 1962 they department stores started putting electronic tags on items and creating alarms to catch shoplifters. As shoplifters kept figuring ways around these precautions, stores had to increase their technology.

It seems as if shoplifting is something that mostly women do. They usually hit department stores for cosmetics, jewelry, clothes and perfume. Men caught up to women in the 1980s though. They began stealing mostly electronics like TVs, VCRs, DVD players and power tools.

In the 1990s, psychologists connected female appetite diseases such as anorexia and bulimia to the tendency to shoplift. They came up with the term CRAVED. It stands for Concealable, Removable, Available, Valuable, Enjoyable and Disposable. The item stolen usually fits one or all of those categories.

The top 10 Items Stolen:

1) Gillette Razors and Cartridges
2) Toiletries and Alcohol
3) Clothing
4) Lingerie
5) Batteries
6) CDs and DVDs
7) Vitamins and Pregnancy Tests
8) Luxury Toothbrushes
9) Instant Coffee
10) Steak

If a loaf of bread is stolen because someone is hungry it is often overlooked. However, when people start stealing steak the stores get really pissed off.

There is also something called Bibliomania which is specifically the stealing of books. "A Gentle Madness" by Nicholas Bashbanes says that Bibliomania is more like hoarding than actual stealing since it is usually done as a hobby and not with intent to resell. Oddly, the bible is the most stolen book in the bible belt of the USA.

Why do people do it? Sometimes it is out of genuine need. Sometimes it for the sheer thrill of it. Sometimes it is a "catch me if you can" kind of attitude. Other times it is an illness or compulsion. Sometimes it is even a political statement—like Abbie Hoffman's book entitled *Steal This Book*.

The Things That Matter

The Things That Matter: What Seven Classic Novels Have to Say about the Stages of Life by Edward Mendelson came out in 2006. Novels, Edward Mendelson writes, should be interpreted and understood from a personal point of view, and not just historically, thematically or analytically. "A reader who identifies with the characters in a novel is not reacting in a naïve way that ought to be outgrown or transcended, but is performing one of the central acts of literary understanding."

Frankenstein represents Birth. *Wuthering Heights* represents childhood. *Jane Eyre* represents growth. *Middle March* represents Marriage. *Mrs. Dalloway* represents Love. *To the Lighthouse* represents Parenthood and *Between the Acts* represents the Future. Although I've read and enjoyed *Mrs. Dalloway, To the Light House* and *Between the Acts*, my interest lay mostly in his discussion of *Wuthering Heights* and *Jane Eyre*.

Frankenstein, which I've also read and enjoyed, deals with a father-son relationship. It is a modern day Prometheus. Mendelson covers the themes of Choosing Beauty, Everything Has a Beginning, Original Virtue, Happiness and Vehemence, The Bonds of Love and The Fatal Wedding Night. Control is the goal of his scientific tinkerings, and to create a life without the communion of sex is to pursue total control. This, of course, leads to its total and disastrous loss.

Wuthering Heights represents the Romantic Childhood. Heathcliff merged with Catherine's soul. This merger dissolved boundaries and abolished their separate identities. And the tragedy was is not because they couldn't marry each other. It is because that they grow into adulthood in which sex and marriage are the closest substitutes that anyone can find for the unity that the adults have lost forever.

The God in Emily Bronte's universe is an inner god, created and worshipped by her own imagination. What cannot be spoken by Bronte or her characters is the idea that "God is within my breast." God is not cruel. It is nature that is cruel. Heathcliff and Cathy are doomed by being into a childhood so glorious and bright in its vision that they prefer death to the uncertainties of growth.

Jane Eyre shows us that nothing can be learned without suffering. Jane Eyre manages the nearly impossible feat of reconciling romantic nature worship with the ethical world of monotheism. Solitude and loneliness are the way to intimacy. Marriage requires individuals to enter into intimacy. However Jane and Rochester's fertile love embraces others as well.

"She felt rather inclined just for a moment to stand still after all that chatter, and pick out one particular thing; the thing that mattered . . ."—Virginia Woolf, *To The Lighthouse*. *Mrs. Dalloway* is a portrait of an ideal but almost impossible adult love, and leads us to a fresh

and fascinating new understanding that novel and each of each of the seven novels, reminding us—in the most captivating way—why they matter.

The Twelve Wild Swans

The Twelve Wild Swans: A Journey to the Realm of Magic, Healing and Action by Starhawk and Hilary Valentine came out in 2001. *The Twelve Wild Swans* is an introduction to a mature level of Wicca called "reclaiming," a model of witchcraft that blends magic, personal growth, and activism.

Starhawk is one of the most respected voices in modern Goddess religion and earth-based spirituality. She is the author or coauthor of twelve books, including the classics *The Spiral Dance* and *The Fifth Sacred Thing.*

Starhawk and Valentine have adapted an ancient fairy tale in which a foolish queen wishes to exchange her 12 sons for a daughter. An old woman "dressed all in black" overhears the queen and makes the wish come true, granting the queen a daughter but turning her sons into wild swans. Their sister weaves magic shirts to turn them back into men.

The twelve sons represent the twelve houses of the zodiac. The Rose is the 13th and completes the lunar cycle. The situation is not Rose's fault, but only she can heal it. What is magic but changing consciousness at will. Drugs and meditation can also create these magical states of mind.

Why is Rose important? Because if we learn to live our lives like Rose, we may find that we are able to solve problems that seemed impossible before. She walked away from the old Castle and we can walk away from unhealthy relationships.

Like the Swan brothers we must break our wicked vows of revenge, anger and unhealthy feelings. The Swan brothers desire to kill their sister—who is a woman like the woman who is the cause of their suffering. But she is also their only hope of escape. In this way they meet their shadow selves.

Rose is carried away in a wicker basket to Avalon, the land of Fata Morgana. She is now in the magical realm. Ecstasy can occur when we let the power move us. Dance the balance between risks and boundaries, between containing our power and letting it loose, between holding a strong intention and letting ourselves be carried away.

The weaving is a symbol of creating a mystery, a circle of safety and spell work. It can create ecstasy like group chanting. Rose now has a challenge. She has to weave the shirt out of nettles. The shirts are symbolic of the souls of her brothers. She takes a vow of silence like a priestess. For great works of magic require dedication. For us we need to have great dedication to our creative work and to healing.

We can hold our center and find our power within like Rose. We can focus on ourselves and our worth despite loss, pain and jealousy. We can maintain our work on our self for our personal growth and healing. We may listen to criticism for criticism can be a gift if we truly listen.

The 12 Swans come to Rose's aid because she was willing to help them, just as the earth and other animals may help us along on our journey. The transformation of the swans back into boys is symbolic of rebirth. We can transform ourselves and be reborn. As we gather power, we must also face our fears though.

The Unsayable

The Unsayable by Annie G Rogers, PhD came out in 2007. A clinical psychologist, Rogers has spent 15 years researching girls and young women, and here she uses those case studies, along with her own experiences details how, as a teenager. Rogers was treated for schizophrenia with weekly electroconvulsive therapy-to demonstrate how discovering the "unsayable" helps unlock the psyche of sexual abuse victims. Today Rogers is a psychoanalyst who treats children traumatized as she was by using a structure for listening developed by the French -clinician-theorist Jacques Lacan in art and other expressive therapies.

As Lacan says that the unconscious is structure like a language and Poet Audre Lorde tells us that poetry is the way we give names to the nameless so it can be thought. Trauma then is like a letter written on the body in invisible ink. Characters of the alphabet seem alone and isolate and impossible to interpret.

Speech markers are repeated words and phrases that can be signifiers. These speech markers can be symbolic in nature and often reveal the subtext. They are the "erasure."

Lacanian work therapists do not interpret what is said. Rather, they underline the signifiers and help the patient make connections to their unconscious.

Freudians, on the other hand, are more like archaeologists of the unconscious. They are trying to "dig up" what is buried. However, Lacanians believe that we do more telling by not telling. In other words, what is left out is more revealing than what is included in our personal narratives.

Victims of abuse have a very difficult time talking about what has happened to them. It is literally unspeakable or unsayable to them. They aren't sure who will treat them as a person instead of an object. Eventually, when trust has been gained, there will be verbal clues even if the truth goes unsaid.

Annie's final words of the book when sum it up nicely, "If your body in pieces has begun to speak, and if you are now brimming with words and their sounds--and you're no longer sure of what you're hearing or saying—you are the one person I've written this for, the one to whom I entrust these words."

The User Illusion

The User Illusion: Cutting Consciousness Down To Size by Tor
Norrentranders came out in 1991, but it wasn't translated from
Danish into English until 1998. I didn't read it until 2000. The **user
illusion** is the illusion created for the user by a human-computer
interface, for example the visual metaphor of a desktop used in many
graphical user interfaces. The phrase originated at Xerox.

He introduced the notion of exformation, which is explicitly
discarded information, in this book. According to this metaphor, our
experience of the world is not immediate, as all sensation requires
processing time. It follows that our conscious experience is less a
perfect reflection of what is occurring, and more a simulation
produced unconsciously by the brain. Therefore, there may be
phenomena that exist beyond our peripheries, beyond what
consciousness could create to isolate or reduce them.

Norrentranders says the puzzle of communication is how it can be
possible. A good communicator does not think only of himself, he
also thinks about whatever the receiver has in his head. It is not
enough for the explicitness of the information to refer to some
information in the senders head if that information does not
somehow lead to the correct associations by the receiver. The words
are merely references to something not present in the words—but
present in our heads. The idea of conversation is to elicit related

states in each other's minds and then exchange the events that take place in our own heads. You don't merely believe what they are saying, you sympathize, you love the person, you miss them, etc.

It is more important to know what is going on in people's heads than to understand the words they speak. But if there is a contradiction between what is said and what is meant, in the long run you'll go mad. It is good for you to get mad at people who say one thing verbally and then say the opposite with their bodies. Conscious language manages very little of what goes on in a social situation. Far too much information is discarded before we get to the information. People who not understand the subtext make fools of themselves.

Take music for example. The main thing in music is not the sound waves. It is that the composer or player converts a number of mental states into a pattern which evokes the same (or different) mental states for the listener. If we want to understand Bach or The Beatles, what we need to look at is not much the information that is conveyed by the notes, but the exformation the notes evoke in the listener.

The fact is every single second millions of bits of information flood in through our senses. But our consciousness process only perhaps 40bits a second at most. Millions and millions of bits condensed to conscious experience that contains practically not information al all. Every single second, everyone discards millions of bit in order to arrive at the special state known as consciousness. Consciousness is not about information, but about its opposite—order.

Symbols are Trojan horses by which we smuggle bits into our consciousness. Our memories are limited by the units or symbols we must master. Thus, it is helpful to organize material intelligently before we try to memorize it. Rote memorization relies on chunking information, or organizing it.

Intelligence is thus not about remembering lots of microstats at once in a sequence. Intelligence is about being able to see what microstats best combine with all the other microstates. Seeing a jumble of confused data into a concise, clear message can be a real turn on. Beauty, elegance, ease and laid-backness are linked. Saying a lot in a few words or signs is beautiful. Everything is not present, but it not gone either. Consciousness breathes information and exhales exformation.

As Schopenhauer said, "Thoughts die the moment they are embodied by words." The picture is very clear—there is plenty that goes on inside of us that we are not even aware of. Consciousness is ingenious because it knows what is important. The sorting and interpretation of data is NOT conscious on our part though. Subliminal perception and sorting is the real secret behind consciousness.

It is a pretty weird notion to realize that we do not live in real time at all. We experience the world on a sort of delay. This, of course, allows us time to keep track of all the illusions and solve all the binding problems, coordinate the many different sensory date that are processed in numerous ways via numerous channels in the brain into one world, one experience, one object. But nevertheless, it means that we experience a sort of lie. Because we do not experience it directly, but filtered through our consciousness our experience lags behind.

The User Illusion is a metaphor indifferent to the actual 0s and 1s. It is, instead, concerned with overall function. Consciousness is not a user illusion for the whole world or the whole of one's self. Consciousness is a user illusion for the aspect of the world that can be affected by consciousness itself. The user illusion is one's very own map of one's self and one's possibilities of intervening in the world.

Civilization is about removing information about our surroundings, discarding information about nature so our senses are not burdened with all that information and consciousness so we can concentrate on other matters. We cut away the loads of information from our surroundings in order to devote ourselves to the inner lives inside our heads and our lives in society. However, our surrounding become so little of a burden to us that we can allow ourselves to relocated consciousness to a ½ a second behind reality so can talk about with other people.

Information in society can seem stressful because it contains not too much information, but too little instead. Sense poverty is on its way to becoming a major problem in society, provoking a cry for meaning amidst the flow of information. Man has moved down to a lower bandwidth and is getting work. "What is done by myself, I feel, is done by something greater than myself in me," said James Clerk Maxwell. He did not suffer from the User Illusion.

The Zen of Oz

The Zen of Oz: Spiritual Lessons from Over the Rainbow by Joey Green came out in 1998. Green asks could Dorothy be trying to convey the idea that Oz is a state of mind or a kind of enlightenment like Nirvana.

The Tornado is bad karma. It represents things spinning out of control. The cyclone becomes a physical manifestation of Dorothy Gale's inner struggle for inner awareness. The results of the "gale" winds storming through her psyche.

Landing in Oz was the rebirth into another life. The Wicked Witch is the bad Karma following her. Dorothy must stop seeking Aunt Em's love so obsessively. Your choices, after all, mirror, how deeply you know your true self. If you make good choices in Kansas then you won't have to go to Oz.

The Ruby slippers, which were silver in the book, actually represent the inner spark of divinity in all of us. Glinda's pink bubble is like a womb. Glinda tells Dorothy never to let the slippers off her feet. The Wicked Witch is jealous of Dorothy's youthful spark and the slippers represent.

Oz is very similar to the word Om, which is used in mediation. And "There's No Place Like Home" shows that you already process the attributes you seek most passionately. Glinda the Good Witch is like a Zen Master and The Yellow Brick Road is the Journey to Enlightenment. The Lion, The Scarecrow and the Tin Woodman all want to flow with the cosmos. "Follow The Yellow Brick Road" is a sort of mantra and meditation.

The path or journey is not simple. There is a fork in the road and there are decisions to be made. It doesn't matter what road she takes, they all lead to self-awareness. If the only decision you make is to keep going forward that can still lead to self-awareness.

The Tin Man is rusted when Dorothy finds him. The Tin man is a second group of people or soul searchers who are paralyzed by indecisiveness. The Scarecrow is nailed to a post and can't go anywhere. He represents the people in live who let others hold them back from realized their dreams and aspirations. The cowardly lion represents those who lack the courage to make the spiritual journey alone.

Knowing others is intelligence. Knowing yourself is true wisdom. Mastering others is strength. Mastering yourself is true power. The Scarecrow also says, *"Of course, I don't know, but I think it gets darker before it gets lighter."* This echoes the Tao teaching that the path into light seems dark.

When the Scarecrow craves intelligence, but it escapes him. When Scarecrow lets go of his preoccupation with obtaining, he becomes a quick thinker and problem solver. The Lao Tzu says, "Free from desire, you realize the mystery." When you look for it, there is

362

nothing to see. When you listen for it, there is nothing to hear. When you use it is inexhaustible.

The Tin Man shows us what comes around goes around as far as love is concerned. The Lion yearns to be King of the Forest, but what he really craves is to be King of himself. Lao Tzu says, "Because of deep love, one is courageous." Your heart's desire is your destiny, for this to be they must to follow the witch's advice and surrender. Why? Because even your worst enemy has something to teach you. What Dorothy surrenders is her desire to go back to Kansas.

Detachment allows the intelligence of the universe to help your intentions manifest themselves. To feel in control, the Wicked Witch is obsessed with controlling others. The need to control demonstrates a lack of self-worth. The Witch's motive is to gain control over herself, in inward power struggle turned perversely outward. Of course, the only way to gain control over yourself is to instill balance and harmony in your life is the inner spark within you. This will unlock the rich creative potential we all have.

In Zen the monkey represents madness. The Witch thus surrounds herself with Madness. The Wicked Witch is then killed by water. In the Tao Te Ching it is said that in the world nothing is as soft and yielding as water, but it dissolves the hard and inflexible. Nothing can surpass it.

The Wizard is a false prophet. He is a good man, but a bad wizard. He sends Dorthy out to confront her fears. The Wizard gives her a spiritual lesson, namely that you already possess the attributes that you seek most passionately. Jeremy Wolf says that experience is not only the best teacher, but the only teacher.

In the end, Pierre Teilhard de Chardin says that, "We are not humans having a spiritual experience, but we are spiritual beings having a human experience." And that is very true. And we can to that there is no place like home—yourself.

Timequake

"A quake in time/Makes you go back past nine/one becomes unstuck/Free to repeat each fuck-up!" A limerick of sorts dedicated to Kurt Vonnegut. I picked up *Slaughter-House 5* due to the reference on *Lost*. While I was at it, I picked up *Breakfast of Champions* and *Timequake*. It was very entertaining read, chocked full of intertexuality.

Slaughter House 5 mentions *Heaven and Hell* by William Blake, *Red Badge of Courage* by Stephen Crane, *The Brothers Karamazov* by Dostoyevsky—just to name a few! *Breakfast of Champions* didn't really name too many. Timequake was the richest source of references. *Our Town* by Thornton Wilder, *A Street Car Named Desire* by Tennessee Williams, *Old Man and The Sea* by Hemingway, *Walden* by Thoreau, *Candide* by Voltaire, *Moby Dick* by Melville, *Frankenstein* by Shelly and *Julius Caesar* by Shakespeare. He also mentioned the authors HC Mencken, AE Housman, William Styron, TS Elliot, Mark Twain, Isaac Asimov, Dick Francis and others! Perhaps most interesting was that Vonnegut list Socialist George Bernard Shaw as his hero. He mentions Nietzsche in passing. Then he mentions Samuel Taylor Coleridge by way of Kubla Khan. Coleridge mentions Xanadu or Shangdu. Vonnegut mentions Joseph Heller's Catch-22. Very interesting indeed!

Although *Slaughter-House 5* was mentioned in the enhanced version of *Lost*, *Timequake* seems more relevant, especially considering its themes of free will versus determinism. Not to mention all the literary crossovers. Vonnegut connects George Bernard Shaw, among many others.

Vonnegut fits into the theme of this diary as well. He was the president of the Association for Secular Humanism.

Secular Humanism embraces morals and ethics without embracing God or the Christian Faith. That is not to say all Secular Humanists are Atheists. Some are Agnostic and others may even be Gnostic. Mostly Secular Humanists place reason and the scientific method above all else. They believe in an objective truth. They also support good will, tolerance and individual responsibility. A Secular Humanist wants to build a better world. Over all, it is a positive outlook and appealing organization!

Kurt Vonnegut is just one of many famous authors on the list of Secular Humanist authors that I found.. Some others I found interesting: Isaac Asimov, Albert Camus, EM Forrester, John Lennon, John Stuart Mill, Phillip Pullman, Gene Roddenberry, Carl Sagan, Bertrand Russell and Charles Schulz.

Secular Humanism grew out of the Enlightenment in many ways. Without Rousseau, Hume, Locke and Paine, Secular Humanism might not exist and neither would many of the characters on *Lost!*

To Repress or Not To Repress

Is repression necessary for a functioning society? Does the individual have to conform in order to be healthy or is conforming merely the appearance of health? Which is more important—the subjective inner truth or the objective truth of society? Perhaps the answer lies in the ever-elusive idea of balance.

What brings up these topics? I just finished reading two very interesting books that seemingly contradict each other completely.

The first book was *The Inanity of Normality* by Arno Grun. Grun is German, which I think is important in as far as his cultural perspective. He tackled not only Nazism but American politics as well. His approach was pretty objective and fair I thought. He neither defended nor attacked any specific authors or theorists. His argument was well drawn and stood on its own without excessive citation, which is more than I can say for the second book. *One Nation Under Therapy* by Sommors and Satel was fatally flawed, yet unfortunately it was the one book that was more widely read and quoted!

The thesis of *The Insanity of Normality* is the idea that society is inherently full of crazy contradictions and that there is more danger in accepting these contradictions than there is in questioning them. "Normal" people tend to kill off any conflicting feelings in order to fit in. In sacrificing their inner truth this makes them more prone to becoming a sociopath or psychopath. Psychopaths mimic emotions and fit into society. They are capable of appearing normal and that is precisely what makes them so dangerous. Schizophrenics are at the opposite end of the spectrum. They cannot accept society in all of its hypocrisy, so they withdraw from it completely. They turn inward in order to maintain a sense of self. Insanity then, is a protest. It is a rebellious way of life. Arno recognizes that schizophrenics are indeed ill, but he believes that so-called normal conformists can also be very ill and because they go largely unrecognized and unhealed, they are worse off. He views self-hatred as the reason for any sort of violence and destructiveness. If a normal person is fairly well adjusted and capable of compassion they are not a threat. A person who is filled with repressed anger or who has completely numbed themselves to their pain is a person who will torture and kill when sanctioned by society. If these so-called normal people are anti-social then they may strike regardless of any moral or illegal implications. Overall, Arno stresses the need for balance. He says, "Truly, responsible actions and genuine humaneness are possible if there is an autonomous self that interrogates the internal and external world. In this possibility lies the hope for our future."

One Nation Under Therapy attacks what they call "Therapism." The authors are responding to legit issues. The crisis of the public schools is one that does need attention. Empty self-esteem does create narcissism and educators who protect student from ANY stress at all are doing more harm than good. The schools have lost their focus on academics and that does need changed. However, I disagree with most everything else that they say! Sommors and Satel believe that repression, not expression, is important. They cite studies showing that dwelling on your past and your feelings can lead to actually feeling worse. While excessive focus on feeling can swing toward depression and even schizophrenia, that doesn't mean one should sacrifice their inner truth either. Repression isn't the right word for what is needed. It is the wrong approach. Repression implies that the inner world is less important. It implies that one can control their feelings or forget them when convenient. This sort of psychic death is what Arno warns against.

One *should* try to refrain from obsessing too much. Getting involved in various extra curricular activities or community activities *is* important for a healthy balance. Emotions do have their time and place though. Rather than repress them, one needs only to find a proper outlet for them. Reading and writing can help someone work through some genuine issues. However, self-pity and focusing on counterfactuals (the what if's) do serve only to perpetuate the negative feelings. Therapy or therapeutic activities can help heal in right time and place—which is probably not during school hours. Sommors and Satel seem to believe that medicine is perhaps a better tool than talk-therapy, but even medicine is met with some skepticism. Although not explicitly stated, they basically believe that philosophy, sociology and religion have a better chance of improving our lives. Christian morals and ethics, or even some sort of secular set of morals and ethics, are better suited for our children than psychotherapy.

They also believe that criminals need to take responsibility for their actions. Understanding the reasons behind their actions is a pointless endeavor in Sommors and Satel's view. Lock the criminals away and forget about them! Punishment seems to be favored over any sort of rehabilitation.

Overall, they have a rather bleak view of society that feels jaded and frustrated at best. I didn't get a good feel for what they viewed as a solution. The book felt like a backlash for the baby-boomer rebellion. It is an extreme reaction without balance in my opinion. I really hope that society doesn't swing to another extreme. We do need a balance, which is what Arno works towards.

Touched With Fire

Touched With Fire" by Kaye Jamison Redfield explores the connection between Bipolar Disorder and the Artistic Temperament. Many authors and artist suffer from what Patty Duke calls A Brilliant Madness. There does seem to be a strong correlation between mental illness and creative genius. The question is why? Is it necessary to suffer in order to be great? Can only the tormented provide insight into the human heart? Does wellness equal a world without literary heroes? Redfield seems to lean in that direction but Kramer—in his book *Against Depression*—leans in the opposite direction. Kramer recognizes the Romanticizing of melancholy, but refuses to believe that artist should have to be afflicted in order to create.

I've heard comments from students, complaints mostly, that all the authors I cover are too depressed. "Oh no! Not another author who committed suicide! Aren't there any happy authors?" they ask. There are plenty of authors who lead relatively "normal" lives. It just seems as if the bipolar lead the most interesting lives or at least the most dramatic.

The question really becomes is illness necessary for a profound and intense experience? Some people can manage great depth and range of emotion without succumbing to a mood disorder. Illness isn't the only way to experience a heightened sense of emotion. You don't have to be suicidal to suffer nor do you have to suffer to be noble.

Normal ups and downs can be enough to inspire creativity.

So why the correlation or the connection? Why romanticize melancholy, depression or bipolar disorder? Well, I think it goes back to what I said before. We are neither emotional animals nor intellectuals alone. It is our ability to understand our emotions that make us superior. A person, who can understand their emotional experiences, be it basic or complex, shallow or deep, unhealthy or healthy, is of a higher order. Authors and artists, by their vary nature, examine and explore humanity in all of its many hues. Their quest for understanding, communication and communion allow for greater depth and range. The illness does not make them great, rather their understanding of it makes them great. Redfield pointed out the Byron, in all of his madness, still managed to write clearly. His lucidness, even in deeply troubled times, made for particularly brilliant work. If he'd been befuddled by his emotions then he wouldn't have been capable of such sharp observations. Virginia Woolf was much the same. An ability to see things from the inside and the outside seems necessary for true insight. Complete madness—insanity to the point of losing one's sense or self-consciousness—rarely makes for a good readable work of literature. It is awareness that is the key.

The problem comes, I think, in being aware, but not able to comprehend. If you are overloaded, overwhelmed and unclear about things then you do become crazy. The fire of creativity is fueled by emotion, but too much or too little emotion is counterproductive.

Creativity and emotion are inexorably linked, but they are not interchangeable. Creation requires energy and emotions ARE energy.

In the end we find that creativity requires a bit of a mystical mind set. Rather the artist acquires this state of hypersensitivity and awareness through meditation, mental illness or drugs it does not matter. There are many paths, but just one goal. The writer and mystic seek the fire of life. *"To know where it all did begin."* Divinity and the collective unconscious are sought by those who desire enlightenment, but also by those who seek to create. Though separate; enlightenment, creativity, beauty and truth overlap. To seek one you must embrace all.

Truth Or Dare

Truth or Dare: Encounters with Power, Authority and Mystery by Starhawk came out in 1987. Truth or Dare is about the roles we play that society places on us.

Magic is a liberation type of psychology. How do we break free from other's control and set ourselves free? Witchcraft is a mystery religion based on ritual and on consciously structured collective materials that allow us to experience the immeasurable.

"If I call myself a witch even though I am fully aware the word often produces fear," says Starhawk. Where there is fear, there is power. Where there is power, there is fear. Until we confront the fears and stereotypes evoked by the word we cannot contact the powers that are also embedded there. To be a witch is to make a commitment to the Goddess and to the protection, preservation, nurturing and fostering of the great powers as they emerge in every day beings.

We are afraid of the pain. We are afraid of seeing how deeply we have been shaped by the system of control. The insides of our minds resemble battlefields and jails. A teacher may have skills to empower us or another may treat in a way to make you feel inferior to them. It just depends on the teacher.

There are three types of power. There is the power over which motivates through fear. There is the power from within which is magic or divinity. There is the power with which is the world pattern of relationships. The power over is based on material goods and the material world. The power from within is spiritual.

Spiritual often promotes passivity when the domain of the spirit is defined by the outside world. When this world is the terrain of the spirit we ourselves become actors in the story and this world becomes the realm in which the sacred must be honored and freedom created.

Language is political. Language can be magical as well. The goal of language and magic is balance. Our way to get out from under other's control is through both resistance and renewal. The truth goes beyond any description of it. Starhawk is daring us to tell the truth and resist the powers that be.

Women once gathered herbs and plants. They learned their uses and were able to heal children and even animals. Shrines to the Goddess turned into temples for the Gods. The matriarchal society all but disappeared and was replaced the current patriarchal one. These healers and worshippers of the Goddess were called witches and condemned out of fear.

Consider these questions: 1) When in my life have I complied or obeyed when I didn't want to. 2) What did I feel at the time? What was I thinking? What choices did I perceive? 3) What other choices might have actually existed? What might have happened if I'd taken them?

Then consider these questions: 1) When in my life might I have rebelled? How and with what success? At what cost? 2) What choices did I see I had? What other choices might have been possible? 3) What might have been different? Withdrawal is another way to something intolerable. When have you withdrawn? How could you awaken and take action? When did you do this and how did you feel?

Often we suffer from self hate. We need to grieve over and cry over missed opportunities. Power over us has life and energy all its own. Patterns of power and control are never accidental. They are manifestations of our self-hate. We need to do a cleansing, grounding and creating of sacred space.

Guilt does not encourage us to change. Instead, it paralyzes us. Guilt is the internalized hatred of one's self instilled through fear of punishment. Guilt is how we punish ourselves. We need to see and value ourselves as well as others.

We can build an alter, draw a circle and banish the power by calling on the four directions. We can invoke a name and give it power over us no more. Starhawk talks about the cone of power, the energy dance, going places, going to place of personal power, feasting and the transition of return rituals.

There are four groups to consider: Myth Making, Personal Myth, Tales from the Elders and Children's Stories. There are three gifts to consider as well: Gift of Power, Gift for the Newborn, Gift of Chance.

Authoritarian figures have been our models in child-rearing. Parents exert power over children in disciplining them. We can easily over power children, but instead we need to respond by communicating, making suggestions and doing some critical thinking instead of lashing out. We value what we protect and we protect what we value.

A person doesn't change after you try to help them. They will only change when they are willing to talk about it and change it themselves. They need to find a voice. They need to break the silence on their own. In truth or dare Starhawk dares you to talk about all those things that are forbidden to talk about and take responsibility for your own personal truth.

War once meant rape. Power has always been tied to sexuality. Men often identified their sexuality with aggression. The master or powerful man became the abuser, rapist or child molester who hates other because he does not see them as having independence or a valid existence on their own. Often these men often had their own needs denied. They felt powerless and were victims themselves. But instead of ending the cycle, they continue it by victimizing others.

Even if you have been a victim of rape or abuse you can reclaim your body. You can cleanse it and renew it and enjoy it once again. Starhawk describes another ritual. She talks about Snakes, Dragons,

Crows and Grace representing each of the four directions. She talks about the Rite of Passage, which includes Preparing for the Struggle, Returning From the Struggle and the Spiral Dance, which is the sacred space.

We can create a new culture of life together if chose to do so.

Twenty-Something

Twenty-Something: Why Do Young Adults Seem So Stuck by Robin Henig and Samantha Henig came out in 2013. Many Millennials are living in their parent's basement, eating ramen noodles and sometimes even on food stamps. Why is this? Are they lazy or are there other things working against them.

First, lets establish the generations. The "Baby Boomers" were born from 1946 to 1954. Sometimes they also consider those born 1955-1964 the younger "Boomers." Generation X came along from 1965 to 1976 for the most part, but some people lump in those born up to 1982 as part of Gen X. Generation Y or the Millennials came along 1980 to 1990.

They are often called Millennials because they came of adult age around the turn of the century.

The Twenty-Somethings want to keep their options open, so they often don't wish to narrow down their focus and choose a major. They suffer from choice overload. The deadline for growing up has changed. Now those people in their twenties are considered being in Emerging Adulthood or Extended Adolescents. And these twenty-somethings know that the internet has changed everything in their world.

In 1968 going to a 4yr University was affordable. A person making minimum wage working only 6.2 hours a week could cover their tuition and fees. Today's student needs a full time job to foot the bill for their education. Student debt has increased dramatically over the past twenty or thirty years. Not only that, but the Master's degree is the new Bachelor's degree. In many areas a Master's degree just isn't enough any longer, which means more debt in trying to obtain a PhD. Even still, people with an MA will earn 25% more than those with just a BA.

Interestingly, your cognitive function drops in your early 30s. You are at the peak of your abilities academically between ages 25 and 34. However, the more education that you have the more likely you are to retain your intelligence and abilities as you age.

You don't have to spend a fortune on your education though. You can do things alternative to college that will keep you sharp and make you smart. Subscribe to the Economist, Memorize the name of every country in the world, Buy a round the world ticket and be sure to stop in Asia and Africa, Read the basic texts of all the major world religions, Read 30 nonfiction books and 20 Classics, Do an Online or CD Language Course and Learn 3 new skills.

Some people do okay to skip college and enter right into the work force. They are able to have a trade or a skill that is marketable and able to get right to work. These people do not delay adulthood. They get married and have kids at an earlier age than their college counterparts though.

What does this mean for a lifetime of earning? Well, only 53% of those age 25-34 earned more in 2011 than they did four years earlier. Rent for these 25-34 year olds was higher than their parent's rent in 1980 though. Some 54% of those surveyed were not working in their field. 33% of those who graduated from a 4yr college weren't working in their field and 29% of those who obtained a graduate degree were weren't working in their field either. Those who fought in Iraq were doing even worse than the rest of those students who did not.

Baby Boomers have an average of 11 jobs before age 44. Most of the changes in jobs occur before the age of 27.

How does this new generation do as far marriage is concerned? Well in 1960 the median age for women to marry was 20.3 and for men was 22.8. In 2010 that went up to 26.5 for women and 28.7 for men. One woman talked about her 2-2-2 formula. Date the man for two years, get engaged and be engaged for two years and then get married and be married two years before having children. Sadly, many people these days get married to the person they are living with because it is easier than moving out.

Women are putting off having children longer than ever. Some of them don't realize that you have only a 20% of having a baby at age 30. By age 40 that drops to only a 5% chance. However, for those women who did wait until they were 34 years old, they were earning 72% than the women who had had babies at age 26.

Sadly, a nanny can cost $25,000 a year or more. Most women aren't making enough at their jobs to justify the nanny expense or general childcare expenses. Raising a kid costs roughly $226,920 from birth to 18 yrs. That isn't even counting college! Housing takes up a huge chunk of one's income these days, but if you have more than 2 children in day care your day care expenses can be more than your housing costs!

Many Millennials are having a Quaterlife Crisis. Like a midlife crisis, it is a time when they reflect on their long term choice and come to regret some of them. It is true that a 16 year old brain is not the same as a 25 year old's brain. So people are still growing and learning and maturing from age 16-25. That is nearly ten years longer than scientists once expected.

Millennials are addicted to facebook. There is no doubt about that. Some of them suffer from FOMO or Fear of Missing Out. Their friends are their new family and they want to keep in touch with them. Kids also want to stay in touch with their actual family— particularly their parents—these days.

What is an adult? It is hard to say. But many people say if you are eating alone and you are using a plate and aren't standing up you are probably an adult. If you are accountable to yourself and even keep things at your house for when your friends visit, then you are probably an adult. If you put your socks in their draw and don't push them under the bed, you are probably and adult.

Some things are the same for Boomers as for Millennials and other things differed. What is NEW? Decision making, Schooling and Babies are all areas that have seen major changes between the generations. However, there are things that are the SAME as ever. What is the SAME? Careers, Marriage, Friends, Family and Health Concerns mostly.

Overall, an informative and thought-provoking book. Definitely check it out.

Zealot

Zealot: The Life and Times of Jesus of Nazareth by Reza Aslan caught my eye at the library, so I picked it up. I was not aware of the controversy surrounding it until after I'd finished and sat down to write. It is just plain silly to think that because the author is Muslim that the book is an attack on Christianity. The author is a biblical scholar and writes like one. It is much less biased than other accounts of Jesus's life that I've read and those were written by Christians themselves.

Yes, he does differentiate between the perception of Jesus the man and Jesus as Christ. Perhaps that is what has all the conservatives all riled up. Aslan, whose name recalls the Jesus-like lion from *The Chronicles of Narnia*, does a terrific job of placing Jesus in his historical context. This is, in fact, a classic way to look at any text when analyzing it. That is nothing new. And neither are the controversies that Aslan brings up in the course of the book.

His main point is that Jesus was part of the Zealot movement. He was supposed to fulfill the role of the Jewish Messiah in that he was supposed to free Jerusalem from Roman Rule. The idea that he was the savior of mankind came much later. His role was very specific to his time and place. Knowing that he was crucified for the crime of sedition is all we really need to know about him. He declared himself the King of Jews, and for that, he committed high treason in the eyes of Rome.

The virgin birth in Bethlehem was retro-fitted to make Jesus more of a Christ figure. The virgin birth was a staple of many mythologies. And it was unlikely that his parents traveled to Bethlehem for any sort of census. The resurrection element of the story of Jesus was new though.

John the Baptist was likely part of the Essene Brotherhood. When he baptized Jesus, he was not doing the traditional washing away of sins. Rather, he was initiating him into his group. Jesus's ministry was very influenced by the Essenes. Later, when John the Baptist was killed, Jesus even took two of his followers as his own. Simon and Philip were originally followers of John the Baptist.

Jesus often spoke of the Kingdom of God and the Son of Man. The Jehovah Witness believe that this Kingdom of God is yet to come and that after a world-wide Armageddon that the chosen ones will remain in an earthly paradise. Aslan's analysis points more toward the fact that Jesus was speaking specifically about his time in history. He believed that the Jerusalem would be The Kingdom of God in his lifetime and that he would rule as "the son of man" and not "the son of God."

After Jesus's death his followers were mostly aligned with his brother James. Saul, who became Paul, began teaching his own version of Christianity. In fact, there is evidence that James and Paul were publically in conflict with one another. James is reported to have called Paul to Jerusalem to recant his deviant teachings. James saw his brother as a zealot and a messiah, but not necessarily as a world-wide Christ.

When James was killed, Peter took over Jesus's movement. Peter and Paul both ended up in Rome, but not much in known about the end of their days. Paul ended up in Prison and Peter preached. Ironically, it was Paul's version of Christianity that gained popularity and ended up being adopted by the Roman Empire.